D0426262

Partner Schools

Russell T. Osguthorpe
R. Carl Harris
Melanie Fox Harris
Sharon Black
Editors
. . . .

Foreword by John I. Goodlad

Partner Schools

· ·

Centers for Educational Renewal

Jossey-Bass Publishers
San Francisco

✦ ✦ ✦ ✦ ✦ ✦ ✦ ✦ ✦ ✦ ✦ ✦ ✦ ✦ ✦

Copyright © 1995 by Jossey-Bass Inc., Publishers, 350 Sansome Street, San Francisco, California 94104. Copyright under International, Pan American, and Universal Copyright Conventions. All rights reserved. No part of this book may be reproduced in any form—except for brief quotation (not to exceed 1,000 words) in a review or professional work—without permission in writing from the publishers.

Substantial discounts on bulk quantities of Jossey-Bass books are available to corporations, professional associations, and other organizations. For details and discount information, contact the special sales department at Jossey-Bass Inc., Publishers. (415) 433-1740; Fax (800) 605-2665.

For sales outside the United States, please contact your local Paramount Publishing International Office.

TCF Manufactured in the United States of America on Lyons Falls Pathfinder Trade-book. This paper is acid-free and 100 percent totally chlorine-free.

Library of Congress Cataloging-in-Publication Data

Partner schools: centers for educational renewal/Russell T. Osguthorpe . . . [et al.], editors.—1st ed.
   p. cm.—(The Jossey-Bass education series)
  Includes bibliographical references and index.
  ISBN 0-7879-0065-6 (acid-free paper)
  1. College-school cooperation—United States. 2. Educational innovations—United States. 3. School improvement programs—United States. 4. School management and organization—United States.
I. Osguthorpe, Russell T. II. Series.
LB2331.53.P37 1995   94-46687
378.1'03—dc20   CIP

FIRST EDITION
HB Printing   10 9 8 7 6 5 4 3 2 1   *Code 9522*

The Jossey-Bass Education Series

. . . .

Contents

· ·

Foreword

. . . .

In the mid 1980s, the concept of school-university partnerships emerged in the rhetoric of educational advocacy with the intensity of an idea whose time was come. Indeed, partnerships were the "in" thing, both within and outside the educational enterprise. Soon, there were sufficient reports in the educational literature and at conferences to suggest that school-university partnerships were springing up all over. Even though very few people could claim any direct involvement in such collaborations, a new field of educational criticism was on the rise. The movement had all the earmarks of a fad.

But a fad it was not. Had those partnerships been prepared only as one more of the many extant proposals for school reform, the idea of school-university partnerships probably would have faded as quickly as hundreds of other proposals that surfaced briefly following the 1983 publication of the report from the U.S. National Commission on Excellence in Education, *A Nation at Risk*. However, other factors were at work. Several major studies of schools revealed a monumental disjuncture between calcified school practices and an extensive body of knowledge pointing to better ways. Some of these studies, along with other reports, raised parallel questions about outdated, unfocused programs for educating those who were expected to renew our schools. Colleges and universities increasingly were seen not merely as disinterested in and removed from the schools but as part of the problem. The idea of joining the renewal of schools and the preparation programs for those who work in them may have been somewhat intimidating for educators on both sides of the proposed partnership, but it made sense to many people in the policy arenas.

It was in this changing context that the concept of professional development, clinical, or "teaching" schools took hold. It was not new. There are clear parallels in the teaching hospitals of medical education and the field stations of agriculture, architecture, and urban planning. And of course, there is the informative history of laboratory schools attached to universities, a history that has probably served as much to discourage as to encourage what some saw as an effort to resurrect them. The laboratory school role that John Dewey had envisioned and tried at the University of Chicago at the turn of the century had by now been largely obfuscated by the intrusion of many other purposes for these schools.

As usually is the case with movements viewed as becoming popular, individuals and groups came on board with many different interests in mind. Professional development schools were quickly and variously seen as vehicles for the inservice education of teachers throughout whole school districts, the research of university professors, innovation in school practices, and more. Sometimes such schools were seen as integral to preservice teacher education programs, sometimes not. Because my colleagues and I saw them as absolutely essential to preservice teacher education—as central as the teaching hospital is to preservice medical education—we sought a designation not yet carrying several other denotations. We chose the term *partner school*.

This book addresses partner schools: schools engaged simultaneously and jointly with colleges and universities in the renewal of both themselves and the educator preparation programs of which they are an integral part. This central function does not rule out several other supportive auxiliary functions for these schools. Indeed, these supporting functions—the continuing education and renewal of faculty members from both the schools and the collabo-

rating universities, research, dissemination of results, and so forth—
are essential to exemplary fulfillment of the central one. Nonethe-
less, the central concept is of schools where efficacious educators
who ordinarily would teach only children and youths and efficacious
educators who ordinarily would teach only adults come together not
only to educate both groups of students but also to create exemplary
schools and exemplary teacher education programs. And, of course,
by definition, they are schools where *all* of the individuals encom-
passed are partners in educational adventures.

This is not a book of advocacy. The writers who came together
to plan its purposes and themes assumed that plenty of persuasion,
exhortation, and exposition had already been spread about. They
assumed a readership of people seeking to get beyond the what to
the how. The best way to do this, they concluded, was to share the
ways they had already chosen and moved forward on various productive roads. Most of them already had visited the settings of some
of the others; most had participated in various conferences on the
subject, not always with the same colleagues. They concluded that
they had much to share with others already on or about to enter on
roads pointed toward the destinations of partner schools.

Although the authors' emphasis is on how partner schools
develop and function, an enormous amount of information on what
partner schools are or should be is woven into the narratives.
Because this essential subject matter is brought so naturally into the
conversations, anecdotes, and reflections that enliven the pages, the
reader will learn more about what partner schools are than he or
she might glean from a more deliberate exposition.

The reader will become increasingly aware that he or she is
being introduced, usually in quite subtle fashion, to the creation of
new settings. A mature, or even maturing, partner school is a quite
different cultural entity than it was before the partnership process
began, and it is unlikely ever to return to its former state. In his
book, *The Creation of Settings and the Future Societies* (Jossey-Bass,
1972), Seymour B. Sarason observes that, in the past, "too many

people spent too much time trying to understand chronologically mature settings and were overlooking how they came into existence." The historical trail of such important human enterprises as mosques, churches, wineries, communes, sailing vessels, business enterprises, and universities is almost always ill-marked with respect to their original settings and very beginnings.

This potential problem is largely overcome in *Partner Schools*. While we must make some assumptions about a person with a vision bringing together others with a stake in education and having something to contribute, we get to listen to the early conversations of these key partner school participants and we see a number of those important beginning steps. Recalling these steps will become increasingly difficult and inaccurate with the passage of time. Consequently, the chronicling of the early stages of developments likely to lead on to significant others constitutes an enormous contribution to the literature of educational change and improvement.

In addition, the accounts that follow are necessarily of work in progress. There are as yet no settings sufficiently mature for the authors to provide us with summative accounts of utopias realized.

Ultimately, our ability to achieve mature partner schools and to renew both schooling and the education of educators depends on our establishing partnerships more tenuous and even more difficult to attain and sustain than the ones described here. We must create these additional partnerships with the political leadership and funding sectors of our democratic society. How serious are we about education, schooling, and the education of teachers for our schools? The gap between rhetoric and reality is formidable.

The moral messages on the pages of this book are powerful. And so are the messages about the additional time and energy required to meet our educational goals. In virtually all aspects of life except education, time and energy invariably are equated with money. If teachers in partner schools are to spend time helping neophytes understand sound teaching principles, there must be other teachers to take over their classes. If university professors, rather than part-time temporary personnel, are to be with their student teachers and interns and engaged in school renewal, the costs of doing business go up. There are innovative ways to redesign the entire delivery system, but they cannot be planned and implemented without the initial expenditure of additional energy, time, and money.

The refinement of partner schools requires a unique blending of resources conventionally located separately in schools and universities. So long as these resources are separately allocated and managed, partner schools are in danger. The many individuals who appear in the pages of this book have contributed their time and energy on the assumption that they are making things better for our young people. If these efforts are not to be in vain, partner schools must be lodged securely in centers with secure boundaries and budgets. In my vision and lexicon, these are centers of pedagogy. Many of the settings described in *Partner Schools* are working toward the creation of such entities. If they are to be successful, they must have a close working partnership with the state structure for policy and funding.

John I. Goodlad   *Director, Center for Educational Renewal*
September 1994   *University of Washington*

Preface

· ·

The educational reform movement of the past decade has been uneven in its progress and questionable in its results partly because different reformers have been aiming at different ends. Some have focused on standardized test gains, some on reducing violence in the schools, some on critical thinking, and some on the inclusion in the regular classroom of students with disabilities. Politicians, parents, and educators have all created their own unique agenda for change, agenda that aim toward an ever-growing number of laudable ends.

But while the goals multiply, the process for achieving those goals seems to be narrowing. The reform movement has generated at least one point on which all can agree: lasting improvement (of whatever kind) in education will come only if all the stakeholders work *together* to achieve it. Whether we want our schools to be safer places, our students to perform better in mathematics, or our teachers to be more knowledgeable, we are coming to believe that the only way to see positive results is to establish enduring partnerships among parents, teachers, students, university educators, and community leaders.

This book is about the places where such educational partnerships are taking root, places this book calls *partner schools*. A casual observer might have difficulty distinguishing partner schools from other schools, but a close examination reveals that teachers and students, university professors and administrators, and parents and community leaders have assumed new roles in partner schools and are pursuing new goals. They have made a commitment to change the way teaching and learning occur. They are not only engaged in delivering education, they are committed to *renewing* it, so that students will learn more and be able to contribute more to the communities in which they live. The purpose of this book is to take a close look at partner schools, to document their current state of development, and to consider the educational possibilities they present for the future.

Audience

This book has been written for teachers, university students and professors, administrators, parents, and community leaders who are collaborating to build a community of learners in partner schools. Teachers will gain added perspective in their roles as instructors of both children and university students. University students will better understand their roles as reflective preservice teachers. Professors will find examples for combining theory and practice in a new paradigm. Administrators will understand their important role in validating and facilitating collaborative efforts of the schools and university. Parents and community leaders will understand more clearly the vision of collaboration and the benefits their children will receive from being in the enriched environment of a partner school.

Questions Addressed

There are many questions that need to be addressed at this stage in the development of partner schools, but three are of particular interest to this book.

Is the partner school concept just another passing fad? Administering a partner school certainly requires concentrated effort, frequent sacrifice, and calculated risk. Before approaching such a task, teach-

ers and administrators must be convinced of the potential of partner schools to effect real change.

Partner schools, like most innovations in education, began as an
experiment. During the 1960s, the *laboratory schools* and *training
schools* that had provided places for prospective teachers to gain
experience began fading rapidly. For nearly two decades, there was
little to take their place in providing structured, supervised classroom experience for prospective teachers. Finally, in the 1980s, college and public school personnel began realizing that, if education
were to be truly reformed, colleges and schools needed to engage in
the formidable task together, working toward goals that would result
in enduring innovations, affecting the ways teachers teach and students learn. In the early 1980s, when John Goodlad began promoting the concept of colleges and schools working as equal partners
in educating teachers and simultaneously renewing schools, some
educators began experimenting with partnerships, even though others dismissed the partnership concept as yet another fad.

By a decade or more of profitable functioning, some of these
early partnerships have now proven that they are, indeed, more
than a fad. School partnerships are growing, evolving, adapting, and
exploring. There are many variations on the partnership theme, but
the underlying rationale of the partner school remains the same. As
the partner school movement continues to gain strength nationwide, it is important to document its progress. One purpose of this
book is to provide that documentation for specific functions and
innovations. The chapter authors present many examples that
demonstrate the areas in which partner schools are meeting a variety of teacher, student, and administrator needs.

*What do educators need to know to initiate a partnership and a part-
ner school?* Those who will be initiating partner schools need examples and cases, but they also need to see the principles and
recommendations that grow out of the successes and frustrations evident in the cases, which ultimately confirm the value of the project.

The contributors to this book blend analysis with specific cases, explaining what is demanded of university and public school educators and of other partners involved in the partner school venture. By carefully considering the analysis, potential partner school participants will gain a basic understanding of what they need to do to make their partner school successful.

What can we anticipate from partner schools in the future? Anyone seriously considering a partnership needs to look ahead and consider both costs and benefits. It would be naive to begin a school-university partnership without considering the challenges and potential pitfalls; but it would also be counterproductive to initiate the effort without anticipating the positive effects that can come from true collaboration. While describing the difficulties all participants face in creating and sustaining partner schools, the chapter authors also emphasize the potential benefits. Thus, when they look to the future, they project with the eye of hope rather than the eye of the hard critic or cynic. The time for hard criticism will come when partner schools are better established; now is the time for examining their possibilities as tools for educational renewal.

A Balanced View

This book emerged from a conference of the National Network for Educational Renewal (NNER), and a variety of NNER participants have collaborated on it. When the first meeting of potential authors was held, during the conference, the only unity in the diversity of those present was that everyone was willing to cooperate. To be sure that the various chapters represented an appropriate balance of viewpoints, each chapter was assigned to a team consisting of both college and school educators, with some of the teams including writers from different geographic areas. Team members were to bring their ideas together to form unified chapters based on specific topics. Such collaboration is not easy, and the project involved some trial and error and a lot of revision, but gradually unified chapters emerged. The striking feature of this collaboration—for which all the editors are grateful—is that in spite of ups and downs, discouragements, deadlines, and revisions, not one incident of anger, defensiveness, or negative relationships among the participants was reported to the editors. Thus the stories of collaboration in this book were contained within a larger collaboration: a variety of authors engaged in a collaboration to examine collaboration.

Chapter authors were asked to avoid naming their partner school sites. Instead, they have described general settings, so that readers can relate more readily to the experiences of each author. The chapters focus on the principles that underlie partner schools and include a variety of examples to give life to these principles, in order to help readers apply the information more easily to create or strengthen their own partner schools. The Appendix contains more detailed descriptions of each school-university partnership in NNER, for readers who may want to contact specific site directors.

Overview of the Contents

Partner Schools is divided into two parts: the first part (Chapters One through Five) describes the purposes of partner schools; the second part (Chapters Six through Eleven) describes how such schools are developed.

Chapter One emphasizes those characteristics that are prerequisites for all partner schools. Chapter Two focuses on the most fundamental purpose of partner schools—improving student learning. In this chapter, we hear the voices of young students and learn how students affect the nature of the partner school in which they are enrolled.

Chapter Three addresses the role of partner schools in improving the preparation of teachers, perhaps the most critical factor in sustaining the improvements in student learning described in Chapter Two. At first glance, we might assume that student learning is the responsibility of the school while teacher preparation is the responsibility of the college or university. However, the first three chapters illustrate how effective partner schools in widely diverse settings cause university faculty to sense a deeper responsibility for learning in the schools and school faculty to sense a deeper responsibility for the teachers they are helping to prepare.

Chapter Four describes how partner schools are committed to improving teaching throughout the lifelong career of the professional educator. This chapter, as clearly as any in the book, shows how partner schools create not only new lines of responsibility but also new roles for school and university faculty and for students. These role changes mean that educators in partner schools no longer spend all their time in the traditional and somewhat rigid roles of teacher, principal, or university faculty member. Instead, school faculty spend more time as mentors to their peers, while university faculty spend more time with young students.

The essential contributions of research and inquiry in partner schools are discussed in Chapter Five. Once the exclusive purview of higher education, research and inquiry are becoming more integral ingredients in teacher education and student learning in the schools. This shift is partly due to the changing definition of research itself, as it comes to be viewed as a useful approach to learning for *all* members of our society rather than only for a select few who have been trained in objective, scientific methods. Examples in this chapter illustrate how the personal questions of students or faculty not only drive personal learning but also drive efforts to improve teaching and learning throughout the partner school.

The authors of Chapter Six draw upon years of experience in partnership work as they describe the necessary steps or phases in creating a partner school. Like the remaining chapters in Part Two, this chapter portrays the pain as well as the exhilaration of the change process of establishing and developing a partner school. Chapter Seven then focuses on the process of expanding the influence of partner schools to an entire school district. In describing how partner schools can strengthen teaching and learning in nonpartner schools, the authors of this chapter directly address the criticism that partner schools (like their predecessors, laboratory schools) are isolated, self-serving organizations interested only in their own well-being.

Continuing to discuss some of the concepts introduced in Chapter Seven, Chapter Eight describes how the effects of partner schools can be extended throughout an entire state. Both chapters introduce creative and successful organizational structures for linking partner schools in a single school district or across a state. Because these approaches have been developed and refined in several states, readers will find the suggestions practical as they create their own partner schools and develop their own systems for linking partner schools to one another.

Chapter Nine explains how partner schools can expand and strengthen their relationships with parents and other community agencies. It also shows how partner schools can address the life-threatening problems that are increasing in our society because of the moral decay that has occurred during the past half-century, decay that is particularly acute in U.S. inner cities. The authors of this chapter make a strong case for expanding partnerships beyond university and school walls to include the home and all agencies designed to serve the needs of students who are at risk.

The worth of any new educational innovation can only be determined if participants are willing to evaluate its effects. Partner schools are no exception. Participating sites in the National Network for Educational Renewal were so convinced of the importance of partner schools that they developed a common set of purposes and criteria for evaluating them. Chapter Ten outlines these criteria and describes how data can be collected to measure the progress of a partner school toward each purpose and criterion. Readers will find this approach useful as they attempt to evaluate their own efforts in partner schools.

The final chapter looks to the future as the chapter authors tie the contents of the previous chapters to trends that are beginning to emerge across our continent. Though tenuous now, these trends will affect the long-term results of partner schools, determining

whether these schools will be simply another short-lived novelty in
the ongoing saga of educational reform or an enduring structure that
will permanently change the ways we teach and the ways we learn.

Provo, Utah   Russell T. Osguthorpe
July 1994   R. Carl Harris
                                                  Melanie Fox Harris
                                                    Sharon Black

The Editors

· ·

Russell T. Osguthorpe, a professor of instructional science, currently serves as associate dean in the College of Education at Brigham Young University (BYU) and as a member of the coordinating council of the BYU-Public School Partnership. He received his education at the University of Utah and BYU, receiving his Ph.D. degree from BYU in Instructional Psychology. Osguthorpe has published widely in the areas of peer tutoring and the use of technology in special education, teacher education, and instructional science, and has served as a reviewer for the *Journal of Teacher Education* and *The Elementary School Journal*. He has directed funded projects in the United States and China and has served as a review panelist of grant applications for the U.S. Department of Education. He has been a visiting scholar at the University of Toronto and most recently at the University of Paris, where he studied educational partnerships in France.

R. Carl Harris is professor of teacher education in the Department of Elementary Education at Brigham Young University. His teaching and administrative experience with youth includes work in the Samoan, Fijian, and Hawaiian Islands as well as teaching third grade in a rural school in Utah. His preparation for teacher education includes a M.S. degree in psychology from Utah State University and a Ph.D. degree in educational psychology from Pennsylvania State University. His experience in teacher education includes over two decades of teaching undergraduate and graduate teacher education courses on campuses in Pennsylvania, Hawaii, and Utah. He also has a decade of experience working in the BYU-Public School Partnership and is currently assigned as the university faculty member in a cluster of four partner schools. Much of his research and writing over the past decade has explored the partner-school effect on teacher preparation, professional development, and school renewal. During the past year he has collaborated with researchers from six other nations on a study of the active learning model in education. His research findings on Motorola University's *Explorations 94 Program* will be reported in a chapter on active learning in a forthcoming book to be published by the Center for Educational Research and Innovation (CERI), which operates from Paris, France, under the auspices of the Organization for Economic Cooperation and Development (OECD).

Melanie Fox Harris is an educator on loan from the Nebo School District serving as assistant to the director of the BYU-Public School Partnership. She has taught preschool, first grade, multi-age groups of third, fourth, and fifth grade students and has mentored student teachers and interns. She holds a B.S. degree in Elementary Education from BYU-Hawaii and a Gifted/Talented Endorsement and M.Ed. degree in Teaching and Learning from Brigham Young University. She has coauthored articles on the simultaneous renewal of teacher education and schooling. Harris is presently working on a certificate for Teaching English as a Second Language.

Sharon J. Black has a dual appointment as an instructor in the College of Education and in the English Department of the College of Humanities at Brigham Young University. She received her B.A. degree in English and her M.A. degree in American Literature at BYU. Black has designed curriculum and has taught in a private school for gifted children. She has coauthored articles in a broad range of areas including literacy, reading, writing, and teaching gifted children. She has a keen interest in adult and family literacy and works with a volunteer family literacy program.

The Contributors

Michael L. Barnhart is director of the office of student services and professional field experiences and assistant professor of teacher education and educational leadership at the College of Education and Human Services, Wright State University.

Monica M. Beglau is former executive director of the Wyoming School-University Partnership.

Katharine Briar is professor and chair of family studies and social work at Miami University, Ohio.

Richard W. Clark is senior associate of the Center for Educational Renewal at the University of Washington.

Donna J. Cole is associate professor of teacher education and foundations in the Department of Teacher Education, College of Education and Human Services, Wright State University.

Beverly R. Cutler is associate dean and associate professor of elementary education at the College of Education, Brigham Young University.

Randall Flora is adjunct associate professor and coordinator of teacher preparation and field relations at Miami University, Ohio.

Patricia Graham is associate dean of the School of Education at Winthrop University.

Kolene F. Granger is assistant superintendent of instructional services for the Alpine School District, American Fork, Utah.

Stevenson T. Hansell is professor of education at the College of Education and Human Services, Wright State University.

Thomas S. Howick is assistant professor of education at the College of Education, University of Southern Maine.

Francis P. Hunkins is professor of curriculum and instruction at the College of Education, University of Washington.

Jan Kettlewell is professor and dean of the School of Education and Allied Professions, Miami University, Ohio.

Walter H. Kimball is associate professor of education at the College of Education, University of Southern Maine.

Patricia A. LaRosa is an elementary teacher at the White Rock School, Gorham School Department.

Hal A. Lawson is professor at the School of Education and Allied Professions, Miami University, Ohio.

Barbara Little-Gottesman is executive director of the South Carolina Center for the Advancement of Teaching and School Leadership and state director for the South Carolina Collaborative to Renew Teacher Education, Winthrop University.

Sally Lloyd is associate dean of the School of Education and Allied Professions and professor in the family and consumer science department at Miami University, Ohio.

Bonnie K. Mathies is associate professor of educational technology and chair of the Department of Educational Technology, Vocational Education and Applied Programs, at the College of Education and Human Services, Wright State University.

Nicholas M. Michelli is dean of the School of Professional Studies, Montclair State University.

Lourdes Z. Mitchel is principal of Harold Wilson Middle School for Professional Development, Newark School District, Newark, New Jersey.

Carol Nogy is associate professor in the Department of Education, Furman University.

Robert A. Pines is director of teacher education at Montclair State University.

William E. Smith, Jr. is superintendent of Trotwood-Madison City Schools, Trotwood, Ohio.

Susan M. Swap is professor of education, director of the Center on College-School-Community Partnerships, and chair of the Department of Professional Studies, Wheelock College.

Richard C. Williams is executive director of the Puget Sound Educational Consortium and professor of educational leadership and policy studies in the College of Education, University of Washington.

Donna L. Wiseman is associate dean of the College of Education and interim department head and professor of curriculum and instruction at Texas A & M University.

James Ziegler is associate professor in the Department of Teacher

Education at the School of Education and Allied Professions, Miami University, Ohio.

Partner Schools

1

Introduction

Understanding School-University Partnerships

Russell T. Osguthorpe, R. Carl Harris, Sharon Black, Beverly R. Cutler, and Melanie Fox Harris

"If we would just look at the literature. After all, if we don't look at history we're destined to repeat it. The whole issue has been treated—"

"But what we're doing isn't history—it's new. What we really need is to look at teaching and learning from a whole different perspective—"

"The perspective is that we're developing teachers for the twenty-first century; we need to recognize the impact of technology—"

"Children are more important than technology. The composition of today's classroom is different; we need more preparation in multicultural issues, more focus on meeting children's social and emotional needs—"

"One way we can get to these needs is through giving more emphasis to the arts. Music is universal; drawing is universal. Children can express what's inside them and learn to deal with it—regardless of language deficiencies or troubled home life—"

The members of this restructuring group were communicating but not really *communicating*. Faculty from a university's college of education; faculty from the same university's departments of music, dance, visual arts, English, linguistics, physical education, and health; teachers and administrators from three school districts; and education students from the university had met to design a new program to prepare elementary school teachers. Each participant had a perspective, a value system, and turf to defend. Although participants listened respectfully to one another, all heard in the comments of the others only the words that triggered reactions in favor of their own self-interests.

They were struggling for a common perspective when the storm hit: a sudden, unanticipated pelting of hail, with winds later reported to be 125 miles per hour. The school darkened as electricity was lost, and the screams of frightened children echoed in the halls. Drawn to the windows as magnetically as the children, the educators at the meeting gasped as trees the height of three-story buildings plummeted to the earth. The storm was soon over, but it did not take long for everyone to realize that the terrain around the school would never be the same again.

Not all efforts to restructure teacher education and strengthen school programs and curricula involve happenings quite this dramatic. Fortunately, the remaining group meetings did not involve external storms, the confusion was not caused by hail or lost electricity, and the barriers that fell were not trees. But when groups composed of university and public school personnel work together *in partnership, within partner schools*, barriers do come down, visions and perspectives do change, and both the schools and the university are opened to permanent change.

This book presents a mosaic of the many kinds of change that are occurring in partner schools throughout the United States. A variety of partner schools will be explored to examine what these schools are, how they have developed, and what possibilities they hold for educational renewal. This initial chapter focuses on the qualitative characteristics that are essential for any partner school to succeed, characteristics that have little to do with funding mechanisms or organizational structure and much to do with the human side of partnering. These characteristics are collaboration, community, and connectedness.

School-University Partnerships

In their simplest form, school-university partnerships are organized collaboratives that bring university and public school teachers and administrators together to promote more effective preparation of preservice teachers and, at the same time, to renew conditions and curricula in the public schools. In some partnerships, parent organizations are included as official partners; in others, representatives of businesses, industries, and social agencies are participants. Some partnerships involve a single college and a few schools; others bring together a number of school districts and several colleges and universities. Some partnerships involve a network of collaboration that functions throughout a state.

For a school-university partnership to effect lasting change, a structure must be created in which all partners have equal status. University deans and school district superintendents must have equal voting and veto power on the board that oversees partnership activity. In partnerships involving additional groups, equivalent representation for these participants must be arranged. Depending on the specific partnership's size and complexity, councils, committees, task forces, and other units may be formed, giving equal voice to all participating partners. Although specific organizational structures and established practices and procedures will vary with the nature and needs of each partnership, these structures and procedures, whatever they may be, must be clearly defined and all participants must agree and commit to them. At the same time, structures and procedures must be flexible enough that partnership practice can adapt to changing needs in the schools and communities, as well as to changing leadership within the partnership itself. A clear definition and flexibility of the partnership function are possible when the participants share both general and specific goals for educator preparation and school renewal, and when they trust and respect each other sufficiently to share decisions and resources. On a practical, day-to-day level, such give-and-take is often difficult.

The restructuring group whose meeting was interrupted by the storm is representative of many partnerships. Their partnership has been in existence for ten years, and many leaders of the restructuring effort were involved in the initial organization; so these participants have experienced a good deal of collaboration. They know the ups and downs of collaborative work; they have experienced its frustrations and enjoyed its victories. Stalemates do not surprise them, nor do exciting moments of consensus, frequent polite clashes of will, occasional flaring tempers, or the exciting "aha" moments in meetings when significant ideas and understandings emerge. That is the way it is with educational partnerships: varied contributions, occasional disagreements, excitement, fatigue, comprehension, mutual appreciation, discouragement, and discovery.

Partner Schools

Collaborative relationships can only endure if they are given a *place* to endure. Partner schools are selected sites where collaborative programs are put into practice. They are located in areas from Maine to Hawaii, urban and rural, homogeneous and multicultural, economically secure and socioeconomically depressed. Partner schools have served as practicum sites for preservice teachers and administrative and counseling interns; implemented extensive inservice education programs to strengthen practicing teachers; and promoted evaluation, study, and renewal of a variety of curricula. Some partner schools have become centers for specialized programs, created laboratories for exploring new uses of technology, served as sites for action research, coordinated social services to meet the physical and emotional needs of students, and initiated community actions that affect students and their families.

Although no two partner schools are completely alike, all school-university partnerships appear to have been formed with two broad general goals: first, to strengthen the preparation of teachers and, second, to renew K–12 education. To advance these goals, four basic areas of partnership activity have been designated—all aimed at increasing student learning. (Figure 1.1 illustrates the interrelationships of these goals and of the participants in partner schools.)

1. *Educator preparation:* collaboration between partners to ensure that those entering the education profession are prepared to serve all students effectively

2. *Professional development:* collaboration between partners to provide opportunities for teachers to strengthen their ability to contribute to the students they serve

3. *Curriculum development:* collaboration between partners to improve the education and school experience of all students

4. *Research and inquiry:* collaboration between partners to raise questions and conduct research that will promote educational renewal at both the school and the university.

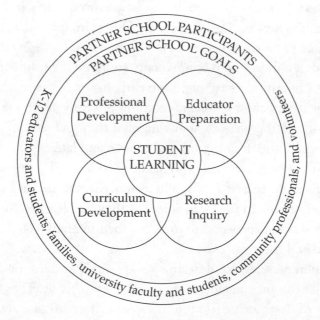

Figure 1.1. Partner School Relationships.

While most participants in partner schools would agree that these are the goals that direct their activities and that student learning is the overriding goal, we know of no partner school that claims to excel equally in all four areas. More balanced and complete approaches will likely develop as partner school participants continue to pursue the image of educational renewal depicted in Figure 1.1. That image is admittedly the ideal—something partner school participants are working toward. It will be important for all involved to keep that image in mind as partner schools are created throughout the nation, but it is also essential that educators learn from what is currently happening in existing partner schools.

The partner school at which the meeting was interrupted by the storm had been the site of much partnership activity in the past. Teachers at this partner school had become accustomed to coaching preservice teachers from the university; they felt responsible for acquainting these teacher candidates with the best practice they as experienced teachers were able to find, and they allowed themselves to learn from the student teachers and from the university supervisor, who was often on-site to discuss ideas as well as to join in mentoring and evaluating processes. The principal had already designated a room at the school in which methods classes would be held for a cohort group of university students the following fall. These students were to spend the early hours of the morning in partner school classrooms; mid-morning and early afternoon in session with their professors, analyzing what they had seen and learning methodology for teaching and coping; and late afternoon back in the classrooms, trying out what they had learned. The inservice teachers knew this strategy would require them to sacrifice some of their autonomy in the classroom, but they had learned from past partner school experiences to trust that their interests would be considered and their voices heard.

When people with differing backgrounds and interests work together toward common goals, sparks inevitably fly. They can be sparks of destructive friction or "sparks of creative electricity"

(Ziegler, 1981, p. 232). But without the relationships that develop through close collaborative work, partner schools cannot exist.

Collaboration

When people are committed to common goals and to achieving those goals by working together, true collaboration occurs. Although the term *collaboration* is frequently used to describe any type of cooperative working arrangement, in the context of a partner school it implies more than simply cooperating with one another. It implies an active, directed form of cooperation that is motivated from within the participating individuals and groups. This type of collaboration can occur only after people connect with ideas, form relationships based upon equity and trust, and develop commitment to shared goals.

Shared goals and commitments emerge more readily among students and teachers working collaboratively than among teachers themselves or among teachers working with university faculty. John Goodlad (1990) describes tensions between school teachers and university faculty as especially prevalent: "Higher education has never been disposed to working collaboratively with the lower schools. . . . University professors [ironically] complain about both the products of the schools coming to their classes and the poor quality of those who taught them. The schools, on the other hand, would have had little reason to celebrate the appearance on their doorsteps of a sometimes-discordant army of crusaders from the universities intent on a pilgrimage" (pp. 102–103).

In order to replace these feelings of tension with a sense of community, university faculty and educators in the schools need to understand each other's institutional cultures, appreciate the demands their cultures place on everyone, and recognize the potential for their cultures to complement each other. It is only when school and university faculty have found *unity* in certain of their goals that a partner school can function effectively (Harris & Harris, 1992). Such unity requires that members of both cultures be willing to enter each other's worlds and to consider the conditions of those worlds specifically and seriously enough to become somewhat comfortable there. For example, in addition to sharing an extraordinary storm, the members of the restructuring partnership shared an experience with each department represented in the group. With the music teacher, they learned to produce musical tone from a string; with the health teacher, they calculated their resting heart rates, jogged, and had juice and fresh fruit for the session's refreshments. The teacher of English as a second language conducted part of her presentation in Spanish so at least half of the participants felt puzzled and left out; the art teacher took the group on a tour of the university's fine arts museum. Meeting for several hours in two public schools, the group heard children sing before they heard the principal, teachers, and parents express their positions and concerns.

The last of the presentations took place in the university's dance studio, where the dance instructor led the partnership participants in a creative movement experience, during which they attempted to understand how others felt by replicating each other's positions and movement patterns. On a physical level, the director of the partnership (a former district superintendent), the chair of the university's elementary education department, public school teachers, university methods professors, university teachers of a wide range of subjects, and preservice teachers walked as others walked, stood as others stood, and changed stances and positions as others changed. The experience culminated as the group learned a folk dance from Israel, a dance which celebrates land, relationships, and people. Finally, the group joined hands in doing this dance, first in a large circle in which everyone faced the center—equal and seamless—then in lines that wound in new and complex patterns.

Members of most school-university partnerships do not physically move in others' shapes and positions, nor do they literally join hands in celebration of their unity in diversity. But figuratively they can, and must, do so if they are to create effective communities of learners among themselves and in the institutions where they teach.

Community

Sergiovanni (1993) explains that schools are typically viewed as organizations, that is, institutions based on individual rights, on bartering, and on contractual relationships. He suggests it is more productive to conceive of schools as communities: "Communities are collections of individuals who are bonded together by natural will and who are together bound to a set of shared ideas and ideals. This bonding and binding is tight enough to transform them from a collection of 'I's' into a collective 'we.' As a 'we,' members are part of a tightly-knit web of meaningful relationships. This 'we' usually shares a common place and over time comes to share common sentiments and traditions that are sustaining" (p. 8).

When one public school teacher's school became a partner school, she also saw this development as a chance for people to find unity: "I saw it as an opportunity to pull education together. I've thought for years that [people in the university and in the schools] were kind of going in their own separate little channels, kind of like water going down a ditch that had sprung a leak and was going in all directions. And I saw [the partner school] as an opportunity for everybody to focus on where education ought to be" (Harris & Harris, 1991, p. 18).

This teacher saw a striking example of partnership members working together to create a community of learners in her school. The special education teacher had become frustrated with the school's partial mainstreaming program. As he expressed it, "Each year I got a few new students who were supposed to be spending at least part of their time in the regular classroom. And frankly, partial mainstreaming wasn't working. The kids were still mocked on the playground, still labeled. I could see the only way to stop it would be to get them in the regular classroom all day, every day" (Chris Roberts, personal communication, 1992).

Because of the collaborative trust that already existed in the school and with its university partner, this special education teacher felt comfortable in sharing an idea that would involve not merely a new arrangement but a systemic philosophical shift. He offered to teach one of the regular classes himself, so that the class size for all of the participating teachers would be reduced, if the teachers would be willing to take on an innovative classroom program in which special education students would become part of the regular classes. Working together, the teachers and the partner school university representative structured a multi-age third- through fifth-grade group of students: no student was to be labeled or segregated, and the teachers would collaboratively teach the group. The university placed preservice teachers in the school to free one of the teachers to develop and coordinate efforts. Parents of both regular and special education students were also integral to the program's success.

Consensus did not always come easily, and the change did not occur without struggle. Some parents of students without disabilities felt that another setting would be more appropriate for their children and asked that their children be transferred to another school, and those requests were honored. But all stakeholders—parents, school and university educators, and the children themselves—were included in planning and implementing the new approach. As the multi-age program matured, parents in other parts of the district volunteered to provide transportation if their children could participate in this program.

Community in such a partnership can extend to become unity in the classroom. Students who do not have disabilities can participate in buddy reading with students who are disabled. In heterogeneous cooperative learning groups, older students can guide younger students in structuring work projects and carrying them through. In heterogeneous pairs, students on all ability levels might find new and interesting ways of assisting each other in understanding and applying classroom content.

Relationships in a partner school are based upon the principle of *dignity*—a recognition that everyone is a person of worth, that all have equal value in the school, and that equity and trust are characteristic of all socially productive relationships (Harris & Harris, 1992).

Connectedness

In a talk on what it means to be an educated person, Ernest Boyer (1993) emphasized the importance of connectedness between people:

> Far too many children do not have intergenerational connections. Margaret Mead said on one occasion that the health of any culture is sustained when three generations are vitally interacting with each other, a kind of vertical connection in which the different ages are connected. And yet in America today we are creating what might be called a horizontal culture, with each generation living all alone, disconnected from the other. Infants are in nurseries, toddlers in day care, older children are in schools, and we layer them by age. College students are isolated on campuses, living in a climate of low grade decadence. Adults are in the work place. And older citizens are in retirement villages living and dying all alone.

Some partner schools have been designed to be places where teaching and learning are shared between literal as well as educational generations: children, college students, parents, school teachers, university professors, grandparents, and volunteers of all ages. In one classroom, a university student doing her practicum teaching may make a special effort to reach out to a little girl who has recently moved into the area and has no close friends. In another, a teacher the age of her students' mothers may give praise and support to a behavior-disordered child whose own mother is too discouraged to provide it. A grandfatherly professor may take a few minutes to discuss an advanced math concept with a gifted child. An elderly volunteer may listen to a learning disabled child who is struggling to read. These connections, of course, can happen in any school. But they are purposefully sought and promoted by the underlying philosophy and the collaborative framework of the partner school situation.

When educators and students on all levels connect and communicate, they can come to trust one another and begin to explore the connectedness of things. As Boyer (1993) says,

> To be truly educated means going beyond the isolated facts; it means putting learning in a larger context; and above all, it means, to return to my favorite word, it means discovering the *connectedness* of things. The Nobel laureate Barbara McClintock wrote on one occasion, "Everything is one. There is no way to draw a line between things." I wonder if Professor McClintock has looked at a school curriculum in recent years with all the separate academic boxes. Frank Press, President of the National Academy of Sciences, said in a recent speech that scientists are in some respects like artists, and to illustrate the point he said that the magnificent double helix, which broke the genetic code, was not only rational, it was beautiful as well. And yet in most schools, science and art teachers live in absolutely separate worlds; they don't communicate with one another [pp. 6–7].

Because partner schools emphasize the relationships between people, they are capable of becoming places where students learn to see the wholeness of the world. This wholeness extends into curriculum areas as well. For example, in one partner high school, a Spanish teacher and a history teacher team teach world history in the Spanish language. In another partner high school, a science teacher and an English teacher teach their topics together. When teachers cooperate and integrate curricula in this way, students are much more likely to see the interconnectedness of knowledge, remember it, and use it in their everyday lives.

Another partner high school has carried connectedness to a very complex level. Their program, called Unified Studies, began when an English teacher and a science teacher found they shared a concern that secondary education had become splintered and impersonal. Leaving the confines of their traditional classroom, these teachers designed a program in which academic disciplines and lived experience would become more "unified" for a selected group of students who would themselves be "unified" in their diversity. A heterogeneous group of students would participate for a full day every other day in a class with these two teachers. Teachers and students jointly defined the curriculum, and students were to have an atypical amount of freedom to determine what they would study and how they would study it.

Because of the holistic approach, learning in this program often occurs outside classroom walls, where students and teachers can be surrounded by nature. Science is often taught and learned beside streams and under trees, integrated with the arts and the humanities. Students may observe insects in a field of June grass, read Thoreau's account of watching ants at Walden, write their reactions to their own observations in a personal essay or a poem, and then paint a picture reflecting aspects of their experience.

Unified Studies actually began before the partnership in which the school now participates, but partnership members recognized their goal of interconnectedness in the course and accepted an invitation to participate in it. A university faculty member began observing the course as an ethnographic researcher—not attempting to change anything, simply trying to understand course purposes and effects. Soon this professor began to bring graduate students with him. Learning was contagious, and professor and graduate students began to participate with the high school teachers and students as fellow teachers and learners. The professor was so enthralled with the learning experience that he began bringing undergraduate student interns with him as well. The interns documented their observations in field notes and shared their insights with the high school students and teachers as well as with the graduate students and the professor (Williams, 1991).

Roles within this community of learners became more and more fluid and interchangeable. At one moment, a high school student might function as a tutor in art, in which he excels; later as an observer of a high school teacher in science, a field that fascinates but frustrates him; and finally as a learner, when he and the teacher work together to complete an experiment. The university professor might observe and jot down field notes on the interactions of teachers and students; later, he might tutor a student who is having difficulty expressing his ideas in writing; and finally, he might become the learner as high school students share with him the results of their discovery learning experience. Learning is less firmly structured and less predictable because it is occurring in a natural environment rather than following the predetermined order of a textbook. Rather than having to focus on discipline or student management, as many high school classes do, this class is free to focus on the learning and growth of all the participants.

Student interns, observing the two experienced classroom teachers, pose questions about pedagogical practice as well as content. In after-class meetings they share observations and insights about each other's teaching. All can discuss process as well as content because all are part of the processes of teaching and learning. When somebody does not live up to expectations, support instead of blame is given because all are part of a connected group of learners, seeking connections within their studies and connections between their studies and their lives.

A memorable project culminated one year of the Unified Studies program as the program participants traveled to Romania to give service by caring for orphaned and disabled children. High school students, university undergraduates and graduates, high school teach-

ers, and university faculty all participated. As they planned their
activities, they learned in an integrated, purposeful way about the
history and current challenges of the Romanian people. While in
Romania, they painted orphanages, assisted with a countrywide
Special Olympics program, and helped care for children—some of
whom had been labeled "irrecoverable." They not only learned
more about the Romanian people, they learned more about themselves and about their individual places in the world. Their experience was consistent with Boyer's (1993) suggestion: that "all
students should be asked to complete a community service project
in order to demonstrate that learning has a practical and applied
side that must be tested." This project could be "in day care centers
or in retirement villages or in tutoring other children." Boyer also
quotes Martin Luther King: "everyone can be great because everyone can serve."

The concept of connectedness is not new, nor is an emphasis on
connectedness exclusive to partner schools. As John Dewey asserted
in 1938, "Amid all uncertainties there is one permanent frame of
reference: namely the organic connection between education and
personal experience" (p. 25). What distinguishes the connectedness in partner schools are the number and the variety of people
who participate in it and the way in which preservice teachers who
live the experiences are able to pass them on to future generations
of participants.

Result: Everyone Teaches, Everyone Learns

In the Harold A. Wilson Middle School, a partner school in
Newark, New Jersey, a slogan appears in large letters on the hallway wall: "Everyone teaches, everyone learns." These words could
be a slogan for any partner school in the country; they cogently
express the partner school mode of conducting schooling. Teachers
and students of all ages seek knowledge together, and they share
what they find. Everyone asks questions, and everyone participates

in finding answers. An episode in a multi-age classroom, part of the program initiated by the special education teacher described earlier in this chapter, illustrates the way learning can happen in a partner school in which collaboration, community, and connectedness are emphasized by all participants. In this and all other examples, the names are pseudonyms. The children are sitting in pairs; the teacher, Ms. Bayles, circulates among them. "Raise your hand when you and your partner have found two and five-sixteenths inches on your ruler," she instructs. In the back of the room, a university faculty member motions to his six observing preservice students to watch carefully—much will be happening below the surface of a seemingly simple lesson for this group. As Ms. Bayles asks the heterogeneous pairs to locate a number of measurements on their rulers, the university students circulate to help the children. All the children are enthusiastically engaged in the activity; there is no off-task behavior. Then, at Ms. Bayles's request, the children move to one end of the room where they gather around her, sitting closely together on the floor. She holds up a dark blue oblong cloth.

MS. BAYLES: This cloth I'm holding was given to us by Gina's mom who works at the hospital. She gave us a whole box of these for our science lab. Now that you know how to measure things with a ruler, we're going to learn about perimeter and area. If I wanted to trim the outside edge of this cloth with another material, what measurement would I need to know? Todd?

TODD, A THIRD GRADER [*pointing to the edge of the cloth*]: You'd need to know how long it is all the way around.

MS. BAYLES: So let's measure it with a ruler. Mike and Lori, will you bring your ruler here and measure it for us?

MIKE, A CONFIDENT FOURTH GRADER [*reading the numbers aloud as Lori, a fourth grader with a learning disability, holds the ruler*]: We've got it, Ms. Bayles! The long side is two feet, seven inches and the short side is one foot, five inches.

MS. BAYLES: So what is the perimeter of this cloth?

LISA, A FIFTH GRADER: Eight feet.
MS. BAYLES [*somewhat surprised*]: That's right, Lisa. Can you tell us how you figured that out?
LISA: Well, I just added two and one; that made three feet. Then I added seven inches and five inches; and that made one foot. Three plus one is four feet; then I doubled that to make eight.

The professor smiles. When he debriefs his students after this session of observation, he will teach them a term for the process they have just observed and tell them where they can find it described in the professional literature. In addition to Lisa's learning experience, the university students will discuss what has happened for Gina, the nurse's daughter, and for Lori, the measuring partner who is learning disabled.

Ms. Bayles moves on. She asks the students to pretend that the cloth is a piece of carpet. She then asks them to imagine that John's dad, who is a carpet layer, needs to know how much floor space this piece of carpet would cover. She teaches the children the concept of area, and John, who has accompanied his father on a number of Saturday mornings, teaches her, along with his classmates and the university participants, part of the process involved in carpeting a floor.

As the children move back to sit at tables in groups of four for the next activity, Julie, a fourth grader who was formerly in a self-contained classroom for children with emotional and behavioral problems, begins to cry. Diane, Julie's partner, raises her hand.

DIANE: Ms. Bayles, I don't think Julie got a hug today.
MS. BAYLES [*not wanting to draw undue attention to Julie*]: Thanks for letting me know, but I think Julie will be all right. Now let's pick parts for our story.
JULIE [*glaring angrily at Jeff, who is sitting across from her*]: Oh, shut up!
Neither Jeff nor Diane says anything.

MS. BAYLES [*continuing as if there had been no interruption*]: Who
would like to take the part of Sam in the readers theater?

Julie raises her hand along with everyone else, tears and anger
gone. Some of the university students had felt indignant when the
teacher did not go immediately to hug the crying child and were
troubled when she ignored the rude outburst. Seeing the rest of the
incident, they now understand why Ms. Bayles gently but firmly
refused to let Julie interrupt the learning community of the classroom. Later, the preservice teachers' professor will respond to their
questions and discuss the effects of this interchange on Diane and
Jeff as well as on Julie. There are some aspects of Ms. Bayles's skill
that have surprised and intrigued him as well. He feels that he and
his students can now more fully understand Parker Palmer's (1992)
concept of a classroom "so rooted in love that it could sustain the
effects of rigor." He is looking forward to the discussion.

Conclusion

Partner schools vary significantly. Some are urban, some rural. Some
are elementary schools, others secondary. All, however, are based
upon mutual trust, understanding, and collaboration among partners. All recognize the importance of making connections in the
learning process: connections between people and connections
within and between knowledge areas. And all are committed to
converting their schools into communities of learners. *Commitment,
collaboration*, and *connectedness*—these are the essential attributes
for any partner school; without these ingredients, no partner school
can achieve its overall purpose of improving student learning. Only
as these attributes emerge can partner schools improve student
learning by addressing the four goal areas of school-university partnerships: educator preparation, professional development, curriculum development, and research and inquiry.

    The following chapters show how partner schools are beginning to address these four goals. The authors of each chapter describe a rich and diverse set of cases and examples to illustrate the current operation of partner schools in the United States. Such illustrations demonstrate the potential of partner schools to effect meaningful change in education; they do not, however, provide definitive data on the comparative benefits of partner schools versus other forms of educational intervention. That data must be the subject of another book at another time. What is needed now, and what the following chapters provide, is a record of our current progress in creating and sustaining partner schools, a record that shows the possibilities these schools have for changing the ways we teach and the ways we learn.

References

Boyer, E. L. (1993, March). In search of community. Invited address at the annual meeting of the Association for Supervision and Curriculum Development, Washington, DC.

Dewey, J. (1938). *Education and experience*. New York: Collier Books/MacMillan.

Goodlad, J. I. (1990). *Teachers for our nation's schools*. San Francisco: Jossey-Bass.

Harris, R. C., & Harris, M. F. (1991). Symbiosis on trial in educational renewal. *Researcher, 7*(2), 15–27.

Harris, M. F., & Harris, R. C. (1992). Glasser comes to a rural school. *Educational Leadership, 50*(3), 18–21.

Palmer, P. (1992, June). The courage to teach: Explorations in spirit and practice. Honors and General Education Seminar, presented at Brigham Young University, Provo, UT.

Sergiovanni, T. J. (1993, April). Organizations or communities? Changing the metaphor changes the theory. Invited address at the annual meeting of the American Educational Research Association, Atlanta, GA.

Williams, D.D. (1991, April). Student teachers as naturalistic inquirers. A paper presented at the annual meeting of the American Educational Research Association, Chicago, IL.

Ziegler, A. (1981). *The Writing Workshop* (Vol. 2). New York: Teachers and Writers Collaborative.

Part One

The Goals of Partner Schools

2

Improving Student Learning

Walter H. Kimball, Susan M. Swap, Patricia A. LaRosa, and Thomas S. Howick

Educational renewal is an urgent need. Almost a third of the students in the United States are at risk for school failure, and many other students do not reach their potential for school achievement. We have not fully acknowledged the necessity of helping all students to succeed in school, regardless of race, class, cultural background, facility in English, or special needs. Yet the twenty-first century will place even more demands on our students. Innovative curriculum and instructional practices will be needed to prepare them for the challenges their lives will bring.

Partner schools promote educational renewal through enhancing and enriching students' classroom experience. With today's educational needs, partnership is not a luxury; faculty and students in schools and universities must have each other's expertise and creativity if they are to break through current and future barriers to student learning. The potential of school-university partnerships in educational renewal has been recognized, and student learning, educational renewal, and partnership are now intertwined in the

The authors gratefully acknowledge the following students, whose work and thinking are at the heart of our discussion: Cara Dennison, Narragansett School, Gorham, Maine; the students of Cheryl Madden and Mary Ellen Moon, White Rock School, Gorham, Maine; and the leadership team of administrators, teachers, parents, parent liaisons, and college faculty at the Martin Luther King, Jr. School in Cambridge, Mass.: Dawn Lewis, Lynn Moore, Carol Basile, Paul Russo, Lena James, Beth Carman, Joan Sulis-Kramer, Jeff Winokur, Ellen Davidson, Cassandra Reese, Cathy Hemenway, Marcie Osinski, and Sandra Spooner.

restructuring literature. For example, Lieberman and Miller (1990) include among the building blocks of restructuring both the activities of rethinking curricular and instructional efforts to promote quality for all students and of building partnerships, networks, and alliances to enhance these efforts. The success of a partnership, then, should be gauged by the extent to which examination and assessment reveal that student learning has improved.

As illustrated in Figure 1.1, the goal of improving the students' learning experience must take precedence over other aspects of partnership function, although this focus may become more difficult as the partnership's structure becomes more complex. The means to an effective partnership can easily become ends in themselves. For example, the energy for change in schools may become focused only on improving working conditions for teachers, establishing more collaborative decision-making structures, or creating more flexible schedules, all of which can be means to the end of learning but should not be ends themselves. Administrative practice can change without passing the advantage to the classroom. Partners must focus on student learning, viewing the partnership as a vehicle to be steered toward a goal that is of greater significance than the vehicle itself.

A partnership to improve student learning can and should extend beyond the faculty of the partner school and the college or university. Partnerships between teachers and families, mentor teaching partnerships with volunteers from the business community, or a partnership with staff from a local museum can expand the principle of collaboration to the benefit of all participants. This extended learning community enriches students' explorations and provides important learning opportunities for college and school faculty as well.

In this chapter we will explore five varied examples of ways in which partnerships have implemented special programs to enhance student learning at sites affiliated with the Center for Educational Renewal, directed by John Goodlad. The partners include students, school faculty, parents, university faculty, community members, and preservice teachers. The examples span work in individual classroom, school, and interdistrict settings. One example shows students reflecting directly on the learning experience, supported by college interns. Another example involves a partnership in a ninth-grade science class where a preservice teacher and an experienced teacher collaborated to implement a variety of methods to support student learning. Further examples demonstrate a partnership that asked hard questions about what and how students were learning, leading to a proposal for rethinking science education at school and college levels. A final example explores the nontraditional approaches to assessment that enabled a partnership to more effectively document and enhance student learning.

Preservice Teachers

Preservice teaching internships are common components of partner school operation which contribute substantially to student learning. They furnish preservice teachers with extended classroom participation and allow practicing teachers more time to participate in research and inquiry. Much of the intern's effect on student learning can be discerned through assessments of student work and through observations by cooperating teachers and site coordinators. But the voices of the students add a rich dimension, a dimension which is, after all, one of the most significant if student learning is to be the major focus of partnership activity. When children at one site were asked how they felt about their interns, their responses tended to address three general categories: the individual learning experiences between student and intern teacher, the continuity offered to the class as a group by the intern's presence, and the impact of special projects or units facilitated by the intern.

Many students focused on personal relationships and shared learning experiences:

SCOTT, AGE FIVE: Mr. Adams helped me on the haunted house project. He talks to me. He likes me.
ANDREW, AGE FIVE: Mr. Adams looked at the picture I drew. He liked it because I did a good job.

NATASHA, AGE NINE: Ms. Finch helped me on my autobiog-
raphy. She would let me edit it myself, and if I didn't know what
a word was she would help me sound it out. She gave me clues
to the answers.

EVELYN, AGE SEVEN: Ms. Tang gave me some clues when I was
figuring out a math puzzle. I did figure it out after a while. If she
had told me how to do it, I wouldn't have learned anything.

Primary age students in partner schools frequently recall experiences in which they received personal reinforcement and feedback
from an intern; many describe times in which the intern helped
them with a project without taking control and doing the project
for them. Their voices remind more experienced teachers and
administrators that interns, with their natural enthusiasm and ability to relate to student creativity, can contribute much to meeting
children's needs for reinforcement and individual guidance.

Continuity in the classroom can become a serious problem in
schools that are in the process of renewal when experienced teachers are often asked to leave their classes to participate in supervision, inquiry, and research. In addition, inquiry often generates
instructional and assessment practices that require more individual
student-teacher interactions and less emphasis on whole-group
instruction. Thus more people than the classroom teacher must be
involved in working one-on-one with the students. Again, the children's voices reveal the human dimension of the intern's participation, a dimension at least as significant as scores or performance
assessment.

ETHAN, AGE EIGHT: We always have someone here, and we
don't have to explain how we do things in this room. Ms. Babb
knows what we are working on, so we can go to her if our
teacher is at a meeting or working with other kids.

MIA, AGE TWELVE: Ms. Worthington came to our class before
she became our intern and asked us if we wanted her to work in

our room. We asked her a lot of questions about what kind of teacher she wanted to be and if she would involve us in decision making in our classroom and in what we learn. When she said she would work with us to learn how our classroom works, we said okay. We work well with her because we had a say in her being in here, and we have been happy to have her because she can keep us going better than a substitute. She knows what we expect, and kids don't try to pull stuff on her, so we don't waste time when Ms. Chambers is out. We don't have to do fill-in-time work and can keep going on our projects.

COOPERATING TEACHER: There is a real tension involved in teacher leadership when it takes you out of the classroom on a regular basis. With Becky [an intern], I feel we can plan for my absences in a real team teacher approach, and the kids will feel my absence much less. When planning for an unknown substitute, I always felt as if I was watering down the whole day.

According to students and cooperating teachers alike, the intern who knows the students and the classroom norms and procedures provides the type of continuity that heads off disruption to student learning when the teacher must leave the classroom.

An additional strength that students appreciate in interns is their ability to develop themes, units, or projects for the classrooms. When these special projects or activities are co-planned by intern and cooperating teacher, they tend to be student centered and active, at the same time reflecting current notions of best practice as presented in university methods courses and modeled in renewing schools. Again, the children's voices reflect enthusiasm:

QUENTIN, AGE SEVEN: We're learning nutrition with Ms. Barker. That is healthy eating and what it does for your body. We built a giant food pyramid and did cereal box math. We invented our own cereal. We made our own play about healthy living, and we wrote the play, and we made the costumes. I was a couch potato in the play. Our parents came and watched the play, and we had a healthy snack party after it.

AMY, AGE ELEVEN: Ms. Ketchum handled our environmental studies unit, and it turned out to be a very important unit. We all had different focus groups, and each group presented to the others. That was good, and we got a lot of information, but what was really important was that it got us involved in our town's recycling project. We now have a petition going for curbside pick-up of recyclables, and we are meeting with the town manager.

The voices of students tell us that an intern who is a contributing partner in the classroom has a positive impact on their learning, an impact confirmed by cooperating teachers.

Classroom Teaching Teams

In addition to recognizing the direct impact of the interns and other preservice teachers, experienced teachers also acknowledge the indirect impact of the partnership between the school and university on their own practice and subsequently on their students' learning. Teachers, students, and preservice teachers benefit from the principles and practices presented by university and school faculty when they serve as partners in teacher education courses.

In a ninth-grade science classroom in a rural New England district, for example, Dan, a teacher education intern, was placed for a semester with Bill, an experienced teacher with over twenty-five years' experience in the classroom. Dan and Bill developed a strong personal relationship, with significant mutual respect. Dan admired Bill's diverse and rich experience teaching marine biology in college for over fifteen years in addition to his ten years of high school teaching experience (acquired at two different times in his teaching career). Bill respected Dan's prior work with the U.S. Geological Survey and his practical experience on an oil rig.

The teacher education program in which Dan was a student is organized around a full-service partner school model (Goodlad, 1990), in which a university intern team teaches with a school faculty member on-site for most classes. (One dimension of full-service partner schools is integrating the education of preservice and inservice teachers.) This design allowed Dan the opportunity to put the theory he was learning in college into practice as he worked with Bill and the ninth-grade students. For example, Dan was required to implement learning models he had studied in his teaching strategies course into Bill's science class as part of his course requirement. Dan and Bill's joint work on integrating learning theory and models into the classroom created a positive learning environment for the students. Their integrative work was exemplified in their use of cooperative learning, specifically the expert jigsaw model. Forming cooperative learning groups for a test review, the students took responsibility for the review, and their voices, in addition to the teachers', were heard. At the end of the class, a student who in the past had appeared less interested than others in learning the material complained that he had not had enough time, that he wished the class were longer.

Bill and Dan also reconsidered the ways in which the students in the class were assessed. They found that essay questions asked of the students tended to require more higher-level analysis and comparison than lower-level knowledge-based questions (based on a taxonomy by Bloom et al., 1956), and that essays should be used to complement multiple choice, matching, and fill-in-the-blank questions. As Dan told his university supervisor, "There was very little way to take into account whether someone could write well or not. I saw that change a little bit because [we] got to know the students better. Because they worked in small groups we gave more individual attention to each [student], and I think that they felt a little bit more special." Dan found that, as he had been taught in his methods classes, having students work in cooperative learning groups provides some important benefits: students develop shared responsibility for learning, shared leadership, positive interdependence, and individual accountability (Johnson, 1984). He observed that social skills can be directly taught, as teachers observe and intervene when necessary and students reflect on the effectiveness of the group.

When Dan's supervisor reflected on Dan's experience, he asked Dan if he thought "there was a triad" of the students, Dan, and Bill. Dan said, "Sure. Bill and I worked [well] together. He would start the lecture, and I would ask a pointed question . . . to try to get the kids into it a little more. . . . He would start asking questions of the kids, not rhetorical questions you would normally ask in a lecture, but pointed questions that the kids would have to think about, write down an answer [for], and get into groups to talk about."

Dan summed up his experience and his relationship with Bill by commenting, "I would not say we were peers, but it was pretty close. I think that he respected my enthusiasm, and I respected him obviously for his abilities and knowledge. I think that we were both conscious of each other's abilities. We both worked and played on each other and used each other for the best benefits." Bill confirmed the positive benefits of the experience, remarking, "This was a good example of teaming at its best, where each of us used each other's strengths, and the students were able to see a greater diversity in the class because of this partnership."

Their partnership affected both Dan's and Bill's thinking about teaching and learning. Their productive relationship is an example of how the varied ideas, perspectives, and contributions of the members of a team can positively influence their students' learning environment.

Additional Partners

Teachers in another school-college partnership were concerned about student learning in science. They feared that their science teaching was fragmented and unsystematic and thought that significant turnover in the school's central administration was resulting in a lack of support for their efforts to develop and implement a stronger science curriculum. The school-college steering committee agreed to assess student learning and to poll teachers, families, and students about what they would consider appropriate future directions for the science curriculum.

Working together, committee members generated these questions:

- What is being taught at the school?

- What is the citywide curriculum, and are there priorities for students' learning as defined by the central administration?

- What resources for teaching and learning are currently available in the school, district, and community?

- How are the children doing? What do test scores look like (in the school, in the district, and on national achievement tests)? Who is succeeding? Who is not? What subjects within science reflect more and less student learning? How is our school faring compared to others in the district? What proportion of students pursue science in high school? How many are in the honors classes?

- What do teachers assess as their current strengths in teaching science? Where do they need support?

- What are the families' priorities, hopes, and concerns? Would families be willing to work with the school on improving student learning in science?

- What are the youngsters' priorities, hopes, and concerns?

To answer these questions, teams of college and school faculty interviewed teachers at all grade levels, the director of science in the district, and science specialists assigned to the school. To discover what resources were currently available, school teachers and college faculty conducted a science fair, asking teachers from the school and throughout the district to display the units and experiments they were using. Guests from local museums were also invited to present materials and books. The assistant principal compiled a list of teachers throughout the district who were doing interesting work in science and were willing to have colleagues visit their classrooms. A questionnaire for families and children was sent out, and a subcommittee was formed to probe the implications of test results and other outcome data.

In these ways, the partnership between the college and the school was effective in focusing attention on student learning in science, as the partners' combined energy and resources allowed educators to ask hard questions about overall student performance, unexpected patterns of achievement, and current approaches to teaching.

The combined voices of teachers, administrators, professors, parents, and students revealed many concerns:

- Throughout the elementary grades, most teachers tended to avoid teaching the physical sciences in favor of teaching biology.

- Most teachers had little knowledge about other teachers' goals and methods in teaching science.

- There was no logical sequence of themes and goals across the grades.

- Many teachers had limited access to human and material resources that could enrich the curriculum.

- Differential patterns of student achievement existed between schools and even within schools.

After people's voices had been heard and the findings analyzed, new directions and opportunities emerged, including the following sampling:

- Almost all teachers were committed to improve science teaching across the grades.

- Parents were willing to participate in their children's work in science, either at home or at school, and to share their own experience in science with teachers.

- Teachers were interested in pursuing schoolwide projects in science.

- A school-college task force was created to plan an integrated science curriculum and coordinate with the central administration.

- A collaborative group agreed to explore how to use science content and methods to heighten the access of all students to precollege curriculum; parents agreed to serve on the steering committee and to contribute data and resources.

Multifaceted Collaboration

One partnership district found that poor science preparation was common among its elementary teachers. Many did not feel confident about their understanding of science concepts; thus they were not able to be flexible in their thinking about science or comfortable with questions that took them beyond memorized concepts. Moreover, the partnership investigation found that local college teaching in basic science was often based on rote learning and single-discipline training and that it lacked an articulated vertical structure, moving from beginning to advanced study. Preservice teachers were receiving limited exposure to experiential learning, and there was little or no articulation between science courses and science education courses. When these preservice teachers entered the profession, they tended to perpetuate the same kind of teaching, particularly in the areas of physics and chemistry.

This school-college partnership has undertaken inquiry into

poor science preparation on several different levels. As this chapter is being written, a program is being initiated to redesign undergraduate courses in science, create strong and lasting linkages between science courses and science education courses, and enhance science teaching at the partner school site. Activities at the partner site are being designed to include a range of opportunities to apply and extend science learning for student teachers and experienced teachers as well. For example, undergraduate students enrolled in the course Teaching Science to Children will be given field placements in the partner school, a leadership team of experienced teachers will work with college faculty to develop consistent and integrated approaches to teaching science across the grades, and school faculty will participate with interns and college faculty in inservice activities during the year.

As a result of this plan, professors in astronomy, physics, and education at the college have undertaken new and intensive collaboration, including observation and participation in each other's classes and revision of the syllabi for two required distribution courses in science. Several college faculty will be working collaboratively with teachers in one of the partner schools to develop science workshops and summer seminars for mutual discovery, to make developmentally appropriate classroom applications of science concepts, and to support student teachers in developing new approaches to learning and teaching science. Members of students' families will be invited to share knowledge and/or participate in workshops or seminars to learn to enrich children's learning with approaches consistent with those that are used in the schools.

Data now being collected about the status of children's learning in science will function as a baseline for assessment of changes in student test performance. Performance-based assessment will also be explored as children develop projects, perform experiments, and maintain logs of their investigations.

In this instance, the school-college partnership supports many facets of student learning. All participants are rethinking what it means to understand and "do" science, and youngsters are contributing to their teachers' understanding of scientific phenomena as well as providing feedback on new approaches to teaching. The school-college partnership supports college and school faculty not only in moving beyond traditional approaches to teaching but also in enhancing each other's experience and expertise in teaching and learning science.

Partnership members have agreed on the following goals:

- Participants on all levels will reexamine their understanding of relevant science concepts.

- College and school faculty will reflect on their own processes of learning, looking for parallels to ways in which children learn.

- Partners will examine and analyze pedagogical approaches and strategies appropriate to science in general and to particular topics, including design of an intellectual and social environment that supports classroom inquiry, exploration of new teaching and learning frameworks, assessment of the multiple roles of the teacher, exploration of the nature of science discourse, identification of viable approaches for diverse learners, selection and adaptation of exemplary materials, collaboration with the local museums and arboretum, and experimentation with a variety of assessment strategies.

- Participants will observe in exemplary classrooms.

- Teachers will prepare, implement, and evaluate micro-units with youngsters.

As this partnership project is still in an early stage, it is too soon to document direct benefits to children. But the situation does illustrate how consideration of children's learning can become the focus of collaboration, exploration, and planning. With its varied voices and viewpoints, the partnership provides a much richer and deeper inquiry into children's learning and a more integrated understanding of the scaffolding needed to support the teaching of science than either school or college faculty could have accomplished separately.

An additional concern of this partnership, which functions in an urban area, is the underrepresentation of women and ethnic minorities in fields of higher education that lead to careers in science. Members of the school-college-community partnership are seeking science content that helps children in urban schools to understand and connect to their urban environment; methods to enhance youngsters' logical thinking skills as a foundation for future academic success in mathematics, science, and technology; and ways to generate among families and educators high expectations and concrete support for the academic success of all children in science.

Meaningful Assessment

Accurate and meaningful assessment is an important element of educational reform (Gardner, 1991; Wolf, LeMahieu, & Eresh, 1992). Partnerships have been successful in developing assessment procedures that more directly reflect and influence student learning than many traditional tools. The following partnership assessment experiences have been particularly meaningful because their primary focus has been on student learning, whether the content area is science, writing, or personal interaction in the classroom.

Observation Notebook

One second- and third-grade multi-age classroom teacher uses a weekly observation notebook to extend her view of the children beyond their academic achievement. At least once a week, she and the students together record significant events in the life of the classroom in a journal that includes space for each student. These observations are shared with parents, other teachers, and teacher education interns. The teacher also asks herself a series of reflection questions: Do I know each child's strengths? What will I change, keep, or improve upon? Do children observe the classroom and assess their own progress? Is the environment one in which kids feel safe to take risks and create?

Her voice is represented in the following entries in her observation journal:

> "First three weeks of school, kids getting back into routine. Reminders of doing best when doing work. Kids new to class fit in very well. Did some group activities—good cooperation. Classes set rules for the year. . . . Very excited about making insects and coming up with facts—high activity learning. Raisin math went well—some difficulty with dividing raisins equally. . . . Trip to art museum—good. There was high interest with paintings of impressionists in class. Kids remember info at museums."

> "A. doing better with sharing—still needs to wait her turn. Did cooperate in creative thinking group. . . . Doing much better getting her work done. Always does a good job."

> "C. working on getting things accomplished—works hard on his spelling, writing—got over being frustrated with me— doing nice job! Worked very well in cooperative group."

Student voices are reflected in the next excerpts, which are from two students' observations regarding a quarter just completed:

> "I feel good about this quarter and my reading, math, and my times tables. What I like the most is the graphs and the poetry—my writing is getting better. I get along with all the other kids."

> "I think my writing is a lot better. Making books is also fun to do. I like sharing books, plays, and posters. I think I made a lot of new friends. I like plant observations and graphs."

The weekly observation system has enabled the teacher to get to know her students on a more individual and personal level. She is now able to provide specific examples and quotations at parent conferences, and she has obtained more meaningful data for reporting on student progress (Madden, 1992).

Charts of Goals and Progress

Another teacher and her students became actively involved in assessing progress toward curriculum goals and outcomes as part of their instructional program rather than pausing for spot-check testing or evaluation. The teacher posts the year's curriculum goals in different areas of the classroom. For example, the curriculum chart for writing includes such categories as penmanship, style, and mechanics. The chart is reproduced on individual recording sheets on which students periodically note the activities and goals they are pursuing for those areas. The sheet includes space for students' self-appraisal of their work and for classifying writing according to different styles: for example, a biography titled "My Dad" or a report on jewelry. Self-assessment is a critical step as students construct their portfolios—not only selecting which exhibits to include but also determining what each exhibit shows about their learning (Moon, 1992).

Project Assessment

A teacher of second- and third-grade students and a consultant from the local Audubon Society obtained a school-university partnership site mini-grant to develop a science unit that used studies of habitats to broaden students' understanding of interdependence among the plants and animals in an ecological community. The students' growth in knowledge and understanding during this unit is assessed in terms of projects completed rather than in terms of scores on tests of facts and information. Students develop a brochure about each habitat they investigate. These projects show that students' knowledge has increased, their concepts have developed more sophistication, and their writing has become more expressive. The following contrast shows the differences. In an early brochure on wetlands, the student author describes chickadees with a few very simple sentences: "The chickadee is the State Bird. It gets about five inches long." In a later brochure on backyards and gardens (see Exhibit 2.1), she is more descriptive in writing about the house finch: "They are five or six inches. The male has red on his head and the female does not. The female is brownish. They love sunflower seeds!"

When asked to describe her own work in the wetlands brochure, the student said that the "pictures are just scribbled." The backyard and garden brochure, however, has "longer paragraphs." She remarked, "I guess I wasn't ready for school [when I wrote the first brochure. The second one has] better pictures. This one's more quality!" This student's appraisal of the projects, including her reasons for her judgments, provides evidence of experience and increased maturity in self-assessment.

"Backwards" Assessment

Three schools in a school-university partnership have developed an alternative assessment procedure applying the "planning backwards" model (MacDonald, 1992) across their programs. Personnel at these schools first consider what students should know and be able to do before they restructure curricula, instructional practices, student grouping, schedules, and other aspects of the learning environment to promote these goals. For example, one of these demonstration schools committed to increase the number of students achieving each proficiency level of the National Assessment of Educational Progress (NAEP) in the target areas of reading, writing, mathematics, science, history, civics, and geography. Although the NAEP proficiency levels provide the benchmarks for assessment, juried panels made up of public school teachers, community and business representatives, and members of a university college of arts and sciences and college of education are developing alternatives to the NAEP test items.

A Community

The house finch needs the ant and other insects to live. The ant needs the rhubarb stalk and other plants and insects to eat. The ant needs the soil to make its hill. The rhubarb needs the sun, water, and soil to keep growing. The decomposing plants, like rhubarb, go into the soil to make the soil richer. All the plants and animals in the Backyard and Garden are a part of a community, because they need each other to live.

Rhubarb

People use the stalks to make pies and sauce. It's leaves are poisonous. <u>Our</u> leaves were about two feet wide!

About the Scientist:

Cara Dennison has done all of the habitats with Mrs. Brann. She enjoys learning about animals. Her favorite study was the Backyard/Garden because she likes doing brochures. Cara is 8 1/2 and will be a third grader in the fall. She loves school!

June 1993

House Finch

They are five to six inches. The male has red on his head and the female does not. The female is brownish. They love sunflower seeds!

Exhibit 2.1. Panels from a Student Brochure.
Printed by permission.

Assessment Conference

One school-university partnership provides specific funding for assessment projects and arranges opportunities for the teacher researchers to share their work. Corporations also participate as partners to provide technical assistance and financial support, enabling educators to develop, field-test, and refine assessment processes including demonstrations, real-life problem solving, port-folios, and community-based projects. The partnership hosts an annual conference, Conversations on Assessment, at which school and university teachers gather to share projects.

All these projects represent the array of strategies being developed by school-university partnerships to improve assessment within communities of learners comprised of professional educators, parents, students, and community members. Conferences, mini-grant programs, networks, and consultations are being used to develop opportunities "for students to demonstrate what they know," where "student work is the centerpiece of discussion and decision-making about curriculum, instruction, and assessment" (Southern Maine Partnership Mission Statement, 1994, p.2).

Conclusion

Amid all the debate over education today, one point is not open to question: relegating almost one-third of the nation's children to school failure is not acceptable. Student learning must be renewed. That renewal is the fundamental concern of partner schools. Concern for student learning prompts inquiry into more effective instructional practices; growth in student learning validates the risks and the innovation innate in the school-college partnership. But processes of inquiry and innovation raise many questions.

It is easy to say that the goal of today's educators is to teach all the nation's children successfully. But what does success for all children mean? The goal of some educators is to make all children more successful in the traditional curriculum. Others seek to develop an enriched curriculum, centered in a learning community (see, for example, Pechman, 1992). Sykes, Judge, and Devaney (1992) call for "not a return to dulling drillwork in the basic skills, but rather, a deft blending of instruction in the dominant discourse norms with opportunities for students to create knowledge" (p. 20).

With new concepts and definitions for *teaching, learning,* and *success,* partner schools are developing new approaches and innovative methods for delivery. Input from varied partnership participants has been vital. When preservice interns have been placed in classrooms, students have benefited from receiving individualized attention, such as increased conferencing, and from the interesting and creative projects these new, enthusiastic teachers bring to the classroom. Students have also benefited as the interns have freed regular teachers to participate in a wider variety of professional activities and inservice opportunities, bringing new insights and ideas into their classroom practice. In some partner schools, particularly secondary schools, preservice teachers have been involved to the extent of becoming team teachers in their areas of expertise. Consistent with a rise in cooperation and collaboration in their schools, classroom teachers have allowed the preservice teachers to apply new ideas and innovations and to become members of a teaching team. Results have been striking and positive in such situations. Moreover, partners beyond preservice and inservice teachers have been positively drawn into partner school programs. Parents, business and professional people, community groups, and the students themselves have contributed valuable insights toward developing, implementing, and assessing renewed programs on both elementary and secondary levels. Experiments in such areas as science education and language arts have employed extended partnerships beneficially.

When new programs are initiated to improve student learning, there is always a question whether they are better than earlier programs or just different. Partner school participants have found that assessment of their programs, like the programs themselves, must go beyond traditional methods and concepts. New programs based on new concepts of teaching, learning, and improvement cannot be measured accurately by old assessments based on older concepts and goals. Assessment methods focusing specifically on the goals of innovative programs, including students' evaluation and perceptions of their needs and progress, are being developed at the partner schools by partnership collaborative teams.

If schoolchildren are to be prepared to live effectively in the twenty-first century, they will need stronger educational programs more specifically tailored to their individual needs and to the demands of the society that they will enter. Unquestioningly maintaining traditional curriculum, instruction, and assessment in today's changing schools is pouring old wine into new bottles. The multiple perspectives brought together in a partner school structure have the potential to create a new vintage combining the lessons of the past with new ideas. Exciting results are now becoming apparent.

References

Bloom, B. S. (1956). *Taxonomy of educational objectives, Handbook I: Cognitive domain*. New York: David McKay.

Gardner, H. (1991). Four factors in educational reform. *Journal of Maine Education, 7*(1), 2–3.

Goodlad, J. I. (1990). *Teachers for our nation's schools*. San Francisco: Jossey-Bass.

Johnson, D. W. (1984). *Circles of learning: Cooperation in the classroom*. Alexandria, VA: Association for Supervision and Curriculum Development.

Lieberman, A., & Miller, L. (1990). Restructuring schools: What matters and what works. *Phi Delta Kappan, 71*(10), 759–764.

MacDonald, J. P. (1992). Dilemmas of planning backwards: Rescuing a good idea. *Teachers College Record, 94*(1), 152–169.

Madden, C. (1992, June). *How changing assessment changes teaching*. Panel presentation at "Conversations About Assessment," a conference sponsored by the Southern Maine Partnership, Yarmouth, ME.

Moon, M. E. (1992, June). *How changing assessment changes teaching*. Panel presentation at "Conversations About Assessment," a conference sponsored by the Southern Maine Partnership, Yarmouth, ME.

Pechman, E. (1992). Child as meaning maker: The organizing theme for professional practice schools. In M. Levine (Ed.), *Professional practice schools: Linking teacher education and school reform*. New York: Teachers College Press.

Southern Maine Partnership mission statement. (1994). Gorham, ME: Southern Maine Partnership.

Swap, S. (1993). *Developing home-school partnerships: From concepts to practice.* New York: Teachers College Press.

Sykes, G., Judge, H., & Devaney, K. (1992). *The needs of children and the education of educators.* East Lansing, MI: The Holmes Group.

Wolf, D. P., LeMahieu, P. G., & Eresh, J. (1992). Good measure: Assessment as a tool for educational reform. *Educational Leadership, 49*(8), 8–13.

· ·

3

Strengthening Teacher Education

Michael L. Barnhart, Donna J. Cole, Stevenson T. Hansell, Bonnie K. Mathies, William E. Smith, and Sharon Black

"It's been a tough day! A high school student pulled a knife on one of our student teachers; she panicked, ran out of the room and ran home. When the cooperating teacher returned to the classroom and found out, she was angry. 'What kind of training do you give these kids?' she demanded as she confronted our university group. 'There's a world out there beyond your fancy textbooks and $100,000 grants. If you plan for these kids to teach in it, you're going to need to do more than fill their heads with theories and thrust them into our classrooms!'"

This incident, quoted from the supervising professor's journal, shocked the university college of education, the school faculty, and those community citizens who heard about it. But such encounters are more common than educators like to believe. Preservice teachers enter classrooms able to cite complex definitions of teaching and learning, list innovative methods for teaching subject matter, and explain the advantages and disadvantages of a variety of seating methods. But they may be unable to translate their definitions of *learner* into terms that fit a violent student or to put their methods into practice for a group other than their peers in the college classroom.

A Professional Conversation

Professional literature amply supports this cooperating teacher's charge. Let's review further journal entries in which the supervising professor relates his personal conversation with some of the professional literature. Then we will examine ways in which partner schools are responding to weaknesses he found in traditional methods of teacher preparation.

Journal: March 29

The knife incident still haunts me. Schools need better security measures. They also need better counselors—get those troubled kids in and give them help before they get to the crisis stage. As a teacher educator, I'm used to reaching for books—"professional conversation," I suppose. Perhaps it's just that "misery loves company." Mr. Herbst is strong on school crises:

> All the money school districts lavish on computer workstations, athletic fields, and fancy auditoriums will accomplish little if the classroom teacher fails his or her students. Insofar as we as a people have the will and the power to influence the destinies of our children in our schools, we do it through our teachers. For ill or good, their defects or their strengths and, by implication, the defects and strengths of the education we provide for them, make the decisive difference [Herbst, 1989, p. 196].

But our teachers are carefully trained, I remind Mr. Herbst—and myself. We're lavishing money on well-trained faculty and state of the art equipment in our colleges of education as well as our schools. Another voice from the literature contradicts—this time caustically:

> *As they exist today . . . schools of education are in a weak position to contribute forcefully to the forthcoming challenge of improving quality* [Clifford & Guthrie, 1988, p. 37].

The authors used italics on that one. They mean what they say! But I've devoted my life to improving the quality of education. Is my position really weak?

Journal: April 1

April Fools' Day, and I feel a little like a fool. I spent some time today with my shaky student teacher. We finally got her back in the classroom after the knife incident. She tried teaching some poetry to her students today, but they laughed at her and told her poetry was for "nerds." She didn't know what to say to them; her methods book didn't tell her what to do about nerds.

I couldn't sleep, so I picked up Clifford and Guthrie (1988) again:

> [Much of today's student teaching has consisted of] the expedient placement of students for observation and practice teaching in local public schools whose practices often contradicted the pedagogical and curricular principles being enunciated in the university, and under the daily supervision of teachers often untrained and unrewarded for these duties. Small wonder then, that education students complained that their university courses were "too theoretical" [p. 183].

"Too theoretical"? I wonder if Clifford and Guthrie have been talking to that troublesome cooperating teacher.

Journal: April 5

I'm still troubled over the accusation that my methods classes aren't preparing my students to really teach. As I again searched the literature, the following survey jumped off the page at me.

> According to one disturbing 1987 report, fewer than half of the education students surveyed felt that their program contributed to their development of "academic scholarly and intellectual qualities," and only 57 percent felt it helped them develop skills in critical thinking [Johnston, Spalding, Paden, & Ziffren, 1989, p. 18].

But why? With all the research into teaching and learning that takes place at the university—with the expertise of the university faculty? We as teacher educators think critically—why don't our students?

Journal: April 10

I picked up *Tomorrow's Schools* while I was waiting for the dean this afternoon. My concern for my student teachers keeps eating at me.

> Colleges of education have seldom created connections to schools that encourage the emergence of shared understandings among university and school faculty. Consequently teacher preparation usually lacks both intellectual and organizational articulation between college and school classrooms. Prospective teachers are left alone to integrate knowledge, to puzzle through applications and to resolve contradictions, ambiguities, and tensions [The Holmes Group, 1990, p. 48].

Again why? Integrating knowledge, puzzling with applications, settling contradictions and tensions—all of these are part of the classroom teaching experience. We send our students into classrooms to teach.

> Teacher education has not been organized to encourage the application of principles to practical experience in classrooms; nor to provide the systematic trial teaching followed by critique that is necessary to improve skills; nor to convey the value commitments inherent in the work of teaching. Educators have been unable to reach consensus on a course of study that draws on and integrates the disciplines and practical wisdom possessed by expert teachers [The Holmes Group, 1990, p. 47].

A More Effective Way

Many preservice teachers *are* struggling in their classrooms, a good number of cooperating teachers are disgruntled, and supervising professors at many universities are losing sleep. As the previous professional conversation confirms, today's schools are not as effective as they need to be, and many teachers entering the profession are not adequately prepared. Serious breaches between our preparatory courses and the real world of classroom practice exist; and all of us lose. Surely there must be a more effective way.

To this discouraging professional conversation, contrast the experience of a preservice teacher from an urban middle school in the Midwest.

> From the first day I walked into the classroom, I was considered a teacher by the students. This made it easier to gain their respect and to keep control. The faculty prepared us well for the first day. Not only was I now teaching, but I was learning a great deal about the art of teaching. I was now experiencing things that no textbook could teach. I was gaining a new appreciation for the teachers who continue to give their all each year.
>
> It is hard for me to express the emotions that I felt during this six week period. They ranged from displeasure to great jubilation (many times within the same day and many times towards the same student). Yet through it all, I learned to stay focused on the task at hand. I watched as the kids grew both in confidence and in ability during our short time together. What a wonderful testimony to this program. This experience will surely last me a lifetime.

If this preservice teacher's attitude toward her teaching and her assessment of her learning are more positive than the experiences alluded to in some of the professional literature, perhaps the reason lies in the type of practicum in which she participated. Though not yet the norm for teacher-training programs, the type of project in which she participated is becoming more common as teacher preparation institutions recognize the advantages of working as partners with local public schools.

Teacher preparation in the partner schools varies widely in its details, as school areas vary in location, demography, and student and faculty needs. Yet the project in which the enthusiastic preservice teacher was involved, though designed to meet the needs of the particular district in which it occurred, illustrates many of the advantages that come to preservice teachers, college professors, public school teachers, elementary and secondary students, and their parents when colleges and schools work together in the preparation of teachers for tomorrow's schools.

If we were to walk into the summer school classroom for inner-city first graders in which this preservice teacher has been completing her practicum, we might not be noticed—everyone is busy, and a variety of activities are going on. Children from the lowest 5 percent of their regular classes are involved in intensive literacy instruction, based on a Reading Recovery program (see Clay, 1978, 1991, 1993).

The most experienced teacher is writing a story on large paper with one group of students. She selects students to write specific words, giving them the kind of support that they need. Three other teachers are working with small groups. One teacher works with three boys who are silently reading different books. The boys take turns reading aloud to the teacher, and he makes written notes about their performances. One of the boys acts out, and the teacher asks a visitor to listen to the others read while he takes the offender outside to discuss his behavior. Another teacher is helping three children compose and write sentences in their journals (see Calkins, 1980). The third teacher is reading to a group of about ten students from a "big book." In another corner, a teenager helps a small group of students read and recite nursery rhymes. Minor behavior problems are handled casually, without distracting the other children.

In this particular classroom, there are thirty children, two city teachers, two preservice teachers, and one city high school honors student who is interested in education. The senior teacher, who designed the program, serves in a double leadership role, as the leader of the city teachers and also as an adjunct university faculty member in charge of guiding the preservice teachers through their participation. A university professor has adapted a group of language arts, reading, and teaching skills courses into the program so that the participating high school student and city teachers can receive university credit. This team, and eleven others like it, conduct these literacy sessions daily.

Programs Tailored to Current Needs

Programs like this summer early literacy intervention course have developed in response to needs becoming evident in partnership communities. As school situations no longer resemble those of the 1940s and 1950s, teacher preparation programs that were developed for those earlier schools are not effective for the schools that they service today. No wonder we are finding significant flaws.

Though reformers have long been calling for updated teacher preparation, only recently have they been calling for official linkages between the institutions that train the teachers and the schools in which these teachers are preparing to work. In recent years more deans are realizing that they will benefit as much as school superintendents if they are willing to sit down at the same conference table with those superintendents. Certainly, a profession centered on learning should be able to adopt structures that will encourage all of its members to learn from each other (Joyce, Wolf, & Calhoun, 1993; Smith & Scott, 1990). As John J. Bostingl (1992) points out, the systems involved in education form a continuum so that improvement of any phase depends on the effectiveness of other phases: teacher education will improve only as it interacts with the needs of many stakeholders in the educational enterprise.

When schools and colleges work in partnership, programs like early literacy intervention are succeeding in bringing together the innovative professional knowledge of the university, the grass-roots experience of public school personnel, and the energy and enthusiasm of preservice teachers and prospective future education students in order to meet the needs of children in the community.

Preservice teachers then benefit from the strengths of all these participating groups, including their peers. The integrated classroom experience prepares them realistically for the best (and sometimes the most frustrating) classroom situations that the profession has to offer, while they are supported by the continual availability of mentors from both the school and the university—mentors who enhance rather than struggle against each other's efforts.

Principles Behind Success

All participants in the early literacy program were enthusiastic about its success. Preservice teachers were enthusiastic about the children, the Reading Recovery program, and the mentors under whom they taught. One of them wrote at the conclusion of his participation, "I learned that I can actually make a difference in a child's life through reading." Public school teachers and administrators lauded the dedication, hard work, and personal qualities of the preservice teachers; one principal was heard to remark, "We probably don't give the preservice teachers enough credit. They fit in so well, we consider them part of the staff." Parents praised their children's gains, and a large percentage requested that their children remain with the program throughout the regular school year. When the lead teacher held a parents' tea on the final day of school, all but two children were represented by at least one member of their family—a remarkable turnout for families of an inner-city school. The children themselves benefited from a well-designed program and lots of attention from caring adults. Their reading and writing improved, and they learned to be excited and confident about their reading and writing skills.

A fairy tale? The drama does seem magical as it unfolds on the stage of the classroom. But behind the scenes, it is evident that such success is the result of dedication, cooperation, sacrifice, and hard work. It is also evident that such efforts and results can be generalized to apply to a wide range of needs of a variety of people in circumstances particular to colleges and school districts throughout the United States.

Partner school classrooms also involve a significant shift in traditional roles. College professors, school teachers and administrators, and the preservice teachers themselves must be willing to act in new roles and assume new relationships in four important teacher and student functions: *organizing, supervising, modeling,* and *facilitating.* These four functions warrant further examination.

Organizing

Although teacher education programs have been largely designed, structured, and legislated by university faculty and administrators, the partnership paradigm encourages schoolteachers and principals to propose programs and assume key roles in carrying them through. The early literacy program was initiated by a teacher who had obtained exceptional results in an earlier first-grade summer school program based on Reading Recovery. She had developed her program under the instruction and supervision of a university professor and a central office administrator from the city—together, the three of them had an eight-year history of literacy instruction. The university professor had worked with key teachers over a period of eight years, five of which had been spent teaching the most at-risk first graders he could find in the district. He knew firsthand the effects of the children's hunger, anger, neglect, and abuse—but he had also shared with these children the joy of learning to read. Professor, classroom teacher, and administrator shared goals and purposes, and they trusted each other. Other Reading Recovery teachers joined the effort until eleven early literacy classrooms in five buildings were participating in the project.

The program was designed so that preservice teachers spent five full mornings in the classroom each week: 7:30 A.M. to 11:30 A.M., the same schedule as the participating inservice teachers. In addition, the preservice teachers met at a city school for four afternoons each week for additional instruction and discussion, each session led by one to three instructors. Problem-solving techniques—including matters of classroom management and discipline—along with elaboration and refinement of instructional procedures made up the bulk of these sessions. In addition, each preservice teacher was required to assess at least two students, keep journals on two students, and teach six lessons. Altogether, the preservice teachers had over 100 hours of classroom time, approximately 80 percent of it spent with children, working collaboratively with other adults in creating meaningful learning experiences.

Supervising

Traditionally, preservice teachers have been supervised by university professors, who often have not agreed with the cooperating teacher on the needs of the children in the class, the most effective instructional methodologies for meeting those needs, or the criteria on which the preservice teacher's performance should be evaluated. In the early literacy summer classrooms, because the teacher who had designed the program was on the adjunct faculty at the university, she worked in collaboration with university language arts teachers to be sure that her program filled the criteria for preservice teachers to receive language arts as well as teaching methods credit, and she herself guided the preservice teachers through the program. She also served as leader for the city teachers who participated, and she herself taught alongside all of them in the program.

In these classrooms, "supervision" did not feel like supervision. As one cooperating teacher remarked, "It was a beautiful experience to see . . . personalities work so well together." Two university faculty visited each classroom twice a week. During the first and second weeks of the session, they spent their visit talking with the preservice teachers, but by the third week everyone was so busy that the university faculty found themselves quickly observing or videotaping the preservice teachers' performance for evaluation and discussion in the afternoon sessions, then pitching in and helping with the children. They were delighted to find that all groups—schoolteachers, preservice teachers, and even the children—viewed them as part of a team of problem solvers, not as final authorities or judgmental assessors.

Though a critic might ask if the absence of traditional supervision pressures might result in laziness or noninvolvement on the part of preservice teachers, in these classrooms the opposite appeared to be true. At the conclusion of the experience, the public school teachers were asked to rate the preservice teachers on a scale of 1 to 5, with 5 being highest, on seven criteria common in preservice teaching assessment: attending reliably, supporting primary students, providing assistance to inservice teachers, being knowledgeable about testing procedures, being knowledgeable about teaching procedures, taking responsibility, and helping to solve problems. No rating other than 5 was given to any preservice teacher on any criterion. The feeling of community was so strong in the classrooms that lines of mentoring and supervision blurred until the operation appeared seamless. In fact, late in the program a visiting administrator from another district was embarrassed when he mistook one of the younger partner teachers for a high school student volunteer.

Modeling

Traditionally, cooperating teachers have instructed preservice teachers on how to teach. In the literacy classroom, modeling replaced this instruction. The lead teacher, university supervisors, and inservice teachers did not lecture the preservice teachers but taught beside them. The preservice teachers' comments at the end of their practicum reveal something of the range and depth of what they learned from their partner school models.

> "I will need a lot of traits to be an effective teacher: listening, patience, sense of humor, flexibility, and more."

> "You need to be a teacher not a friend to a student."

"I need to give children more credit for what they know."

"Students can learn if you just work with them."

"Some can be pushed, while others need to be supported."

"I learned that you need to have everything prepared ahead of time. You need to be organized and have some backup projects in case something goes wrong."

"Discipline is the first step of teaching a large group."

When the participating city teachers commented on their experience, it was apparent that modeling worked in two directions. One teacher remarked, "I have learned so much from watching Kristin integrate her ideas and thoughts into our program. Kids know that she cares." Another expressed admiration for a preservice teacher's ability to work personally with the children: "Sam relates to the children and their individual needs well. He is able to find their strengths and interests and build upon them to support their weaknesses. Children are drawn to him."

Facilitating

Traditionally, preservice teachers were instructed didactically: they were considered somewhat blank slates on which their instructors both at the college and at the school marked out the methods and procedures they were to follow—occasionally, these methods and procedures were congruent. In the early literacy classroom, however, college and school personnel took a constructivist approach to preservice teachers' learning: preservice teachers were expected to construct their teaching skills and capabilities by applying their prior knowledge and experiences to the actual teaching-learning situation (this distinction between approaches is made by Winitzky, Stoddart, & O'Keefe, 1992, p. 6). They were to learn to teach through active involvement in the processes of teaching.

During the six weeks that the preservice teachers participated in the literacy program, they experienced the full cycle of the school year: the chaos of the first day, the initial instruction in classroom rules and procedures, the development of student-teacher relationships, and the record-keeping and clean-up at the end of the session. They were treated as responsible for student learning and discipline, and they accepted that responsibility. The lead teacher, university professors, and city teachers viewed themselves not as dispensers but as facilitators of the learning experiences. Sometimes stepping back into a facilitator's role required courage: for example, the more experienced teachers and administrators were shocked by some preservice teachers' naïveté about multicultural characteristics and concerns.

Holding one's experienced tongue can be difficult. As one university participant recalled, "We felt the frustration of not being able to communicate our understanding of teaching in specific situations, and we felt the joy of seeing the preservice and inservice teachers as well as the primary students construct their own insights into teaching and learning." One preservice teacher confirmed this insight with a statement that was heard a number of times in several variations among her peers: "I now know that I can't expect anyone to tell me how to teach. I have to make my own decisions using my own best judgment at that moment."

Principles Further Applied

Though the early literacy program included many situational components that cannot be easily generalized to a variety of teacher preparation programs, the four program aspects of supervising, modeling, and facilitating do seem to be common to all successful partnership efforts and further general principles can be deduced in each of these areas.

Organizing

Organizing teacher preparation in partnership programs involves an outlook and processes different from those that guide the organization of traditional programs. In order for theory and practice to be effectively merged, individuals with an in-depth, specialized knowledge of theory and individuals with a broad-based, highly developed, and sometimes highly intuitive understanding of practice must merge their strengths and contributions. In a society characterized by mounting problems with broken families, substance abuse, communicable diseases, international unrest, and continual violence in homes, schools, and communities, teachers must be prepared to deal with these problems as they affect children in the classroom. Today's teachers must be equipped with an array of thinking and problem-solving skills greater than those of any past generation of teachers. Neither today's university professors with their knowledge of principles and patterns nor today's teachers with their experience in daily crises have the entire picture. When preservice programs can merge these two areas of knowledge, they can come closer to preparing young teachers to meet students' myriad needs.

In a school-university partnership structure, school and university personnel are equal participants—open communication and shared decision making are stressed. For example, on the governing board of a partnership consisting of one university and five school districts, the dean of the college of education has one vote—equal to the one vote of each district superintendent. Decisions are made on the basis of six equal voices. In a partnership, teacher preparation programs not are "owned" by either the college or the school district. For example, a task force designing a program for preparing school principals must include professors of educational administration *and* seasoned, experienced principals with years of experience administering public schools. Partners share resources, expertise, and commitment, with agreements that extend over a substantial period of time.

As they did in the literacy classroom, proposals for generating, adapting, or strengthening teacher preparation programs can come from teachers in the schools as well as from professors at the university. In one partnership, an entirely new method of collaborative mentoring was initiated when a cooperating teacher drew attention to the fact that her preservice teacher was having to rewrite lesson plans in order to submit them to both the university and the school because different formats were required and different—and not necessarily complementary—aspects of teaching were being evaluated by the cooperating teacher and the professor. When the teacher brought this problem to the attention of the partnership, meetings were held, and partner school instruction and evaluation models were created, containing elements from both school and university perspectives. Jointly, school and university personnel created the Partner School Lesson Plan, which preservice teachers could use in designing their lessons, and an evaluation form to be used by all who were to observe and critique preservice teachers' work (Harris, 1991). In this case, a need was identified and dialogue initiated by the teacher, and both school and university personnel worked together to form effective solutions.

When public school teachers are encouraged to voice their concerns and initiate partnership investigations and projects, their initiative and self-esteem are enhanced, along with their participation. A study comparing teachers' perceptions of themselves and their work in a partner and a nonpartner school found that teachers' feelings of efficacy and self-confidence were greater when they were teaching in a partner school (Lofgreen, 1988). A teacher from a partner school expressed her sense of efficacy when she said, "Because of the partnership I feel I can say what I think is needed, and it will be regarded as valuable" (Harris & Harris, 1992, p. 578).

At other times, university faculty may begin the work of change. Another partnership undertaking was initiated by faculty in a college of education and human services who felt that their teacher preparation program needed closer articulation with the schools in which preservice teachers were receiving their practicum experience. These professors chose a local school that was large enough for all members of a teacher preparation class to practice teach at the same time if some of them doubled up two to a class. Arrangements were then made to hold the teacher preparation class on-site at the school; this made it more practical for some school faculty members and administrators to be guest lecturers for the college students, and it raised the level of preservice teacher involvement in the classes. Although the schoolteachers had to share their parking lot, and some adjustments had to be made in the use of the lunchroom, the experiment was successful, as reflected in the attitudes, skills, interpersonal relationships, and even test scores of the preservice teachers. As these examples suggest, when partner schools function as training areas for preservice teachers, ideas and initiatives *should* and *must* come from all partnership participants.

Supervising

Supervision of preservice teachers has long been a sensitive area of teacher preparation. Preservice teachers have complained that their college courses have not adequately prepared them for the challenges of the classroom (Clifford & Guthrie, 1988; Johnston, Spalding, Paden, & Ziffren, 1989; The Holmes Group, 1990) and that supervising professors fail to provide the systematic feedback preservice teachers need in order to improve their classroom skills (The Holmes Group, 1990). Professors also find the situation trying, as clinical supervision is regarded as a "low status task" (Clark, 1988, p. 7), obviously labor intensive, yet not recognized professionally for what it is—"the most important and challenging task of professional education: creating the effective and influential teacher" (Clifford & Guthrie, 1988, p. 325). Many supervising professors feel that the creating and influencing they do are unrecognized and unappreciated. Cooperating teachers have added their objections to student teaching supervision, claiming that too much time is required to train preservice teachers to the proficiency level at which they can actually make a contribution to the class. "It seems nice at the end when they're leaving and they're conducting your class, but an awful lot goes into getting to that point " (Johnson, 1990, p. 176). Teachers blame "poorly structured relationships between their schools and sponsoring colleges and . . . disorderly processes of assignment and supervision" (Johnson, 1990, p. 178) for the difficulties they experience.

In designing more effective forms of preservice teacher preparation and supervision, school-university partnerships must begin with those poorly structured relationships. Since preservice teachers have affirmed that they profit most from supervision when supervisors combine expertise in subject matter with proficiency in pedagogy (Moore, 1994), partner school participants now realize that their equal sharing of resources and responsibilities must be applied to preservice teacher supervision: professors contribute their expertise in subject matter; practicing teachers contribute their proficiency in pedagogy. Some partnerships have adopted the term *triangulation* to describe the mentoring that occurs in their supervisory programs. Use of this term, which indicates multiple measures or views, reflects the belief that more valid evaluation or feedback can be accomplished when observation occurs from multiple perspectives (Mathison, 1988).

But equal contributions do not ensure an effective blend. And multiple views can be incompatible, particularly if one of them is distant or uninvolved. Studies have shown that preservice teachers are strongly influenced by their cooperating teachers, who are right in the classrooms beside them, but not significantly affected by their college supervisors, who seem more distant and less personally involved with the classroom situation (Moore, 1994). Similarly, one partnership has found that triangulation mentoring is most effective when the triangle is equilateral—the preservice teacher, cooperating teacher, and supervising professor are equal participants in the processes of supervision and evaluation. In many of the schools in this partnership, to achieve this equality the professor goes into the classroom and teaches alongside the preservice and cooperating teachers. Three roles are designated for such observation sessions: the *teacher*, who presents the lesson; the *mentor*, who points out things that went well during the lesson; and the *evaluator*, who looks for things about the lesson that could be improved. The three partnership teachers take turns functioning in each of the roles. This means that the professor must sharpen his or her pedagogical skills and display them in front of the other two. Sometimes the preservice teacher will be the mentor, looking for strengths in the professor's teaching, and at other times the preservice teacher will be the evaluator, pointing out ways in which the professor could improve. Similarly, the preservice teacher has opportunities to act as both mentor and evaluator to the cooperating teacher. In conferences after each observation session, the three teachers frankly and openly discuss what went on in the classroom. One preservice teacher described this meeting, saying, "I was nervous at first about evaluating my university supervisor. But when we met later, he was really responsive to the suggestions I gave him. . . . Having to evaluate made me pay more attention to what was going on too, since I was looking for things and taking notes. Then when I took my turn presenting, I wasn't as nervous. . . . The feedback I got was very specific" (Harris, 1991, p. 65).

In other schools in the same partnership, a peer component has been added to the triangulation. Classroom schedules are arranged so that each observation-supervision team includes at least one other preservice teacher assigned to the school. When this model is used, preservice teachers report that watching their peers gives them new ideas for methods and management as well as greater awareness of the strengths and weaknesses in their own teaching. They also report that the feedback they receive from the peers who observe them is often more relevant than the feedback from the more experienced cooperating teacher and university professor because peers are struggling with some of the same needs, anxieties, and challenges that they are; preservice teachers also indicate that the responses of their peers carry high credibility as they work on improving their classroom techniques (Moore, 1994).

Modeling

Supervision in partner schools often blends into modeling. Although the prevalent pattern outside partner schools is for university people to supervise and school people to model, the triangulation approach involves *all* participants in modeling as well as analyzing performance. Because modeling and analyzing are planned collaboratively by university and school personnel, the cooperating teacher does not have to worry whether appropriate criteria will be used in judging her preservice teacher (who may be using the cooperating teacher's own favorite methods), and the professor does not have to worry whether the preservice teacher will be observing and imitating a model whose teaching methods are opposite to those he has been attempting to teach to the neophyte.

In one partner school, modeling begins before the preservice teachers enter the classroom. For the two weeks prior to the student-teaching practicum, school personnel in cooperation with the college supervisor conduct intensive training sessions for the preservice teachers. During these sessions, the college coordinator and the teachers from the school present formal lessons and simulations on the pedagogy associated with math, science, reading, and spelling. Preservice teachers are then taken to classrooms where they watch demonstrations on which they reflect before they write a structured analysis. Finally, the college supervisor meets with the preservice teachers to further reflect on and discuss what they have observed and learned. The preservice teachers observe many classrooms during the two-week preparation period, and they are allowed some choice of the cooperating teacher with whom they will be placed. Under this program, when they enter the classrooms, these preservice teachers are familiar with the curriculum and vocabulary used in the school, they have a repertoire of ideas from the modeling they have seen, and they know a little about the teacher and the children with whom they will be participating—they are ready to teach (Green & Harris, 1990).

Effective modeling enables preservice teachers to take over classrooms sooner, which, in turn, provides opportunities for even more effective modeling to take place. In a study conducted in a rural partner school, preservice teachers put in a total of 14,131 hours during one semester, with 5,172 of those hours being teaching time

(Green & Harris, 1990). During those thousands of hours, the class-room teachers were able to upgrade their own knowledge and skills by attending partnership inservice sessions, visiting schools in which exemplary and innovative programs were taking place, participating in research projects with university professors and graduate students, reading professional literature, and spending time with special needs students who required individual help. Returning to their classrooms, these teachers were able to model exciting new programs and skills for their preservice teachers as well as other teachers throughout their schools.

When preservice teachers and cooperating teachers work well together, modeling can work in both directions. Interviewing cooperating teachers, Moore (1994) found that they described using ideas and plans that they had seen their preservice teachers use: one teacher described the combination of "youth and ideas" as being valuable to practicing teachers; another brought out that preservice teachers have current materials not available to the practicing teachers during their college years. An experienced partner school teacher discussing a particular intern with a university supervisor said, "[I have] been more spontaneous with ideas she has brought from the university. I have tried more reading and writing workshop ideas than ever before. . . . I'm not sure I could have said this before [our school became] a partner school, but maybe there is hope in bringing about change in education through collaboration" (Harris & Harris, 1992, p. 578).

Facilitating

In partner schools, the constructivist approach is applied to preservice teacher education in ways unique in teacher education programs. Preservice teachers, cooperating teachers, and university faculty are all in a continual process of constructing more and more advanced and effective knowledge and practice.

Because knowledge and skills are constructed from the raw materials of each individual's experience, the more varied the experiences, the richer and more advanced the potential products. For this reason, some partner schools have adopted models whereby each preservice teacher is mentored by several experienced teachers. These teachers share the responsibility for observing and giving feedback to the trainee; they invite her or him to visit many different classrooms; and each provides formal or informal training sessions in her or his particular area of expertise (Green & Harris, 1990).

In addition, to eliminate the inconsistencies in preservice teachers' building materials that might make construction frustrating and difficult, professors involved with some partner schools are consulting cooperating teachers on content as they design their methods courses. As one university coordinator remarked: "It makes sense to adjust the requirements of my classes after seeing my students at work in a real classroom. In fact, I now ask cooperating teachers to review my lesson plans. It is this constant interchange which gives partnership activities continual renewal" (Green & Harris, 1990, p. 14). To further refine the fit between preservice teachers' experiences in their college courses and their public school classrooms, the partnership in which this professor participates holds frequent "linking workshops," in which college personnel and teachers and administrators from the partnership's five participating school districts meet together in presentation sessions and discussion groups to share and compare their experiences in mentoring preservice teachers as part of their work to upgrade education in the schools.

This effort to pull educational resources together, so that each preservice teacher has a broad base of mentor knowledge and experience from which to select materials to construct his or her own teaching, is one of the most significant strengths of the partner school. However, those who structure and administer teacher preparation programs realize that not every preservice teacher will use the available materials in the same way. Each prospective educator will approach the construction effort with a different background, different strengths, and different needs. Because differences between an individual's circumstances and the traditional structure of preservice programs can prevent some who have outstanding teaching potential from entering the profession, some partnerships are offering alternative preservice programs.

One alternative program that has proved beneficial not only to preservice teachers but also to cooperating teachers and partnership administrators is a one-year internship offered to strong teaching candidates who need financial support during their practicum period. Rather than student teaching without financial compensation, some prospective teachers who have demonstrated competence during earlier practicum participation teach their own classes for the full school year, receiving half of a starting teacher's salary and full benefits. The administrators have a capable teacher at half cost, and the intern receives a salary for completing the university's student teaching requirement.

Other alternative preservice programs have been designed for individuals who want to teach but have already graduated from a university in a field other than education. Some make the decision that they want to teach relatively soon after their graduation; others work for many years in another field before making a decision to change careers. To prepare such individuals to teach in classrooms without requiring that they return to college for several years, a fifth-year program has been adopted by some school-university partnerships. Under these programs, students who have a four-year degree in another academic discipline attend a series of classes to develop pedagogical knowledge and skills while they participate in intensive practicum work. Most of the courses are taught on-site at the partner schools, so these preservice teachers are constantly observing classrooms and applying theory as they learn it. The coordinator of the fifth-year program at one partnership keeps in close contact with his graduates and reports that the retention and success rates for these teachers are unusually high.

Conclusion

So much of today's educational reform seems to center in administrative procedures and children's varied needs. Herbst (1989, p. 190) reminds us of another dimension: "The forgotten person . . . in the onward march of professionalization in American public education has been the American . . . school teacher. Though in the past, administrators and teacher educators purported to speak for her, she came to realize through bitter experience that if she were ever to be recognized as more than a temporary employee in a large bureaucratic system, she would have to rely on her own resources to assert her professional competence."

Have American teachers been forgotten? Are they swallowed up in a system in which they receive no recognition or power? Do teacher educators and administrators really make bland promises that will ultimately do nothing to increase teachers' ability to make the contributions to tomorrow's citizens they have the desire and ability to make? Teacher educators and public school administrators and teachers who collaborate through school-university partnerships respond to such questions with a firm, "No! Not in our colleges! Not in our districts!" Preparation and empowerment of teachers are among the top priorities in partnership work.

Preservice teachers in the early literacy program are being prepared to teach by teaching—alongside their lead teacher, their university supervisors, experienced literacy teachers from the city schools, and younger volunteers. One preservice teacher who comes from a middle-class, mainstream family has long had a nagging fear that she will not know what to do for an at-risk child whose background and challenges she has not experienced herself. Today, six-year-old Amanda arrives at school with bruises on her arm and terror in her eyes. She cannot remember the letters and sounds she used so easily yesterday. The young preservice teacher holds Amanda in her arms and invites her to choose a story she would like to hear instead of reading today. The act of compassion is spontaneous; one of the city teachers cuddled and read to frightened J. J. several days ago.

In a nearby city, a preservice teacher is completing his first teacher preparation class at the school that is collaborating with his college in holding preservice coursework on-site. Today as the school principal took his turn teaching the college students, he explained how important extracurricular activities can be in building the self-esteem of children who receive little attention or encouragement at home. There are enough fifth- and sixth-grade boys who love soccer to form a city league team from the school; Jason and Ben, whose parents are in the process of getting a divorce, would be two of the strongest players. The preservice teacher goes to the principal's office to volunteer to coach a team.

In a partner school in another area of the country, a young preservice teacher giggles with slightly nervous anticipation as she watches her university supervisor teaching a math lesson to third graders. She can see how absorbed the children are with the new materials he is using and plans to make available to her. But she also notices that three young boys in the back are not listening and may be plotting a little mischief. The supervisor asked for her feedback and suggestions when he joined her cooperating teacher and her in the classroom. All are teaching, and each is supporting the others and making suggestions. She may have a suggestion that will help the supervisor with the boys; her cooperating teacher showed her a little "trick" about a week ago.

At another partner school in the same district, a preservice teacher is participating on an observation-evaluation team with the cooperating teacher and the college supervisor of Jennifer, one of his peers. Some of the fifth-grade girls are refusing to cooperate in an activity; they are saying loudly that it is "stupid," and Jennifer cannot get them to quiet down and participate. A similar student insurrection happened in his sixth-grade class last week. With a little shock, he realizes that he is not the only one who sometimes has this kind of problem. Jennifer is trying to meet the children's challenge head-on, as he did. Now, as an outsider, he can see why this approach did not work.

At another partner school, a middle-aged preservice teacher observes a classroom in which a master teacher is reading and writing poetry with fourth graders. This nontraditional university student has found that his career in small business is not meeting his personal and family needs; feeling that teaching will be more meaningful to him personally, as well as allowing him to spend more time with his children, he has enrolled in a fifth-year intensive certification program. He never thought much about poetry before his professor explained some of the ways it can contribute to language skills as well as the self-esteem of children and adolescents. He is excited about teaching poetry when he will have his own class—he might try some of these ideas now with his sensitive but troubled twelve-year-old daughter. Near him sits a young woman who graduated just two years ago with a degree in humanities. She always wanted to work with children, but her love of the arts and desire to study them in depth won out when she selected her college major. She is excited to realize that when she receives her teaching certification she will be able to share her knowledge and enthusiasm for poetry with the children she loves.

Because these preservice teachers have been prepared by both universities and public schools, when they enter their own classrooms they will be prepared to be effective. They will have shared the knowledge and experience of professors and teachers whom they admire—professors and teachers who consider and treat each other as members of a team and who welcome preservice teachers into the team as well. From this shared knowledge and experience, these beginners are constructing their own ideas, theories, and practices. As they try out their exciting new constructs, they receive support, suggestions, and occasionally consolation. As new teachers, in several months' time, they will be prepared to handle a crisis, meet a need, or share a joy because they have participated in handling crises, meeting needs, and sharing joys with their mentors beside them.

Partner schools do not have all the answers to the pessimism apparent in some of the professional literature. Children will still have difficulty learning—so will college students, professors, and even schoolteachers. But partnerships have found some answers, and they are actively seeking others. Neither universities nor public schools alone have been adequate in preparing teachers to meet the needs of society's children. Together, we have a better chance.

References

Bostingl, J. J. (1992). *Schools of quality.* Alexandria, VA: Association for Supervision and Curriculum Development.

Calkins, L. M. (1980). Research update: Children learn the writer's craft. *Language Arts, 57*(2), 207–213.

Clark, C. M. (1988, March). Asking the right questions about teacher preparation: Contributions of research on teacher thinking. *Educational Researcher, 17*(2), 5–12.

Clay, M. (1978). *The early detection of reading difficulties.* Portsmouth, NH: Heinemann.

Clay, M. (1991). *Becoming literate: The construction of inner control.* Portsmouth, NH: Heinemann.

Clay, M. (1993). *An observation survey of early literacy achievement.* Portsmouth, NH: Heinemann.

Clifford, G. J., & Guthrie, J. W. (1988). *Ed school: A brief for professional education.* Chicago: University of Chicago Press.

Green, E. E., & Harris, R. C. (1990, January/February). Creating long-term collaboration: The BYU/Public School Partnership experience. *Tech Trends, 35*(1), 12–16.

Harris, R. C. (1991, Summer). Educational renewal: Not by remote control— Work of a university professor in a partner school. *Metropolitan Universities, 2*(1), 61–71.

Harris, R. C., & Harris, M. F. (1992, April). Preparing teachers for literacy education: University/school collaboration. *Journal of Reading, 35*(7), 572–579.

Herbst, J. (1989). *And sadly teach.* Madison, WI: University of Wisconsin Press.

The Holmes Group. (1990). *Tomorrow's schools: Principles for the design of professional development schools.* East Lansing, MI: The Holmes Group.

Johnson, S. M. (1990). *Teachers at work: Achieving success in our schools.* New York: Basic Books.

Johnston, J. S., Spalding, J. R., Paden, R., & Ziffren, A. (1989). *Those who can.* Washington, DC: Association of American Colleges.

Joyce, B., Wolf, J., & Calhoun, E. (1993). *Self-renewing schools.* Alexandria, VA: Association for Supervision and Curriculum Development.

Lofgreen, K. B. (1988), *Teacher efficacy in a partner school.* Unpublished doctoral dissertation, Brigham Young University, Provo, UT.

Mathison, S. (1988, March). Why triangulate. *Educational Researcher, 17*(2), 13–17.

Moore, B. (1994, February). Inservicing through the back door: The impact of the student teacher upon the cooperating teacher. Paper presented at the Association of Teacher Educators, Atlanta, GA.

Smith, S. C., & Scott, J. J. (1990). *The collaborative school.* Eugene, OR: ERIC Clearinghouse on Educational Management, University of Oregon; Reston, VA: National Association of Secondary School Principals.

Winitzky, N., Stoddart, T., & O'Keefe, P. (1992, January/February). Great expectations: Emergent professional development schools. *Journal of Teacher Education, 43*(1), 3–18.

4

Promoting Professional Development

Robert A. Pines, Lourdes Z. Mitchel, and Nicholas Michelli

The building was not remarkable. With its low silhouette and absence of windows, it seemed just another of the commercial and industrial buildings that dotted a cityscape still recovering from civil disturbances of twenty years before. It did not even *look* like a school. Like the building itself, the members of the student body, largely African-American and Latino, were victims of the urban density and diversity, the prevalence of crime, and the family dislocation that characterized the area. These sixth-, seventh-, and eighth-grade students reflected in their conduct and attitudes the loss of identity, sense of powerlessness, and lack of personal control faced by the adults in their neighborhood. It hardly seemed a setting at which teachers from newer, better equipped schools, in more pleasant and optimistic neighborhoods, could come to upgrade their knowledge and skills. "Renewal in public education?" Surely not here.

This chapter presents an example of an inner-city partner school that became a center for teachers' professional development. We look first at the program through the eyes of planners and participants and then at the principles that can be drawn from it. Over a number of years, hundreds of teachers from surrounding school districts have approached this modest building, some eager, some skeptical, some hesitant. This chapter follows a typical teacher and her companions through their professional development experience at this site. Thoughts, motivations, perspectives, and reflections of a variety of participants are revealed, along with changes that occurred in their thinking during the process of participation. The second half of the chapter discusses and expands on principles that underlie these experiences and perceptions.

Participants

Many people are involved in a successful professional development program. Each participant brings to the experience a unique point of view and each gains from the experience according to personal need.

Marilyn Bey, Visiting Teacher

Marilyn Bey, a middle school teacher of English and reading with more than twenty years' experience capped by an award as district-wide "Teacher of the Year," was not optimistic about what she might learn in the five weeks she was to participate as a "visiting teacher" in this "partner school experience." Her colleague, Yvonne Richardson, also an experienced English teacher, had been similarly skeptical when the two of them had been invited to join two mathematics teachers from their school as part of a fourth and final group of teachers to complete this professional development cycle this year; fifteen additional mathematics and reading teachers from five other middle schools would be joining them.

Driving into the partner school parking lot with Yvonne beside her, Marilyn reflected on the wisdom of consenting to this "experience." When her school principal, Rosalyn Greer, had suggested that she participate, Marilyn had been surprised. Her experience and her honors, she thought, should attest to the fact that she was one of the teachers in her school who least needed professional development. Should she really leave her students for five weeks in the hands of an "exchange teacher" (a teacher originally from the partner school), especially now when they were preparing for the newly mandated state testing? She had worked so hard to bring their problem-solving skills to the level where they could represent them-

selves well. Her school was in a more homogeneous, higher socioeconomic area of the city. Could the exchange teacher relate to her
students' backgrounds and their needs? Her concern had faded
somewhat when the exchange teacher had arrived in time to spend
a full week consulting with her and observing her with her students
before assuming responsibility for her class. At least he would continue with what she had been trying to achieve.

Marilyn had to be honest with herself. Much of the problem did
not lie with the exchange teacher or with her students. Much of it
was caused by her own negative feelings about what was optimisti-
cally called "professional development." As a novice teacher in the
mid-1960s, she had been subjected to "inservice education"—
sporadic, one-shot sessions in which outside experts had lectured on
issues more frequently dictated by fashion than by individual or institutional need. Teachers were expected to adopt the new methods
with no opportunity for prior observation or involvement, and with
very little supervision or assistance. Marilyn had been frustrated. In
the 1970s, "staff development" had managed to link the suggested
and mandated changes to schoolwide programmatic goals, but teachers were still expected to passively *accept* and *do*. Marilyn and
Yvonne often winced over the time and energy they had invested in
"individualizing instruction around behavioral objectives"—when
that methodology had been mandated schoolwide and then discontinued as "unworkable" after only one academic year.

Rosalyn Greer, Principal

Principal Rosalyn Greer was excited over the opportunity to have
four of her teachers participate in the partner school experience.
She herself had attended a half-day orientation session, which had
introduced her to the objectives and procedures of the partner
school experience and explained her role in helping her participating teachers create personal action plans. She knew that her teachers would be observing exemplary classroom programs, attending
presentations and demonstrations, participating in discussions and

seminars, and ultimately practicing in hands-on teaching clinics. During these clinics they would learn and practice new strategies in settings where they would join other highly skilled and experienced teachers, giving, receiving, and responding to valid feedback. She had selected Marilyn Bey and Yvonne Richardson, her strongest teachers from the English Department, and Ken Amos and Jana Biggs, two of her most innovative mathematics instructors. She knew they would benefit personally from the experience, represent their school well, and provide strong role models for the rest of the faculty when they implemented change in their own classrooms upon their return.

Rosalyn also looked forward to her own participation in the follow-up seminars for principals held at the midpoint of the five-week cycle and at its conclusion. The first seminar would focus on leadership strategies, which would be valuable to her as she worked with her faculty, individually and in groups, to reflect on their teaching and complete plans for renewal in their classrooms. The final seminar would provide an opportunity for her to meet individually with Marilyn, Yvonne, Jana, and Ken to develop their follow-up action plans for implementing some of the classroom methods and techniques they would have learned. She was glad that an "instructional clinician" from the partner school would also work with the teachers in implementing their plans.

Mike Benston, Partner School Resident Teacher

Mike Benston, a language arts teacher on one of the seventh-grade interdisciplinary teams at the inner-city partner school, looked forward to meeting each new group of visiting teachers for whom he was to serve as liaison for the partnership experience. He had been particularly impressed with Marilyn Bey, a teacher who shared his subject matter and many of his professional goals. Because his schedule was arranged so he taught only in the mornings, he had been able to spend most of five afternoons with Marilyn, acquainting her with the specifics of the program. She had seemed especially interested when he had mentioned the obligatory sessions on understanding adolescents and teaching for critical thinking; she had lately been emphasizing critical thinking among her own students and appeared to have goals very compatible with partner school priorities. Mike had worked with Marilyn and her principal, Rosalyn Greer, to structure a "personal action plan," a personal blueprint for Marilyn, based on her own desires for professional growth. He had noticed that Marilyn and two others from her school had chosen the series of sessions on stress reduction as part of their optional activities. The stress sessions were usually among the most popular for urban teachers, regardless of the area of the city in which they taught.

Mike had sensed in Marilyn and Yvonne a slight skepticism toward professional development programs, although they had both seemed compatible with the values and objectives underlying the program. Perhaps they, like many, had chafed under the pressures of "teacher development" and "school renewal" programs that had been imposed on teachers prior to the formation of the partnership between the school and the university. Such programs had minimized the feelings, initiative, and involvement of the teachers, and Mike did not blame teachers for disliking them. He had tried to stress to the incoming teachers that the partnership was emphasizing the empowerment of classroom teachers, soliciting their input, and respecting their suggestions. Although a nearby state university was one of the participating partners, teachers were the heart of the operation. Teachers were respected by the university professors and administrators, not condescended to or looked down upon. Both the university and the public school contingent, Mike had explained, agreed that teachers are the key to school renewal. When teachers learn and practice exemplary techniques, schools become exemplary places to learn. And of course the strengthening becomes cyclical: when schools become exemplary settings, teachers are better able to develop and practice additional skills.

Perceiving Marilyn's concern for developing students' critical thinking, Mike had also explained the partnership's position on reflection for teachers themselves. Teachers were not expected to accept new ideas passively; they would be encouraged to engage in reflective inquiry—to critically analyze what they observed and what they in turn would practice together with their mentors and their colleagues. Marilyn and her friends had seemed to accept his assurances; he hoped they would respond positively to the partner school participation.

The Partner School Community

Entering the community room at the partner school for their first orientation session, Marilyn and Yvonne discovered that the shabby dullness of the partner school building was only on the exterior. Inside, the partner school was immaculate and inviting. The walls of the orientation area were covered with intriguing pictures and bright, colorful posters. Large plants and a variety of flowers gave an added warmth to the large assembly room. Behind the podium a prominent banner declared, "Everyone teaches, everyone learns." Marilyn and Yvonne selected bagels and drinks, joined Jana and Ken, then turned to look at the assembled participants. The nineteen visiting teachers they had expected were all present, and Marilyn knew some of them personally. But there were a lot of others in the room—almost twice as many as Marilyn had expected. She recognized some of the professors and administrators from the state university where she had completed her master's degree several years before. Some officers from her teachers' union were also scattered throughout the group. Her attention was drawn to the podium as a speaker explained that many parents of the students and other members of the community had been invited to join them as part of the "partner school community." Professors seemed to be in personal conversation with groups of individuals whose ethnic diversity suggested that they might well include parents as well as minority teachers. A union vice president was speaking with a university administrator. As the keynote speaker began, Marilyn recognized him from pictures in the union newsletter as Dr. Robert

Cordoza, principal of the partner school. Marilyn began to feel that she was part of a larger unit of concerned individuals. Community? Yes, that was it: a feeling of community.

Robert Cordoza, Partner School Principal

> We are striving to become an exemplary middle school. We want to better understand our adolescent students and their cultural differences. We want to explore not only the ways in which they learn, but also more authentic procedures for evaluating what they have learned. We want to refine the interdisciplinary dimensions of our curriculum; we want to improve our teacher-based guidance process, and we need to learn how to better collaborate with parents and take advantage of the resources for learning which exist in our community. In all of these efforts, we look to you, our visiting teachers, to help us.

There—he had said it. In the first minute of his speech, Robert Cordoza had laid out some of the main themes he hoped to develop through the partner school experience, and he had appealed for the input and cooperation of all members of the partner school community. He noticed surprise on a few faces, bewilderment on a few, approbation on many. Teachers new to partnership work were not accustomed to being asked for their input; parents, particularly minority parents, were used to being told—not asked—by teachers and administrators what would be best for their children. It was important to help them all realize the focus areas of the partnership, areas dear to him personally: the professional development of inservice teachers, the training of preservice teachers, and the commitment of all to professional inquiry and collegiality. Because of his enthusiastic personal and professional support of these objectives, he had participated in a number of innovative projects prior to the partnership and had been instrumental in the organization of the partner school, becoming its first administrator.

Robert recalled the struggles involved in turning an inner-city school beset by motivation and discipline problems into an exemplary learning center for present and future educators. Contractual discussions between district administrators and union officials regarding teacher mentoring and peer coaching had provided impetus for broader discussions, and these talks had revealed a need for a partner school that would focus on the professional development of district teachers. The professional development model for the partner school had begun to take shape around this need, requiring exemplary resident teachers to devote their time to it and to assume mentoring roles in relation to their peers, mentoring roles that in other schools in the partnership might have been devoted to university students. Robert had been working to find ways of accommodating the needs of university students for clinical experience within the framework of his model, and he would continue to do so. Perhaps classroom teams of resident teacher, visiting teacher, and preservice teacher could be formed as a basic teaching and learning unit. He could feel the sense of community in the diverse group assembled for this orientation session as he concluded his prepared remarks.

> I spoke of the culture of our school. [I hope] we're well along in creating both a culture and a community of inquiry. Teaching and learning are active and, of course, complementary processes, in which we are, all of us— middle school as well as college teachers, students and administrators—simultaneously involved. Sometimes the setting is one of our classrooms; sometimes it is a teaching clinic for visiting teachers or an on-site seminar for preservice teachers from the university. We are hands-on researchers who are trying to improve student learning, teaching, and teacher preparation and development—all at the same time.

The applause seemed genuine, not forced. Randomly scanning the crowd, Robert noticed one of the new visiting teachers who seemed to reflect particular warmth as she nodded vigorously and spoke rapidly to three colleagues surrounding her. She seemed vaguely familiar. Yes, he had seen her picture as the district's Teacher of the Year two or three years ago. She would have much to contribute within the partner school plan. He was glad she would be participating with them.

Turning his attention to the sequence of the orientation, he introduced the next speaker, Brenda Olden, an outspoken representative of the teacher's union.

Brenda Olden, Vice President, District Teachers Union

When she heard Robert introducing her as "one of the other two principal stakeholders in the partner school," Brenda Olden chuckled to herself. As if there were *principal* stakeholders. Everyone in the room was a stakeholder: teachers, administrators, parents, concerned members of the community—even the university people. Brenda's life's work—including years as a seventh-grade social studies teacher and much time as a union representative and officer—had been devoted to being sure that stakeholders recognized the stakes they held, including the benefits and responsibilities. The union had participated in the establishment of the partner school, shifting its historical emphasis from the traditional language of contracts and conditions of employment to language of professionalism and conditions for teacher development.

Sensing the attention lag that audiences often accord to historical details, she addressed this professionalism more directly: "Professionalism for teachers involves *decision making, empowerment, leadership*. The schoolroom isn't a baby sitting service or a retention facility; it's a complex employment situation. School administration isn't line authority; it's participative leadership. But only when teachers are willing and prepared to participate in school organization and governance can school self-renewal become reality. The partnership experience has been designed to develop that preparation and promote that willingness. I congratulate you on your decision to participate."

Scanning the room to acknowledge her applause, Brenda noticed Marilyn Bey, a frequent union participant. She was glad Marilyn would now be using her teaching expertise and her ability to relate well with people in partnership as well as union functions. She turned her attention to the next speaker, officially the third principal stakeholder, Dr. Norman McVay, dean of the School of Education and Human Development at the nearby state university. Variously, Norman had been her undergraduate professor, graduate study mentor, professional adversary, and now close colleague and friend.

Norman McVay, Dean of the School of Education and Human Development

If he were going to speak on the same orientation program with Brenda, Norman McVay was grateful that the sequence gave him the last word. Certainly he never had the last word at any of the partnership meetings and discussions. He had trained her well—too well. But the dialogue was good—everyone was enriched by the diversity of perspectives, interests, and viewpoints that were freely expressed in the partner school.

And the effects of the dialogue went beyond the conference room door. As he now told the audience, almost two dozen faculty members from both the professional education and the arts and sciences departments at his university were actively participating at the partner school. He was proud of the contributions they were making: some as instructors and mentors, some as members of the partner school's interdisciplinary curricular teams, some as consultants to individual faculty members on a range of curricular and instructional issues. A few were serving on management and policy-making bodies and one was on-site every day as the college's administrative liaison, working hand-in-hand with Robert Cordoza to put the conference room decisions (or tolerant allowances) into daily practice. Norman was currently working hard to obtain approval for revisions in his university's reward structure so that these partner school participants would be more consistently acknowledged for their contributions.

The decisions and recommendations of the partnership were not always easy for Norman to put into practice. Traditionally colleges of education and public schools had had little tolerance for one another. A wry smile escaped him as he recalled times when Brenda had accused his faculty of being elitist, stuffy, and aloof from the real world of teachers and the real demands of teaching. On the other side, he had once had to reprimand a professor who referred to Brenda's group as "the rabble."

He refrained from mentioning "the rabble," but he did tell the audience proudly that one of their number, Lorraine Braden-Rounds, was now participating in the university's new "visiting clinical professor program." For this academic year, Lorraine was spending her mornings teaching children at the partner school and her afternoons mentoring prospective teachers and serving on committees at the university. Some of her college students were observing in her partner school classroom and reporting on their experiences during the afternoon seminars. (If the university could not come to the trenches, the trenches could at least come to the university—maybe he had better not put it quite like that, but he had felt that way at times.) He described how Lorraine was accepted and treated as a member of the campus community, with access to the library and computer labs and to campus activities and special events. She had even been given that most coveted possession, a parking pass. When he asked Lorraine to stand and be recognized, the applause was genuine. Lorraine had been one of his students, and he was proud of her, as he was of Brenda and many of the others he recognized among the assembled teachers.

But Lorraine was not the only public school person who was making a difference at the university. Norman concluded his remarks by acknowledging a number of teachers and administrators from the partner school who were working on task forces at the university to implement a series of major curricular initiatives in the teacher education program: "They are helping us to decide how best to prepare our students to carry out the special enculturating role which the schools must play in our democratic society. They have also taken a hand in our efforts to identify and infuse the moral dimensions of teaching across our preparatory curriculum, including the ethical obligations of teacher stewardship. Of course, they are helping us to decide how to better prepare future teachers to work in urban settings like your own."

Yes, their contributions were invaluable. And acknowledging them, even in front of Brenda, felt good. The partner school experience felt good. Contributing to the renewal of education contributes likewise to the renewal of the individual—they are inseparable. He concluded in a positive tone: "Every time one of my colleagues teaches at the partner school or works with one of your interdisciplinary teams, he or she grows professionally. The same is true, I believe, when those of you who work here get directly involved in our programs at the university. I invite your involvement."

As he said the word "invite," Norman's eyes met those of another of his former students, Marilyn Bey. Her face was thoughtful. As a participant among the visiting teachers, she would benefit from the involvement of university and partner school faculty; he hoped she would someday choose a deeper involvement for herself.

Marilyn Bey

Marilyn pushed back her chair and followed Yvonne to the corner of the room where their assigned group was assembling for a tour of the partner school building. As the group launched into the tour, Marilyn no longer noticed the absence of windows or the narrowness of the halls. She saw only faces—students, teachers, administrators, professors, union representatives, business leaders, parents. Their ages, races, life-styles, and ethnicity varied, but all were part of the partner school community. The project coordinator who was conducting the tour said something about the "offices of the visiting teachers while they are participating at the partner school."

Offices? Marilyn had never had an office, unless her classroom could be called an office. "Every staff member at the partner school is a professional, and every professional will be furnished with office space," the guide continued. The school was small, and there were ten desks and one telephone in each of the two rooms allocated to the visiting teachers. But on one of those desks was a plaque reading "Marilyn Bey." Marilyn smiled. Her decision to participate in the partner school experience had been a good one. She was now a functioning member of the partner school community.

Principles

Although the participants' names have been changed, Marilyn Bey's partner school experience is real. The old, scarred building with the fresh interior paint blends into the territory and life-style of a Latino/African-American neighborhood in a large Eastern city. Along with the faculty, administration, students, and parents of the school, the local teachers' union and a nearby state university hold stakes in the partner school program. The participants' viewpoints are real; and Marilyn's experience is typical of that of many visiting teachers who involve themselves with the program.

Although the school and the program are specific, they are representative as well. Personalities, demographics, and program details vary, but successful partner schools are now serving as teaching-learning laboratories nationwide. Several components are necessary to their effectiveness.

Commitment

As Robert Cordoza told the visiting teachers, in partner schools teachers are recognized as the key to educational renewal. The professional development of teachers, principals, and other administrators has often been undervalued or neglected (Lortie, 1975; Goodlad, 1988); the negative experiences of Marilyn and Yvonne are typical for many teachers. Some partner schools place their primary stress on educating preservice teachers, but for Robert and principals like him, the need for continuing professional education and development of inservice teachers has been the impetus for the design of partner schools. Whatever a partner school's specific focus, inservice or preservice teachers, the commitment to educating teachers distinguishes the partner school concept from many other projects aimed at educational renewal.

Many partner schools deepen their commitment to teacher education by a further commitment to *inquiry* as the means for teacher development and continued effectiveness (Levine, 1990; The Holmes Group, 1990). Theories, concepts, research data, and even technical skills can be studied in isolation, but they become more meaningful as college administrators like Norman McVay work in tandem with school administrators like Robert Cordoza who can provide the human resources and the setting to enact the ideas and concepts in real-life situations. Many current educators are coming to espouse the necessity of this real-life view (Goodlad, 1988; The Holmes Group, 1990; Lieberman & Miller, 1992). Yet a further dimension in teacher training occurs when teachers who are striving to incorporate the ideal of *active learning* (Goodlad, 1990) in their classrooms experience it themselves in the partner schools where they learn.

Because of this inner-city partner school's location, history, and participants, its program has some unique features; every partner school's program does. But there is a unity below partnership diversity, both in the commitment to the learning of our nation's teachers, and second, in the commitment to active, theory-into-practice inquiry. All partner schools have such commitments as a means to accomplish their goals.

Beliefs

The critical thinking model used in this inner-city partner school states: "Professional development must be coherent. It must be based on a particular set of beliefs, including a clear sense of what an excellent teacher looks like" (Michelli, 1993, p. 4). A number of important beliefs and assumptions underlie the success of this and other functioning partner schools:

1. The overlapping missions of schools and colleges and universities should be reinterpreted as shared missions in the setting of the partner school (Goodlad, 1990). As Goodlad has suggested, colleges and universities "have played a significant role . . . in designing mechanisms for linking theory, research and practice," and yet "the schooling enterprise is at best only weakly characterized by these essentials of renewal" (p. 10). The partner school, by providing a laboratory to test the validity of theory and to explore the techniques and ramifications for administering that theory, acts as a bridge uniting the contributions of inquiry and practice.

As Brenda Olden, the union vice president, affirmed in her talk to Marilyn Bey's group, the teacher professionalism that results from public school teachers working closely with university personnel in the schools is closely associated with increasing the stewardship and empowerment of teachers (Goodlad, 1990). Instructional supervision in which either the inservice or preservice teacher is merely critiqued and directed and not given decision-making opportunities is, in the view of partner school personnel, simply incongruous (Joyce, Wolf, & Calhoun, 1993).

2. Both preparatory programs and continuing development opportunities for teachers should be knowledge-based. As Gideonse (1989) points out, knowledge is essential to such programs in several ways.

a. Knowledge serves, of course, as curriculum content for teacher education. Classroom management programs, for example, must be known before they can be implemented.

b. Knowledge provides a rationale for what is taught. A knowledge of local and national conditions is caught up with the need for programs to teach teachers their enculturating role in a social and political democracy.

c. Knowledge provides a basis for decisions about how to teach. Understanding transactional models of teaching increases the options available to a teacher looking for a new and effective way to teach a given topic.

d. Knowledge is necessary as a base for reflection, and the ability to blend knowledge and reflection is a measure of professional practice (Schön, 1983; Darling-Hammond & Goodwin, 1993). To reflect on the success of an activity in promoting intercultural understanding, for example, a teacher must know the cultural differences that apparently have been bridged.

3. Reflective, critical thinking is important to the learning of both teachers and students. The philosophy and goals of Dean Norman McVay's school of education and human services structured a vision of "effective teaching" around critical thinking as an educational ideal. As university personnel espousing this ideal blended their conceptions of good teaching with those of the middle school personnel, teaching for critical thinking became part of the knowledge base of the teacher development program and at the same time a foundation element in the middle school curriculum.

As teachers like Marilyn and Yvonne attended content-based seminars during their five-week program, they were encouraged to select thinking processes and skills that would deepen their understanding of the concepts, processes, and ideas they were learning in their discipline of language arts; teachers like Jana and Ken were urged to do the same with content knowledge and skills in mathematics. In addition to choosing processes for reflection and contemplation, all the teachers were encouraged to consider what components of the knowledge base of their disciplines were really worth thinking about—what would most readily transfer to real-life issues and what might be considered "problematic" (Barell, 1991, p. 109). As they thought about thinking as well as about content, the teachers attended related clinics in which they had an opportunity to teach content lessons to sixth-, seventh-, or eighth-grade students and to have their performances critiqued by partner school staff and their fellow visiting teachers. The critiques were structured in terms of models for *active learning:* problem analysis, discussion, group investigation, cooperative learning, and other appropriate methodology.

4. Those responsible for professional development of teachers should be prepared to model what they recommend (Goodlad, 1990). Mike Benston, the resident teacher at the partner school, was personally enthusiastic about new pedagogical policies, procedures, and materials associated with the partner school experience—particularly those related to teaching critical thinking skills. When Mike was asked to guide a student teacher from the university in presenting the school's thematic emphasis on critical thinking and active learning to his seventh-grade class, he used a cognitively oriented coaching technique (Costa & Garmston, 1985), which took the student teacher through many of the critical thinking skills that he would present to the seventh graders.

In addition, throughout the partner school curriculum it was stressed that teachers should maintain in their classrooms the climate of openness and trust that characterized the seminars and discussion groups the teachers had been attending, a climate which Lieberman and Miller (1992, p. 107) have characterized as "a culture of support for teacher inquiry."

Time

One of the weaknesses of traditional inservice development programs for teachers has been the expectation that teachers would learn, comprehend, and be ready to adopt new ideas and policies after one afternoon of instruction. Partner schools, in contrast, develop their programs with the realization that worthwhile and constructive change requires time—"time for reflection, thoughtfulness, and growth" (Michelli, 1993, p. 4).

In reviewing the processes involved in preparing teachers to acquire and apply new classroom skills, Joyce and Weil (1986) list a number of common elements teachers need: study of the underlying theory and rationale, the opportunity to observe experts, practice in limited conditions, feedback on that practice, coaching by peers, companionship of peers, and group exploration of the use of the model and of appropriate responses to students. Joyce and Weil estimate that teacher trainees require fifteen to twenty demonstrations of an unfamiliar teaching model and more than a dozen opportunities to practice it before they are able to use it effectively in the classroom. In light of this finding, Joyce and Weil affirm that the one- or two-day workshops provided by many school districts "simply do not provide enough time to develop the degree of competence necessary for most trainees to be able to apply a new skill in the work setting" (p. 479).

In planning the teacher development sequence at their partner school, Education Dean Norman McVay and Principal Robert Cordoza provided eight weeks for the self-assessment (off-site) and direct involvement (on-site) program components. Follow-through (off-site) monthly coaching visits by partner school staff would continue indefinitely. Such a schedule allowed time for the developmental elements posited by Joyce and Weil as necessary to produce demonstrable change in teacher knowledge and for skill to unfold in the training process. Consideration of theory and research, as well as demonstration, was included in the seminars, and in each partner school experience the designers incorporated time for reflective consideration, to maximize the strength and lasting impact of the learning process. Additional demonstrations of methodology and materials took place in the classrooms of resident teachers like Mike Benston, who modeled the methods and encouraged reflection. When the teaching clinics were held, the visiting teachers had opportunities to practice the techniques with real students in a typical middle school classroom situation and receive peer feedback. The most crucial feedback, perhaps, occurred during the follow-through visits, as the teachers received observation and feedback in the individualized worlds of their own classrooms.

It is true that many teacher development programs attempt to allow sufficient time for teachers to experience as many aspects as possible of the processes involved in learning and change. But it is difficult in any functioning school to find this time, even when intentions are good. When partner schools are specifically structured for professional development, they can schedule staff, resources, and facilities to allow for sufficient teacher development experiences. With their flexible time and continual dialogue among participants, partner schools are able to promote the type of school culture that Lieberman and Miller (1992) suggest supports the philosophy of teacher development as *a process of continuous inquiry into practice*, a schoolwide attitude that "adults are expected to go on learning too" (The Holmes Group, 1990, p. 7).

Applicability

One of the most significant benefits of the learning-reflecting process is the resulting likelihood that knowledge gained through this process will be applied in actual classroom practice. As administrators in Marilyn Bey's district stated: "Professional development must link research and practice. We have made great progress in understanding what works in education and what doesn't" (Michelli, 1993, p. 4). In short, the work of the partner schools is designed to inform theoretical and empirical insight with the wisdom of practice and to strengthen practice with additional options provided by current professional research. Thus the partner school creates what Goodlad calls "a long-term contract between a university and a school district for the renewal of employees and institutions" (Goodlad, 1988, p. 11).

Levine (1992) has recommended the specific research bases, or categories, that should underpin the training of teachers, particularly in partner school settings.

The first category would be what we know about how individuals, and specifically children, learn. The second area is what we have learned about the conditions that support learning, including the research on effective schools and effective teaching and especially the types of pedagogy that are related to teaching in restructured school environments (e.g., cooperative group learning, use of educational technologies, peer tutoring, and coaching).

A third distinct research base, important to the practitioner, is growing out of an examination of the pedagogical requirements of specific content areas. This research focuses on identifying the effective ways of teaching the main understandings or concepts of a particular subject area such as physics or history [p. 15].

In the seminars at the inner-city partner school, Marilyn, Yvonne, and the other teachers were exposed to schema theory as one option for problem-based learning (research base 1). They were taught the insights of Johnson and Johnson (1979), that students develop intellectually as they negotiate situations which challenge their established expectations. The teachers learned that an open and accepting relationship must exist between teacher and students so that students do not feel threatened or defensive when they are confronted with an idea or happening that is not congruent with what they expect or perceive to be correct (research base 2). In exploring their content area, they learned that one way to help seventh-grade students appreciate free verse more easily is to approach specific poems through language, imagery, and symbolism (research base 3). An understanding of these three characteristics might constitute a knowledge base for preparing a lesson to help seventh graders think critically about the values in a selected group of poems written in free verse.

In many knowledge bases, research data would reinforce the base components. To other knowledge bases, specific distinctions in practice between novice and master teachers might be added. As they observed the carefully selected partner school resident teachers,

along with visiting teacher colleagues with varying forms of training and experience, Marilyn and Yvonne became acutely aware of
the ways in which experience and education manifest themselves
in teaching expertise. Nowhere was this expertise more evident
than when teachers were putting something they had recently
learned into practice. Kennedy (1992) refers to expertise in application as "deliberate action." In this action, "content is not auto-
matically applied to situations; instead . . . deliberate actors seek
optimal matches between concepts and principles, on the one side,
and the situations they encounter, on the other. . . . Deliberators
must have access to content, but they also must know how to examine the content, how to examine the situation, and how to examine
the match between the two" (p. 66).

For her lesson using free verse and schema theory, one of the less
experienced teachers in Marilyn's group chose poems that had been
her favorites in college. They were poems with beautiful language and
meaningful symbolism, but the match between the difficult poems
and the multicultural group of thirteen-year-olds was awkward; losing interest, the children were bored and disruptive. Reflecting on
what she knew about seventh graders, Marilyn began with humorous
and satirical verses of e.e. cummings, who—like the seventh graders
themselves—had not much use for punctuation and other conventions. Marilyn's match was more accurate. The children decided that
free verse could be a "fun kind of weird." When Mike Benston commented on Marilyn's lesson, he quoted Levine's statement (1992) that
a teacher should not be "merely a technical expert who uses knowledge, but an individual who transforms a knowledge base, reflects on
practice, and generates new knowledge" (p. 10).

Involvement

The policy recommendations of the inner-city partner school stated
that the content of professional development programs "cannot be
imposed, but must reflect the real needs of practicing teachers"
(Michelli, 1993, p.4). And the teaching profession as a whole is

moving toward programs that actively involve teachers and teacher trainees in decisions about program content and process (Education Commission of the States, 1990; The Holmes Group, 1990; Murphy, 1991; Livingston, 1992; Darling-Hammond & Goodwin, 1993; Joyce, Wolf, & Calhoun, 1993). This position is consistent, of course, with the drive for professionalism among teachers—professionals being those who recognize needs and make decisions accordingly. It is also consistent with what is known about adult learners: adults need to be personally involved in the learning process, and this involvement occurs most effectively when they identify specific problems and marshal educational resources in service of those needs (Knowles, 1970, 1973). To facilitate this involvement among teachers in the professional development program, resident teacher Mike Benston had spent the better part of five afternoons with Marilyn and equivalent time with each teacher in his group, getting to know them personally and working with them to identify needs and interests that would become the core of their personal action plans. The members of school-university partnerships from many states who participate in the National Network for Education Renewal have provided for this and similar procedures in their *Compact for Simultaneous Renewal* (Clark, 1993), stating that "continuing education for educators is collaboratively defined based on the needs of students served by the educators. Continuing education begins from an analysis of the needs of students being served by the school. Based on this analysis, university and school faculty plan continuing education which serves [their] mutual needs and interests" (p. 5).

Conclusion: Marilyn Bey, Program Graduate

Outside, the school was drab—almost grim. But inside, the meeting room was a potpourri of vivid flowers, festive decorations, and varied gifts. Marilyn Bey, along with her colleagues Yvonne, Jana, and Ken and her principal, Rosalyn Greer, had joined the other visiting teachers, principals, partner school staff, and college participants for a lunch and a celebration of teaching and learning. Marilyn thought of the pep rallies at her middle school, even though here the celebrants walked a little more slowly. The after-lunch program would feature keynote speakers and musical, poetic, and other presentations by visiting teachers and by school and university staff. Yvonne, with her flair for satire, had written and directed a sketch on what the eighth graders had taught *her* about Romeo and Juliet. Her performers, including Marilyn and Ken, thoroughly enjoyed acting like middle school students instead of teachers for a change.

As the program drew to a close, the mood shifted as union officer Brenda Olden reminded teachers of the professionalism all of them had displayed throughout the program, of the new professionalism with which they would return to their former classrooms. Yes, Marilyn reflected, the teachers were different—they were more professional. When Brenda used her favorite words, "empowerment" and "renewal," these concepts meant more to Marilyn than they had when Brenda had used them just five weeks before. She thought of her autonomy as a teacher, her ability to make decisions, and the leadership she now felt prepared to assume.

As a professional Marilyn Bey had gained much; and as a professional she had given in return. Both partner school and visiting teachers had commented during the clinics on some of Marilyn's teaching ideas that they would like to incorporate into their own classrooms. After one seminar, a slightly timid young teacher had asked Marilyn a number of questions about her methods of classroom management. Mike Benston had said he planned to try her idea for a thematic unit around the novel *To Kill a Mockingbird*. Only yesterday Mike had told the visiting teachers who had gathered to clean out their office area how they had caused him to reexamine his own teaching practices—and to make some improvements. Each group did this, he had affirmed. He was probably "the most reformed, refurbished, recycled teacher in the district."

Marilyn was drawn back from her musings as one of her fellow visiting language arts teachers stepped to the podium and began to read a poem she had written, reflecting on her partner school experience (Pettigrew-Lane, 1993):

> Like the rain falling
> Softly on the petal of a rose,
> Providing the essence of its beauty.
> You teacher with your tender sharing
> Awaken the beauty of the souls
> Of those entrusted to your care.

References

Barell, J. (1991). *Teaching for thoughtfulness: Classroom strategies to enhance intellectual development*. New York: Longman.

Clark, R. W. (1993). *Compact for simultaneous renewal*. Bellevue, WA: National Network for Educational Renewal.

Costa, A., & Garmston, R. (1985). Supervision for intelligent teaching. *Educational Leadership, 42*, 70–80.

Darling-Hammond, L., & Goodwin, A. L. (1993). Progress toward professionalism in teaching. In G. Cawelti (Ed.), *Challenges and achievements of American education: 1993 yearbook of the Association for Supervision and Curriculum Development* (pp. 19–52). Alexandria, VA: Association for Supervision and Curriculum Development.

Education Commission of the States. (1990). *School restructuring: What the reformers are saying*. Washington, DC: Author.

Gideonse, H. (1989). *Relating knowledge to teacher education: Responding to NCATE's knowledge base and related standards*. Washington, DC: American Association of Colleges for Teacher Education.

Goodlad, J. I. (1988). School-university partnerships for educational renewal: Rationale and concepts. In K. A. Sirotnik & J. I. Goodlad (Eds.), *School-university partnerships in action: Concepts, cases, and concerns* (pp. 3–31). New York: Teachers College Press.

Goodlad, J. I. (1990). *Teachers for our nation's schools*. San Francisco: Jossey-Bass.

The Holmes Group. (1990). *Tomorrow's schools: Principles for the design of professional development schools*. East Lansing, MI: The Holmes Group.

Johnson, R., & Johnson, D. (1979). Conflict in the classroom. *Review of Educational Research, 49*, 59–70.

Joyce, B., & Weil, M. (1986). *Models of teaching*. Englewood Cliffs, NJ: Prentice Hall.

Joyce, B., Wolf, J., & Calhoun, E. (1993). *The self-renewing school*. Alexandria, VA: Association for Supervision and Curriculum Development.

Kennedy, M. (1992). Establishing professional development schools for teachers. In M. Levine (Ed.), *Professional practice schools: Linking teacher education and school reform* (pp. 63–80). New York: Teachers College Press.

Knowles, M. (1970). *The modern practice of adult education*. Englewood Cliffs, NJ: Cambridge Books.

Knowles, M. (1973). *The adult learner: A neglected species*. Houston, TX: Gulf.

Levine, M. (1990). *Professional practice schools: Building a model II* (Monograph No. 2). Washington, DC: Center for Restructuring, American Federation of Teachers.

Levine, M. (1992). A conceptual framework for professional practice schools. In M. Levine (Ed.), *Professional practice schools: Linking teacher education and school reform* (pp. 8–24). New York: Teachers College Press.

Lieberman, A., & Miller, L. (1992). Teacher development in professional practice schools. In M. Levine (Ed.), *Professional practice schools: Linking teacher education and school reform* (pp. 105–123). New York: Teachers College Press.

Livingston, C. (1992). Teacher leadership for restructured schools. In C. Livingston (Ed.), *Teachers as leaders: Evolving roles* (pp. 9–20). Washington, DC: National Education Association.

Lortie, D. (1975). *Schoolteacher: A sociological study*. Chicago: University of Chicago Press.

Michelli, N. (1993). *The agenda for teacher education in a democracy project: Summary of New Jersey policy recommendations*. Upper Montclair, NJ: School of Professional Studies, Montclair State College.

Murphy, J. (1991). *Restructuring schools: Capturing and assessing the phenomena*. New York: Teachers College Press.

Pettigrew-Lane, E. (1993, November). "Teacher." Poem presented at Celebration of Teaching Meeting, Harold Wilson Middle School for Professional Development, Newark, NJ.

Schön, D. A. (1983). *The reflective practitioner: How professionals think in action*. New York: Basic Books.

5

Supporting Collaborative Inquiry

Francis P. Hunkins, Donna L. Wiseman, and Richard C. Williams

TEACHER EDUCATOR: I would like teachers at the school to become more involved in the research that is coming out of this partnership. They need to understand that research is a way of learning *about* what's happening in the schools and of learning *from* what's happening in the schools.

PUBLIC SCHOOL TEACHER: My first research priority is a given—the program I'm working with, including my students and their needs. The second priority is to develop my own curriculum within my own classroom.

These opinions represent the traditional dichotomy between the ways teacher educators and public school faculty perceive research and inquiry. Although the gap between educational research in the colleges and inquiry into its practice in the schools is less strained today than it has been in the past, tensions still exist between the cultures in the ways they view research (Cuban, 1992; Leinhardt, 1990; Richardson, 1990). Teacher education faculty are participants in a profession in which respect and rewards are subject to university research values and procedures; school faculty are members of a culture in which "an action plan, advice on what will work, and evidence that the plan will solve their practical problems" (Cuban, 1992, p. 5) are of primary concern.

However, by their very nature, school-university partnerships alter the "rules, roles, and relationships" of the partners so that important purposes may be served more effectively (Schlechty, 1990, p. xvi). Research and inquiry are areas in which traditional roles and the relationships leading to and from them are being altered. The partner school is becoming an important arena in which such alterations can constructively occur. Though differences will still be prevalent, both schools and universities will benefit from the union of reflection and action that partner schools can provide (Goodlad, 1988; Schlechty & Whitford, 1988). Universities emphasize inquiry into practice, a perspective often missing in the schools (Goodlad, 1988), while school personnel remind university faculty of the importance of focusing inquiry to solve practical problems. Challenges also lie in maintaining communication during inevitable conflicts of interest and in balancing reflection and action so that mutual benefits continue to emerge from the union. This chapter will address the ways in which the partner school functions in uniting theory and practice.

Approaches to School-University Research and Inquiry

In the past, most educational inquiry and research was conducted by universities; now all partnership members are becoming jointly involved, but there is a scarcity of guidance for such joint inquiry. The specific circumstances and challenges of each partnership will vary; however, a consideration of the contexts in which collaborative inquiry has been tried in existing partnerships reveals ways in which effective collaborative inquiry may be developed.

Laboratory Schools

Laboratory schools, which have been in use for over one hundred years, offer one model for joint inquiry by school and university (Hendricks, 1980). They allow university faculty to interact with skilled professionals in an environment more carefully controlled and monitored than the "real world"; thus they would seem ideally suited for gathering insights into the renewal of schools. Typically located on or near the university campus, they provide easy access to clinical settings that university faculty and students can use for preservice training or curriculum development and research; they also allow easy access to university expertise for teachers and administrators desiring special assistance and advice. The overall environment of these schools has been strongly conducive to inquiry.

The nature and role of inquiry in the laboratory school is shaped by the school's setting, environment, and student population. Since the laboratory school is typically owned by the university, the mission and focus of the school are determined by university interests and priorities. On the one hand, colleges and universities that emphasize professional training usually operate laboratory schools that emphasize teacher training, instructional methods, and curriculum development. On the other hand, research universities usually view the laboratory school as largely a research facility (Williams, 1992).

Student populations in many laboratory schools are highly homogeneous, having been drawn largely from the local culture and thus having a high percentage of children of university faculty, staff, and students. However, student populations in some laboratory schools have been specifically selected to represent the heterogeneity of a regional population or to emphasize students with particular characteristics, such as learning disabled or gifted children.

Laboratory schools present many advantages for collaborative school-university research. In addition to selecting the student population, the laboratory school can also control such variables as school programs and instructional methods. Because they are private schools, laboratory schools can conduct studies without getting external approval from a school district. In addition, the proximity to the university campus allows easy access for researchers and assistants.

Despite these advantages the number of laboratory schools in the United States has steadily declined since the mid-sixties; today only about one hundred remain. Various reasons have been suggested for the decline. Researchers are recognizing some of the inherent weaknesses that limit generalizability of laboratory school studies: for example, the characteristically atypical populations and the residual effects of six years of frequent experimental treatments on the children. Also, because the laboratory school is owned by and subordinate to the university, university faculty usually control the research agenda. At research universities, heavy pressure on the faculty to publish is likely to distort the school's educational programs. Goodlad (1980) places the blame for the decline of laboratory schools on the differences in participants' underlying values: "The student teacher wants to get employed; the laboratory school teacher wants to demonstrate pedagogical expertise; the experienced teacher, visiting in the school, hopes to see something he or she can use next week; the professor in a campus department wants access to a research facility with a minimum of hassle; the director of the school probably wants good teaching, experimentation and innovations, and a vigorous research program—all simultaneously. Something or someone has to give. Too often, everything gives and the school ends up doing little or nothing well" (pp. 48–49).

Data Collection in Public Schools

As the university-owned laboratory schools declined, some colleges of education took their research into public schools in proximity to the university. Although these schools and universities may have appeared to work together for inquiry into mutual interests, the interaction was generally between individuals and not between institutions (Goodlad, 1993). University professors used these schools as data collection sites for their research, but school personnel rarely participated in planning the inquiry process or in considering the results. In fact, professors seldom communicated their findings to those who had furnished the data; thus the impact of university research on the schools was limited. The school was no longer under the control of the university, but the separation had gone too far: the school was now a completely separate entity, not benefiting from the process of the inquiry or the results of the experiment.

Laboratory Research in Partner Schools

The term *laboratory* is often used in discussing the research done in partner schools, but a different kind of laboratory from the laboratory schools or data-collection schools is being addressed. Goodlad (1990) uses the word to denote "the availability of a wide array of laboratory settings for observation [and] hands-on experiences" (p. 61). Under the concept of collaborative inquiry promoted by the partner schools, both university and school personnel are invited to participate in educational dialogue, reflection, and inquiry. Experience has shown that the more people who are involved, the richer and more dynamic the educational culture will be.

The concept of partner schools as laboratories or centers for collaborative inquiry rests on several assumptions:

- All members of the school community are learners.
- To function as a center of inquiry, a school must be committed to explore new roles and responsibilities for all members of the school community.
- The school should create contexts that foster innovation as a regular part of teaching.
- All participants—university coordinators, school-teachers, and preservice teachers—share responsibility for creating knowledge and modeling good practice.
- Dialogue and reflection are central to the life of a school which functions as a center for inquiry [Gehrke & McDaniel, 1989].

Collaborative Inquiry

Collaborative inquiry attempts to make meaning out of human actions through a holistic approach in which individuals work together to understand their situation and their roles within it. Such inquiry requires that individuals identify those challenges that demand attention so that human welfare can be advanced (Reason, 1988). To identify challenges, participants ask questions, plan actions to explore these questions, and schedule time to reflect on their observations. The process might include formulating field notes for a story, reflecting on the notes, and writing the story in order to objectify participants' interpretations of what they observed.

Hallmarks

Several hallmarks distinguish collaborative inquiry (Lincoln & Guba, 1985). First, research is accomplished in a natural setting: individuals study an environment while immersed in it. Second, researchers believe in the human instrument: investigators use themselves and others as the primary data-gathering instruments, rather than resorting to paper-and-pencil instruments. When individuals function as research instruments, they can observe and interpret while interacting with others in the inquiry process. They can use tacit knowledge during inquiry, knowledge that does not need to be articulated prior to the study. Third, investigators allow the design of the inquiry to evolve from the needs revealed as the study progresses. They do not impose an a priori plan that may or may not be appropriate to the individual situation. A final hallmark of the collaborative inquiry approach is that it fosters excitement in pursuing questions that may be unrelated to any of the primary research projects underway in the partner school. At first glance, this might seem problematic, as participants from university and public school cultures may well become interested in differing questions. However, in pursuing such questions, participants take ownership of their studies and assume responsibility for completing them; such ownership and responsibility are important aspects of collaborative research (Oja & Smulyan, 1989).

Inquiry in Partner Schools

The shift from the laboratory school concept to the cooperative but separate research approach and finally to the collaborative laboratory is paralleled by shifts in the focus of the inquiry process, the locus of control, and the audience for research results. Partnerships require that schools and universities participate jointly in all parts of inquiry: asking the questions, formulating the design, implementing the process, analyzing the data, and disseminating the results. As advocated by Goodlad and others, inquiry in partner schools is in the tradition of the inquiry advocated by Keislar (1980), with ties to Peter Senge's work (1990) and Schön's work (1983). Such inquiry is driven by an organization's need to examine its goals and purposes; to decide on programs, curricula, and instructional practices that will advance its ability to realize its examined goals and purposes; and to evaluate whether or not it has been successful in achieving its goals. The traditional audience for university faculty research has been colleagues who read refereed journals; the audience for partner school inquiry is the entire professional community, including the faculty of the partner schools themselves.

This shift in focus is critical. It parallels the shift from education as answer driven, with students as passive recipients, to education as question driven, with students, teachers, and sometimes university professors as co-inquirers. All parties then learn to think of education as dynamic, uncertain, playful, contextual, and emergent. The locus of control for learning shifts as roles change; educators are no longer teaching certainties, but rather questioning and inquiring, pushing outward on the boundaries of scholarship, and students become responsible for pushing as well. School personnel are more likely to embrace the inquiry process if they can see that spending time in reflection will help them gain insights that will affect the quality and effectiveness of their practice. All parties—university faculty, schoolteachers, administrators, and students on all levels—are invited to relinquish their uncritical following of past traditions to participate in choosing directions and practices to renew both school and university education. The shift in audience widely expands the audience: teachers, students, and members of the academic and general community are being invited to participate in forming inquiry communities. The patterns of partner school inquiry are blurring the distinction between teacher and learner, between teacher and professor, between educator and parent, between administrators and staff, between school people and community. Educators at all levels are being asked to collaborate on a scale never considered in earlier forms of educational research. Not everyone who has been invited has accepted, but numbers are increasing. In fact, the collaboration which has resulted in producing this book on partner schools is part of an invitation to all educators to "come on down!" All stakeholders in education need to get involved, be active, be assertive, be reflective, and be playful in the school, for it is an arena for inquiry, and all are part of that inquiry. The paradigm is changing, and that change is exhilarating for all.

Cases of Collaborative Inquiry

The concept of partner school research and inquiry requires that the definitions of research and inquiry be expanded to include alternative models in which university and school-based researchers can work together in developing and practicing the inquiry process. Though these expanded models are in their infancy, evolving activities provide insights into the nature of research and inquiry processes. Examples of the range of possibilities have been developed in three categories of inquiry: inquiry into the partnership process, inquiry into the professional development of educators involved in partnerships, and inquiry into best practice in the schools.

Inquiry into the Partnership Process

Adding to the body of information regarding collaboration itself has been a new focus for inquiry (Cole & Knowles, 1993). Systematic study of the patterns, promises, and pitfalls of current partnerships can contribute substantially to the success of partnerships of the future. Inquiry of this type is providing both formative information that contributes to revising and improving partner school processes and summative information that allows institutions to evaluate the outcomes of partnership activity. For example, inquiry at one university posited that interactions between partners constituted the basic units of collaborative activity (Wiseman & Nason, 1993). Participants in the ensuing study described and categorized the interactions between school-based faculty, university professors, and preservice teachers during the first two years of the school-university partnership. Four categories of interaction emerged. From analyzing the interactions within these categories, researchers found that most discussions focused on the partners' self-interests, with only a few instances of discussion that focused on differences between partners' institutions. Partners showed the greatest commitment to each other's interests during interactions that centered on curricular restructuring. The results of this study demonstrated to the participants that members of partnerships need more understanding of the nature of their interactions in order to improve their ability to be mutually supportive in partnership function.

As more school-university partnerships are formed, members of these partnerships need to monitor their developmental processes in order to more fully understand the patterns that emerge (Auger & Odell, 1992). Because describing the interaction that occurs in discussions can reveal patterns for educational reform (Cuban, 1992) and bring about a greater understanding of the process of change, participants should continue this close monitoring throughout partnership development and maturation (Slavin, 1989).

Another study that focused on the partnership process analyzed inquiry projects and enabled participants to distill some of the characteristics of inquiry in collaborative efforts (Wiseman, 1993). This study revealed that although the input of school faculty was more evident in partnership than in prepartnership research, the university was still the major influence in establishing research activities and agendas and that university personnel generally initiated the planning, formulated the questions, and analyzed the data. The exception was a site-specific curriculum study initiated to meet expressed school faculty needs; this project exhibited a more balanced school-university interaction than the other projects. The analysis in this study pointed out that even with expanding definitions of partnership research and inquiry, a balance between the research demands on the university faculty and the needs and desires of public school educators is difficult to achieve. The curriculum inquiry, which was important to school personnel, rewarded the university faculty with intrinsic satisfaction and an individual sense of personal development, but it was not recognized or rewarded by the university. School faculty were acknowledged by their central administration for their participation in research, but they did not receive monetary or concrete rewards of any kind.

Action research, in which teachers record and explain their own experiences, is one of the most effective ways in which teachers can participate in inquiry, Such research has the potential to directly effect changes in the context and practice of education in the schools. When teachers become involved in "systematic and intentional inquiry" (Cochran-Smith & Lytle, 1990, p. 3), school-university tensions are eased as participants come closer together along the continuum that runs between research and action.

Inquiry into Professional Development

Partner schools involved in collaborative inquiry contribute to the professional development of individual teachers while also adding to collective knowledge about teaching and learning (Darling-Hammond, 1993). Professional development can include both inservice and preservice activities, and the measured changes produced by professional development activities are demonstrated in the personal reflection and growth of the educators involved. As preservice teachers, veteran teachers, and university faculty become involved in partnership inquiry, they learn more about the theory and practice of teaching. As their knowledge base expands, they become more reflective in their practice. The benefits of this reflective inquiry are evident in the following examples of comments written by teachers who have been involved in partner school research.

TEACHER WHO HAD PARTICIPATED IN A RESEARCH CLASS: This class has immersed me in the professional literature. I can't believe I had neglected the excellent resources available to me. By keeping abreast of current research and results, I began to change many of my teaching methods in language arts to test the research myself.

TEACHER WHO HAD BEGUN USING REFLECTIVE METHODS: It is my opinion that reflective assessment of one's teaching practices and ability to expand the knowledge base is necessary when considering changing one's instructional methodology.

University faculty who participate in partnership inquiry recognize the need for their own professional development. Thus, cataloguing the professional development of university faculty can be important in promoting renewal efforts for the schools. As one teacher educator said after being involved in partnership activity, "I need to take additional steps to meet my expectations of the partnership. I need to personally try to get a closer match between what I do and what I attempt to have the future teachers do in preparing them to teach mathematics and include what's happening in the classroom. That's really the bottom line."

Partnership activities can also benefit teacher preparation by focusing on methods that have been shown to be best practice in teacher education. Comments by preservice teachers who had just completed field-based teacher-guided learning experiences in a partner school demonstrate the strength of collaborative efforts.

"The collaborative gave us an early-on experience in teaching, and we had four or five teachers that gave us input, not only in classroom management . . . so we had a distinct advantage [during preservice teaching]."

"We were familiar with the physical layout of the school [and] the discipline plan. We knew the faculty, and we were much more at home in the school. I've been able to teach since the second week of school."

"The collaborative is more of a hands-on experience than taking the same classes would be at the university where it is purely academics, and I feel that it would be in the best interest of all students in education to benefit from a program similar to this."

"When you look at the overall picture and see all the different opportunities that students in that collaborative have, then it is easier to understand why we then are more comfortable in the classroom environment."

These and similar comments were collected as preservice teachers were interviewed following their student teaching experience. As such reactions are collected and examined as part of an ongoing inquiry into preservice preparation, partner schools are able to assess what is going well in their programs and what needs revision and adaptation. Restructuring activities based on collaborative research often treat the logistics of field-based courses, the organization of methods courses, and the impact of interdisciplinary teaming by the school faculty, the university faculty, and the preservice teachers.

Inquiry into Best Practice

A very beneficial area of research and inquiry in partnership schools focuses on how teachers and teacher educators can improve their practice. Much of this work takes the form of studies of curriculum and evaluations of classroom methods. The following case demonstrates the range and power of some of the inquiries that focus on best practice.

For the past four years, a university professor has been working with the staff of a partner middle school located in a middle- and upper-middle-class suburban district that might be considered a bed-room community for Seattle. The school serves seven hundred seventh- and eighth-grade students. It is staffed by forty-four energetic professionals who have now accepted the professor as a member of their school community. But that acceptance did not come immediately: it took at least one quarter of his first year at the school before the teachers realized that he was genuinely interested in working with them on their research concerns. In the initial phases, he had to establish trust and become part of the school staff. He had to share his own experiences and expectations. He also had to show his acceptance of the school environment and culture; he even had to learn the language of the school, including the meaning of popular acronyms such as ME (mastery and enrichment). With trust and camaraderie in place, he was then able to create boundaries for his own involvement and to negotiate research (Oja & Smulyan, 1989).

As the professor became acquainted with some of the members of the middle school staff and they discovered his interests and areas of expertise, inquiry questions began to surface and people asked to learn more about issues with which he had been involved. In this way, he found individuals who would be interested in working with him.

Discourse Analysis in Two Science Classes

An eighth-grade science teacher approached the professor with a concern about the language levels she was using in two of her classes. One class was what teachers referred to as a "good" class, while the other had been identified as a "problem" class; the teacher feared that she might not be treating them equitably in terms of challenging language as well as science content. The teacher and the professor worked out a way to analyze what she said in both classes in light of her lesson plans and goals. Then the professor observed both of her classes twice a week for an entire quarter and made a transcripts so that specific language instances and patterns could be studied. Together, the professor and the teacher analyzed her language for content, conceptual level, proportion of student talk to teacher talk, and number of topics addressed. While the professor was doing the observations, he and the teacher worked together to devise the plan for the inquiry, determine their respective roles, interpret the necessary tasks, and analyze and interpret the data. As they analyzed the transcripts together, the teacher was able to discover that she was not shortchanging the problem class in the number of topics covered, in the conceptual level of the discussion, or even in the amount of time she allowed for the students to participate in discussion. In this way, a classroom concern was answered with inquiry that was truly collaborative at every stage.

Developing and Testing Integrative Curriculum

Becoming interested in the notion of integrated curriculum, an art teacher and a home economics teacher decided to develop an integrated unit together and test it in both of their classes. The idea of "investigation" was initiated by the teachers; the professor expressed a willingness to work with them. After this group of three had discussed what *integrated curriculum* could mean, each teacher explained his or her curriculum for the quarter, and the group decided on a useful vehicle to integrate the two courses into a blended experience. The integrated unit was organized around the concept of pattern and a special project of making a quilt. The art teacher developed lessons on design, focusing on the experience of creating quilt sections and incorporating information on past and present quilt making as well. The home economics teacher helped the students translate their art designs into fabric designs and taught them to compose the batiks they had created in art class into an overall quilt. A doctoral student from the university also volunteered to help in creating the integrated unit.

There was a sense of emergence to the integrated unit. Although the teachers taught specific lessons on batik designing and sewing, the students created their own designs, "writing" their own stories into their quilts. When the students finished their quilts, they were asked to explain the symbols and patterns that they had used.

The professor met with the teachers weekly, discussing their emergent curriculum, the ways they were delivering it, and the experiences they wanted their students to have. Through this inquiry, the teachers assumed a *questioning* approach to their teaching, reflecting to determine what had worked well in a specific unit and what conclusions they could make regarding integrated curricula and team efforts in general. Although the effort did not result in a published report, the teachers gained important insights into ways of making a curriculum relevant, meaningful, and enjoyable to their students. As the teachers, along with the professor, became involved in a professional dialogue, their participation brought new energy to their teaching.

As a professor-in-residence at the partner school, this university faculty member has been involved in many other inquiry efforts. For example, he assisted one teacher in working her personal interest in teachers' and students' questions into a design for a master's thesis. Although the professor was not on her thesis committee, he helped prepare her for her master's work by engaging with her in ongoing dialogue regarding the nature of questions and ways to get students more engaged as they question.

Other Collaborative Investigations

At this same suburban partner school, there have been many other collaborative investigations. Another professor, a science teacher, and two student teachers collaborated to investigate ways in which computer networking can help students learn science; this group presented their research findings at a recent national convention of the American Educational Research Association. Two other teachers have engaged in action research on the teaching of writing in their classrooms. Another teacher has done qualitative research on teaching problem solving. A language arts teacher conducted reader response research, doctoral students compared teacher education in partnership schools to that in traditional programs, and counseling psychology faculty have measured the effects of their home-school intervention activities. As needs and interests differ, inquiry is generated and designed to meet each participant's circumstances and desires. As more teachers learn to consider their schools as centers for inquiry, we hope that increasing numbers will make inquiries into the dynamics of education.

Inquiry is often multidimensional. One school-university partnership held a semester-long seminar in which preservice teachers, school faculty, and university professors participated in a middle school curriculum study focused on both the school curriculum and the university teacher preparation programs. The seminar members met regularly to engage in readings and inquiry; all participants were encouraged to formulate questions, review literature, and reflect on personal experiences to explore possible solutions. Discussions of middle school interdisciplinary teaming and implementation occurred in the context of a complex collaboration between varied partners, resulting in major conceptual growth for all parties. At the end of the semester, the inquiry group presented a document summarizing its findings, conclusions, and recommendations to the central administration and to the local school board.

As these examples suggest, the view of educational research and inquiry traditionally accepted by universities must expand so that a wider variety of questions can be asked, and richer and more complex answers can be explored, tested, and shared. As collaborative investigators focus on true parity between parties to an inquiry, new questions will emerge, new methods and designs will be created, and reporting systems will expand to include a wider and more varied audience. The results should be increased knowledge and better teaching in both schools and universities.

Complex Networks of Inquiry

As the examples in this chapter have shown, partnership research and inquiry is expanding and changing the nature of traditional university research models. Inquiry, investigation, reflection, and analysis no longer take place in isolation. As new methods reflect the partnership and parity of school-university collaboration, research can be nested in and interrelated with practice in ways not evident in the past.

Additional nesting, interrelating, and expanding take place when partnerships link together into larger and more complex partnerships, as common data are collected and shared by several smaller inquiry collaboratives. One partnership, for example, is involved in three expanded collaboratives on state and local levels and one national network. One of the local units is a three-university research collaborative that explores the processes and outcomes of partnership development at each of the three institutions and collects comparative data. Research for this group, which evolved from the agenda of the university faculty, includes a three-phase plan: first, descriptions and comparisons of the partnerships at the three universities (Knight, Wiseman, & Smith, 1992); second, interviews with the major partnership participants; and third, a questionnaire that will be developed based on the findings of the first two phases. Both school and university faculty have participated in the in-depth interviews and have supplied other information about their school-university collaborations.

The same partnership participates in a statewide collaborative centered around implementation of a curriculum restructuring effort, the Accelerated Schools Process. Fourteen universities from across a very large state have joined a network to support this process. Initially, the focus was on teacher and administrator education and curriculum development; however, as inquiry proceeded, participants felt the need to collect data on student achievement as well. Then, as discussions proceeded on research design, university faculty began to design methods of collecting information on the processes of school-university collaboration as well. At the present time, the collaborative is collecting baseline data at all fourteen universities on both the outcomes of the Accelerated Schools Process implementation and the function of school-university partnerships.

Members of the network support each other by sharing inquiry methods, data collection procedures, analysis support, and dissemination processes. The group has presented together at state and national conferences and discussed joint monograph production.

These partnerships have joined with others nationwide as members of the National Network for Educational Renewal (NNER) (Goodlad, 1993). The state's partnership contributes examples, status reports, and other qualitative data to the ongoing studies and monitoring efforts of this national consortium.

Due to the extensiveness of most collaborations, it is not unusual in partnerships for data generated in one research project to be used in another as well. Collaborative processes allow data to be used on a national scale or in one individual's project. Material collected for a faculty member's research report or a graduate student's dissertation may be jointly analyzed by several university and school faculty members and presented to a number of schools or aggregated between members of large collaboratives. The in-depth interviews collected by the three universities to compare partnership perceptions and processes were also used in a study of school-university interactions at one of the local sites. In addition, they formed part of a graduate student's case study of school-university partnerships. Collaboratives, indeed, use the resources of all members for the benefit of all.

Partnership Inquiry Issues

Partnership inquiry, like any change involving new paradigms, requires new perspectives, particularly regarding allocations of time, personnel, recognition, and remuneration.

Rewards and recognition

If changes are to occur in the process of research and inquiry, changes must also occur in the systems by which research and inquiry are recognized and rewarded. Unfortunately, the reward system at many universities discourages the field-based applied research that is generated by partnership participation (Winitzky, Stoddart, & O'Keefe, 1992). Also, some faculty prefer not to engage in inquiry that does not have as its first priority publication in journals or reports that meet the standards of university review. It has been suggested that the lack of university recognition of partnership inquiry may actually be used by some faculty as an excuse for not becoming involved in partnership work (Soder, 1991). However, others who do wish to participate in partnership inquiry feel that, with effort, faculty can frame research that will address both the professional questions for which the schools want practical answers and the academic challenges valued by universities, while results can be presented in a variety of ways to meet the needs of multiple audiences. Yet others believe that university tenure and promotion processes need to be adapted to take collaborative inquiry and research into account.

For the schoolteachers who participate in collaborative inquiry, there are rarely extrinsic rewards or recognitions. Of course, those who participate receive intrinsic rewards in the form of professional expertise, increased knowledge and efficacy, enhanced collegial interaction, and strengthened positive attitudes toward teaching.

Time Constraints

The roles of school faculty have not traditionally included research and inquiry activities. Typically, teachers' time is absorbed in the demands of effective teaching; if teachers are also to participate in extensive research, partnerships must find creative and effective ways to give them the necessary time.

A number of time-enhancing strategies have already been devised. Many school-university partnerships make effective use of preservice teachers to support inservice teachers' research activities. For example, some partnerships arrange for student interns to oversee classroom activities so that teachers can be released for short periods of time to work on research and inquiry. Such arrangements must be worked out through clearly stated agreements between the school and the university.

Another approach that has worked well calls for university undergraduates engaged in the field activities that precede student teaching to participate in the inquiry and research processes. These students are paired with teachers to act as research assistants, helping with such data collection activities as completing observation checklists, conducting student interviews, or composing journal entries. The data collection is considered part of the pre–student teaching experience since it provides the students with powerful opportunities to observe classroom procedures and interact with the children. During one such inquiry activity, students in a preservice reading methods course kept running records of children's oral reading miscues for teachers who were testing the impact of an instructional method on oral reading miscues. The undergraduates learned not only about oral reading miscues but also about interacting with children and about taking part in a collaborative inquiry process.

Teacher time for research is also increased and enhanced when teachers join research teams. One successful inquiry team consisting of school and university faculty and graduate students reviewed the impact of teacher education programs on the instructional processes in a partner school. Working together, the team formulated questions, designed a research methodology, and analyzed the data. Each component of the team was assigned a particular task: university faculty compiled the related research review, preservice teachers and graduate students collected the data, and school faculty wrote the implications section of the report after the data were analyzed. Because the team shared the project tasks, the teachers' time commitment was reduced, yet they were able to contribute to and benefit from the results of the inquiry.

Experience and Training

Many teachers in the schools are hesitant to participate in inquiry projects because they are not familiar with research techniques. One way to provide the necessary instruction for these teachers is to offer graduate study opportunities at the partnership school campus so teachers can attend conveniently and in a group. Participating together, they can offer each other support and assistance during the process of gaining research expertise, a process that may seem intimidating at first. This site-specific instruction also allows them time together to plan inquiry activities that use common data to answer difficult questions or to compare results of their data collection across classrooms or teaching methodologies.

Dissemination

Teacher-initiated research is usually disseminated differently from the research traditionally associated with university faculty. Teachers can contribute articles to journals or papers at conferences, but they may also report their findings to school boards, local educational groups, or peers within their own schools. The most important dissemination of teacher inquiry, however, occurs when what teachers learn from inquiry is applied to instructional practices. When teachers have ownership of the inquiry processes and of the knowledge and understanding that are gained, the findings are often more directly applicable to classrooms and children. Of course, this is what teacher research is all about: the education of children and youth.

Results of partnership inquiry and research should be shared with colleagues, central administrators, and other educators. Administrators at the school and district levels will be convinced of the value of providing time for research and inquiry when they see changes in instructional approaches, teacher development, or student achievement in the classrooms. Inquiry results, generalized from data gathered in classrooms, should cycle back to those classrooms in the form of improved teacher understanding and practice. Collaborative approaches in research and inquiry can then become associated with creative and innovative instruction and with professionals who continually learn from and improve on their classroom performance.

Political and Financial Stability

Even when the interests, priorities, and approaches of the school staff match those of the university faculty, conflicts may occur because the school is ultimately responsible to the school board. Unlike tenured university faculty, school boards are not stable over time. Publicly elected school boards can reverse policies and programs with the turn of an election—and they often do. Additional instability occurs as the district and the school experience shifting levels of state and local financial support. When its educational financing goes down, a district may decide to cut the budget by discontinuing support for the partner school.

An additional instability that discourages some schools and districts from participating in partnership work is generated, ironically, by the same impetus that originally caused partnerships to be established: the propensity of the American people for educational reform. In the past, education has experienced a series of reform movements that have not been effective in changing the nature of schooling (Cuban, 1984). Educators at all levels want to participate in innovation, but they are often hesitant to invest their time, energy, expertise, and financial resources in what may turn out to be one more fad. When the foundation of a partnership is laid over a terrain of doubts and suspicions about the longevity and effectiveness of the arrangement, the resulting collaborations may give an illusion of meeting public or legislative needs, but these particular collaborations are in danger of being futile expenditures of energy and resources.

Cultural Change

The partner school concept asks all parties to participate in cultural change: to alter their practices and, essentially, to change themselves. Such changes are difficult, particularly for those who have not reflected on their current practice sufficiently to understand themselves. Some schools may need to generate a very different kind of school organization; others may not. Colleges and schools of education must also become involved in change decisions. The societal context within which schools and colleges exist is undergoing cultural modification; most aspects of society are now revealed as dynamic and increasingly complex. As college professors, as schoolteachers, as administrators—all participants are being asked to alter their perceptions of research and the roles that they have played in research of the past. Teachers, who may have felt that research was distant and not relevant to everyday actions, are now becoming key players in ongoing research efforts. College professors, who may have hidden on university campuses, are going out to live and work in the world of the schools, and they are actually becoming comfortable in doing so. The collaborative research approach requires that teachers perceive themselves as researchers, performing important and legitimate inquiry. It insists also that professors perceive themselves as teachers as well as scholars and researchers. Though professors and school teachers may have been suspicious of each other in the past, under the partnership approach they are colleagues, exhibiting mutual trust and respect.

Conclusion

A partner school is a center of inquiry engaged in *ongoing* actions. The changes needed for schools to reach this goal can sometimes seem overwhelming. Schools have, until recently, been largely places where knowledge and culture were *transmitted*. Now they must become centers where teachers and students of all ages and positions work together to *construct* and *reconstruct* not only the curriculum but the very lore, the grand narrative of education itself.

Nevertheless, despite all the difficulties, substantial change has begun. Professors and schoolteachers and administrators in partnerships are conversing *with* not *at* each other. They are examining new possibilities. They are even inventing new titles to go with the new roles they are defining: *supervising teacher, action research coordinator, site manager, school lesson person, professor in residence, teacher researcher, adjunct personnel.*

Today's world is experiencing changes in perspective and thought.

New patterns are emerging out of chaos; innovation swirls through the thinking and doing in national and world communities. The very purposes of education are being challenged, examined, discarded, and reconstructed. School-university partnerships represent an attempt to make harmony from the rising cacophony of diverse voices in education, many of them previously mute or suppressed. Ideally, these partnerships are formed to recompose and reinvent—while acknowledging and affirming the need for continual reinvention.

References

Auger, F. K., & Odell, S. J. (1992). Three school-university partnerships for teacher development. *Journal of Teacher Education, 43*(4), 262–268.

Cochran-Smith, M., & Lytle, S. (1990). Research on teaching and teacher research: The issues that divide. *Educational Researcher, 19*(2), 2–11.

Cole, A. L., & Knowles, J. G. (1993). Teacher development partnership research: A focus on methods and issues. *American Educational Research Journal, 30* (3), 473–495.

Cuban, L. (1984). *How teachers taught: Constancy and change in American classrooms, 1890–1980.* New York: Longman.

Cuban, L. (1992). Managing dilemmas while building professional communities. *Educational Researcher, 21*(1), 4–11.

Darling-Hammond, L. (1993). *Professional development schools.* New York: Teachers College Press.

Gehrke, N., & McDaniel, J. (1989). *Toward teacher leadership: Planning a multisite professional development center* (Report to the Ford Foundation on a planning grant). Seattle: College of Education, University of Washington.

Goodlad, J. I. (1980). How laboratory schools go awry. *UCLA Educator, 21*(2), 46–33.

Goodlad, J. I. (1988). School-university partnerships for educational renewal: Rationale and concepts. In K. A. Sirotnik & J. I. Goodlad (Eds.), *School-university partnerships in action: Concepts, cases, and concerns* (pp. 3–31). New York: Teachers College Press.

Goodlad, J. I. (1990). *Teachers for our nation's schools.* San Francisco, Jossey-Bass.

Goodlad, J. I. (1993). School-university partnerships and partner schools. *Educational Policy, 7* (1), 24–39.

Hendricks, I. G. (1980). University controlled laboratory schools in historical perspective. *UCLA Educator, 21*(2), 55–59.

Keislar, E. R. (1980). The inquiry-oriented laboratory school. *UCLA Educator, 21*(2), 26–31.

Knight, S. K., Wiseman, D. L., & Smith, C. W. (1992). The reflectivity-activity dilemma in school-university partnerships. *Journal of Teacher Education, 43*(4) 269–277.

Leinhardt, G. (1990). Capturing craft knowledge in teaching. *Educational Researcher, 19*(2), 18–25.

Lincoln, Y. S., & Guba, E. (1985). *Naturalistic inquiry.* Newbury Park, CA: Sage.

Oja, S. N., & Smulyan, L. (1989). *Collaborative action research: A developmental approach.* New York: Falmer Press.

Reason, P. (1988). The cooperative inquiry group. In P. Reason, *Human inquiry in action.* Newbury Park, CA: Sage.

Richardson, V. (1990). Significant and worthwhile change in teaching practice. *Educational Researcher, 19*(7), 10–18.

Schlechty, P. C. (1990). *Schools for the 21st century: Leadership imperatives for educational reform.* San Francisco: Jossey-Bass.

Schlechty, P. C., & Whitford, B. L. (1988). Shared problems and shared vision: Organic collaboration. In K. A. Sirotnik & J. I. Goodlad (Eds.), *School-university partnerships in action: Concepts, cases, and concerns* (pp. 191–204). New York: Teachers College Press.

Schön, D. A. (1983). The reflective practitioner: How professionals think in action. New York: Basic Books.

Senge, P. M. (1990). *The fifth discipline: The art and practice of the learning organization.* New York: Doubleday/Currency.

Slavin, R. (1989). PET and the pendulum: Faddism in education and how to stop it. *Phi Delta Kappan, 70,* 752–758.

Soder, R. (1991). The wealth of higher education, reward structures, and school-university collaboration. *Metropolitan Universities, 2*(1), 93–100.

Williams, R.C. (1992). The Corinne A. Seeds University Elementary School at the University of California, Los Angeles. In Moller, B. (Ed.), *The logics of education: Education as an interdisciplinary subject* (Vol. 4, pp. 65–76). Oldenburg, Germany: Bibliotheks und informationssystem der Universität Oldenburg.

Winitzky, N., Stoddart, T., & O'Keefe, P. O. (1992). Great expectations: Emergent professional development schools. *Journal of Teacher Education, 43*(1) 3–18.

Wiseman, D. L. (1993). Inquiry processes in the Texas A&M University-Jane Long Middle School Partnership. Paper presented at the annual meeting of the American Association of Educational Research, Atlanta, GA.

Wiseman, D. L., & Nason, P. L. (1993). Patterns of interactions in school-university partnerships. Paper presented at American Association of Colleges of Teacher Education, San Diego, CA.

Part Two

Developing and Implementing
Partner Schools

6

Launching and Sustaining a Partner School

R. Carl Harris and Melanie Fox Harris

A journey to renewal is a journey into the unknown. The voyager knows some of the conditions and benefits of the destination, but not all of them. Most travelers have considered the price, but only a part of it. Most who set forth are aware of some of the dangers and pitfalls, but only those that can be inferred from journeys to other destinations. Reading the maps and logs of similar voyages undertaken by others can substantially increase anyone's personal knowledge about destination, price, and pitfalls. For that reason, the authors of this chapter offer excerpts from the documents and transcripts that were the maps and logs of the participants in the launching and sustaining of partner schools in the five districts that our school-university partnership comprises. These excerpts present important aspects of the realities partnerships encounter. They are drawn from six areas of the partners' experience: sensing a need, assessing prerequisites, establishing structures, identifying roles, sustaining the progress, and allocating resources.

Sensing a Need

Successful innovations begin with a desire to go someplace different and experience something new.

Listening to Each Other

Our school-university partnership began as we learned to listen to each other's voices:

EXPERIENCED PUBLIC SCHOOL TEACHER: All three first-grade teachers at our school are using different approaches to reading—phonics, whole language, basal. How can we learn which approach *really* contributes to our students' fluency? Where can we learn about how the approaches really impact our kids?

COOPERATING TEACHER WHO MENTORS UNIVERSITY STUDENTS: My student teacher feels she is trying to serve two masters. People from the university call some aspects of teaching one thing, and I call them something else. I use our district assessment plan to evaluate her while university people use their own department model. At the school we use one format for planning lessons, and her unyielding supervisor asks her to use a different one. How can we work together to support these teachers in training and not neutralize each other's efforts?

NOVICE THIRD-GRADE TEACHER: Our district inservice is a dump model. A visiting guru expounds his specialty in a one-day endurance workshop and then leaves. We are left to use what we can or not at all. If some of these new ideas can impact the whole school, how can we find them and really use them?

TENURED PROFESSOR OF TEACHER EDUCATION: Through research we build a theoretical base for certain forms of pedagogical practice. Our students learn this material. Then when they go into the schools to student teach, they aren't allowed to use it—the school "doesn't do things that way." What hope do we have for building the expertise of our graduates?

UNIVERSITY DEPARTMENT CHAIR: Associate Professor Jones is one of my most talented and hardworking faculty. But how can I send a recommendation to the university committee for his rank advancement when he hasn't published very much during the past three years? His teaching load includes the time-intensive work of supervision in the schools. He also provides inservice [training] for teachers and principals. How can I help him balance the needs of the field with the needs of the campus?

Different personalities, different positions, different needs—very different. Each of these individuals sensed a problem and felt a need for renewal, either in teacher education or in educational practice. Since these two areas are interdependent, it was easily evident that public school and university groups could profitably integrate their efforts (Darling-Hammond, 1994; R. C. Harris & M. F. Harris, 1992). But we needed guidance in bringing our needs and resources together.

Finding a Way

A decade ago, in the work of John Goodlad (1984), we found the ideas and methods that we needed. The dean of our college of education requested Goodlad's assistance. In response Goodlad met separately with public school teachers and administrators in one group and with university administrators and faculty in another group. Then he met with the groups together, demonstrating to them as well as telling them that what was needed was not merely side-by-side cooperation, but symbiotic collaboration. He guided the separate groups in listing their needs and self-interests. Then he guided the combined group in identifying shared interests, overlapping interests, and areas where each could afford to be selfless in yielding to the needs of the other.

As participants met to share, plan, and collaborate, the validity of Goodlad's perspective became more and more evident. The following conversation from a workshop to link school and university educators reveals the understanding that began to emerge as formerly distant associates in the public schools and the university's college of education began to meet as equal stakeholders in the enterprise of renewal.

PROFESSOR: The quality of university learning depends on the preparation of the students who come to us. We can improve what our students learn only as you give them the knowledge base and the skills to handle it.

TEACHER A: But school learning improves only as teachers and administrators are better prepared to improve it. There are a lot of great methods out there, and we need to learn what they are.

PRINCIPAL: Yes, we need to get effective professional development opportunities in place for our teachers. University scholars are uncovering more information on how the brain works and how people learn. They're also learning how to meet the human need for relevance in the educational experience. If our teachers can share this knowledge, they'll find better ways of reaching the kids.

TEACHER B: And today's kids have needs that are different from the needs children had when many of us had our training fifteen or twenty years ago. They're growing up in an information society; they live daily with technology we only dreamed about. And there are equity issues and multicultural issues that many of us have not been prepared to handle. Teaching and learning will improve and become more relevant only if the new teachers coming into the field learn to deal with the technologies and the issues.

PROFESSOR: You're right. We're responsible for getting relevant, up-to-date training for new teachers. But in today's diversified world, information comes from so many sources. We as teacher educators need the cooperation and input of almost every department on campus to keep our students current.

TEACHER A: While we're all shouldering our share of the responsibility, I guess I'd better take mine. The theory and knowledge are important, but if the new teachers can't put them into practice, renewal isn't going to come. We need to provide the kind of observation and practice sites in the schools where student observers can see things happen and student teachers can practice making things happen.

Investigating needs, producing knowledge, sharing it, practicing it, giving feedback, receiving feedback, trying out new options, assessing results, asking questions, investigating need, producing knowledge—as this group of education professionals recognized, improving teacher education and renewing the schools are bound into a cycle in which teachers, professors, and administrators are all participants (Levine, 1992; Harris, 1991). The partner school has emerged as the site at which this cycle can occur (Goodlad, 1990). Perhaps it could be said that the partner school is the starship through which the journey to renewal takes place.

Assessing Prerequisites

From the perspective of a decade of voyaging, we find three factors to have been critical in the launching of our own partner schools, all of them factors that were involved in the launching of the partnership itself. First, there must be enough discontent with the present status of teacher preparation and public school function to motivate all parties involved with the school to participate in renewal. Second, leaders at all levels must be capable of labeling the discontent and looking toward options for changing what needs to be changed. Third, school and university leaders must be willing to accept a new paradigm concerning knowledge, teaching, learning, and leadership.

Discontent

All changes require a price, and participants are rarely willing to make sacrifices when they are already comfortable. If a school's fourth-grade teachers seem to be getting satisfactory, if not stunning, results from the phonics-based methodology they have been using for years, then they will find it easier to continue copying workbook pages than to research and experiment with a literature-based program. If parents continue to think that their neighborhood school is better off than those in distant communities (Bracey, 1993), they will not be motivated to participate with the teachers and children in finding new ways of supporting their children's reading at home. If district leaders feel that their teachers are basically competent, they may provide a little piecemeal inservice professional development, but without seriously listening to teachers' concerns about inconsistency in the reading methodology and without considering follow-up support for teachers who might decide to experiment with something like whole language principles. If college teachers receive basically comfortable feedback from their lectures, they will find it easier and easier to rely on their lecture files. Similarly, contented superintendents support only safe ventures, ones that will not raise controversy with their boards of education, while contented principals control their schools and preserve tradition.

Unfortunately, the result of all this contentment is that the students may continue to mark their worksheets thoughtlessly, left on their own to find (or not to find) meaningful reading experiences outside the classroom. As the old axiom goes, "If you always do as you've always done, you'll always get what you've always got." When we began to launch partner schools, it was in response to a degree of discontent in all stakeholders. The reading program, in particular, was a motivating discontent in one of the schools.

Leadership

A leader in educational renewal, at any level, must be able to designate the objectionable aspects of the current situation and initiate a process of change (Palmer, 1992). Sometimes leadership begins when someone is officially designated as a leader. One partner school principal had a desire for his students to have an international experience. In consultation with the university's center for international studies and with professors in the college of education, he assumed leadership in setting up a sister schools program with three impoverished schools in Mexico. His students helped the Mexican children to raise money to build bathrooms and fences for their schools and to purchase supplies like pencils, notebooks, and a basketball. Correspondence between U.S. and Mexican children followed, and with the consultation and support of university people and the participation of parents, a visit to the Mexican schools was arranged for a number of children, parents, schoolteachers, and university advisors. During this trip, the U.S. visitors installed the necessary wiring for electricity to be brought into one of the schools.

However, leaders do not need to be appointed. Any participant in a partner school may emerge as a leader when a need is discerned and ideas are generated to meet it. For example, a special education teacher who saw significant weaknesses in the resource room policy of an elementary partner school took his findings to administrators and fellow teachers. When they understood his position, they supported his leadership in designing and implementing an inclusion program that has created significant benefits for the school and has become a model for other schools over a wide area. With input from university professors, the program has been refined, and presentations at national conferences and publications in professional journals have been arranged (M.F. Harris and R.C. Harris, 1992).

Preservice teachers are also participants, and their leadership should be respected and supported as well. One student teacher discerned a need for more appropriate, up-to-date use of technology in the partner school in which he was doing his student teaching. Donations were arranged from a large software corporation based nearby, and this preservice teacher assumed leadership in setting up a new computer lab for the school. University and school district personnel with expertise in technology have advised and aided him in this project.

Although the desire for partner school innovation can be generated by the enthusiasm of any teacher, parent, student, principal, or professor who emerges as a grass-roots leader, it must ultimately be channeled and directed by leadership at the higher levels of school administration. As W. Edwards Deming (1986), advocate of Total Quality Management, has affirmed, the chief executive officer of any organization must set the tone for change if successful change is to become a reality. Once the deans at the university and the superintendents in the districts recognize the need for renewal and approve partner schools to participate in it, decision making should be evaluated and redirected to the level of the professors, teachers, and principals at the partner school site.

Paradigms

In his book *The Structure of Scientific Revolutions,* Thomas Kuhn (1963) affirmed that paradigms constitute the structure or lens through which an individual perceives and makes meaning of the world. What is admitted into our vision and how we perceive and interpret what we admit will be greatly influenced by what fits within the parameters of our personal and institutional paradigms (Smith, 1990).

Traditionally, professors on the university campus and teachers in the public schools have viewed themselves as separate, each group going about its own job within a designated sphere. School-teachers have often secretly, or not so secretly, regarded professors as overly theoretical and impractical, removed from the "real world" of the classroom and the current characteristics and needs of the children. Professors have regarded teachers as perhaps well meaning but stagnant, unable to see beyond the daily grindstone and unwilling to question their own practice and to learn new theories and ideas. When it comes to preparing teachers, the general paradigm has been for both groups to tolerate each other—because student teaching opportunities do have to be given to the preservice teachers—but at the same time, each group does its best to counteract the "damage" being done by the other side. This paradigm causes both groups to focus only on the damage and to miss the strengths that the "opposition" has to offer.

A change of paradigms is necessary if true partnerships are to be formed and partner schools are to be established (Wheatley, 1992). The education of teachers and the education of school children must be viewed as interactive processes. Professors need to change their paradigms to recognize that theory that cannot be translated into classroom practice during preservice teachers' college experience will not be translated into practice during their inservice teaching. Teachers in the schools need to guide the preservice teachers in applying what they learn. Teachers with their day-to-day classroom experience also have much to explain and communicate—many insights into children, classrooms, and group dynamics that are not to be found in the professors' reading. Professors need the teachers in order to make the preparation of preservice teachers effective.

Classroom teachers also need to change their paradigms. They need to recognize that many of their timely practices have become timeworn. Professors, with more time and resources for research and professional reading, are able to learn of innovations that can make significant improvements in day-to-day classroom practice. And university students, with fresh idealism and new viewpoints, have much to contribute in their own right. These changes in paradigms are essential if the partner school, once launched, is to sustain its progress. Table 6.1 shows the paradigm shifts that the authors of this chapter view as critical in the school-university partnership in which they have been participants.

Formal Structures

Once the desirability of change has been acknowledged, leadership has begun to emerge, and prospective partners have accepted a shift in paradigm from separation to collaboration, a formal organization for the partnership and its supporting partner school can be selected. For maximum involvement of practitioners and professors, the initial partnership organization must be lean and flat. A governing board, of course, must be selected, and partner school committees should be established in the selected sites. Additional partnership initiatives beyond the partner schools may be facilitated by committees or task forces for special interests, such as teacher education, special education, gifted/talented education, or administrator preparation. Figure 6.1 illustrates the partnership governance established for the school-university partnership described in this chapter.

Table 6.1. Paradigm Shift in Teacher Education and Schooling.

Educational Domain	Dominant Pattern	Paradigm Shift Pattern
Knowing and Knowledge[a]	Objective knowledge lies beyond and independent of the knower. Analytic approach reduces events to their component parts. To know the parts is to know the whole. Use of experimental method to manipulate events to discover if they respond as theory predicts they will. Possessed and owned by others, especially "experts."	Subjective knowledge relates a knowledge of self to a knowledge of events and other knowers. Integrative approach strives to understand larger whole. Knowing how to think metacognitively about knowledge. Knowledge is owned and honored by self. Knowledge is useful in obtaining quality goals.
Learning and Learner[b]	Mastery of a vision of reality developed and maintained by others who may be known as experts. Process of mastery is usually a solitary and competitive process. Learning through exposure to simple representations followed by memorization, conceptualization, imitation, repetition, feedback and testing.	An ongoing process of construction, generation, and creation of meaning. Enhanced by interaction with other learners in cooperative, interdependent, synergistic, and co-creative effort. Validity of learning constantly tested against an internal sense of reality and worth. Self-regulation of learning through questioning and applying.
Teaching and Teacher[c]	Center of the classroom, prime source of wisdom, and the holder of power. Manager of students and resources. Source of information and judgment of right and wrong.	Cognitive coach who functions as a resource and guide for student exploration. Models the problem inquiry process and helps provide the "scaffolding" for students' construction of knowledge.

	Makes all important decisions such as pace, content, and activity. Does most of the talking while prohibiting student talk.	Teachers are learners also and collaborate with students and other teachers in their own learning process.
Leading and Leaders[d]	Transactional leadership or leadership by bartering: the leader and the led exchange needs and services in order to accomplish independent objectives. Leaders and followers assume they do not share a common stake in the enterprise and so they must strike a bargain. Good work is exchanged for positive reinforcement, merit pay for performance, promotion for increased persistence.	Transformational leadership: leaders and followers are united in pursuit of higher-level goals common to both. Leaders and followers raise one another to higher levels of motivation and morality. Leaders provide followers opportunity for esteem, achievement, autonomy, self-actualization, purpose, and significance.
Curriculum Design[e]	Teacher proof. Major decisions about content, sequence, evaluation, critical learning activities, and pacing decided by the "expert" designers. All needed information provided. Practice problems are highly simplified approximations of real world problems. Cover large amounts of information.	Major concepts and themes are provided which represent the valued educational outcomes held by the community. A rich array of sources and ideas allow for teachers' professional decision making given learner needs. Practice problems are authentic and real-world in nature. Additional information must be found by students.
Organization and Structure[f]	Guided by scientific management applied to production practices of factories around the end of the nineteenth century.	Brain-compatible learning environment. Teachers collaborate with parents and students to determine allocation of time, type and place-

Educational Domain	Dominant Pattern	Paradigm Shift Pattern
Organization and Structure (*continued*)	Learning takes place in a formal classroom setting, for a set period of time, with a single subject being taught. Students are assigned their groups on the basis of age/ability. A bell (like factory whistle) signals change of topics and/or classrooms.	ment of content, time spent. Students are grouped to maximize heterogeneity and/or interest. Home and family the preferred metaphor rather than factory and assembly line.
Supervision and Supervisor[g]	Technical rationality the source of authority for policy and practice. Use research to identify best practice. Standardize the work of teaching to reflect best practice. In-service teachers. Monitor the process to ensure compliance. Figure out how to motivate teachers and get them to change.	Promote reflection and dialogue among educators that makes professional values and tenets of practice explicit. Translate the dialogue into professional practice standards. Provide educators with decision-making power. Require that educators hold each other accountable. Make assistance, support, and professional development opportunities available.
Professional Growth[h]	Learning, growth, and career development a personal rather than institutional responsibility. Occurs largely at the margins of educator's work. Inservice imposed by administration and mostly irrelevant. Evaluation and supervision by administration has little impact on classroom practice.	All youths and adults associated with an educational institution are learners and involved in personal/professional growth. Good teaching and leading is a creative process, demanding the constant injection of new information, new perspectives, and new psychic energy. Teachers and administrators collaborate in selecting and designing in-service and other professional development.

Assessment[i]	Paper and pencil, short answer, fill in the blank, sentence completion, circle the right answer, multiple choice, use a #2 pencil to fill in the space.	Downplay psychometrics in favor of real performance.
	Standardized, norm referenced tests compare students to each other with emphasis on memory, imitation, and skills out of context.	Teacher judgment essential but must be informed by regular exposure to models of desired performance.
	Performance reduced to members, bottom line mentality.	Authentic simulations of how knowledge is tested in adult work and civic settings.
		Employ portfolios which are jointly created by students and teachers.
Inquiry[j]	Dominated by university professors who need research publications for rank advancement and continuing status.	Shared responsibility of university and school faculty as a fundamental and integrated part of professional life.
	Research questions frequently do not deal with the problems encountered by practitioners and learners in school.	Includes action research as well as sophisticated, highly disciplined studies.
	"Project orientation" rather than long-term involvement.	Tool for finding answers for real problems as collaboratively defined by school and university educators.
	Teachers are objects of study.	Long-term involvement.
Technology[k]	Paper and pencil.	Liquid crystal displays (LCD) from computer to large screen.
	Chalkboards and charts.	Compressed disk (CD) and laser disk random access to sight and sound and vast data bases of content and lesson guides.
	Two-dimensional printed materials for narratives and illustrations.	Wide area networks (WANs) connecting teacher and student operated computers across schools,
	Desks arranged in egg-carton patterns comprise work sites.	
	Overhead projectors, film projectors, film strip	

Educational Domain	Dominant Pattern	Paradigm Shift Pattern
Technology (*continued*)	One telephone for teacher use and one for student use.	projectors. Every student owns and uses a calculator and has daily access to computer assisted, interactive, individualized work stations.
Administration[l]	All important decisions about calendar, finances, textbook adoption, resource allocation, problem solving made by central administration without teacher input. Hierarchical organization with more power and more pay the further removed the individual is from teaching and learning. Teachers work in isolation.	districts, states, nations. Lean structure, flat organization, and decision making pushed to lowest possible level. Middle managers or district staff act less like controllers and more like colleagues and collaborators. Teachers invited to help inform administrators on needs and new directions and processes. Teachers work as colleagues to support and critique each other.
Social Studies[m]	Memorization of facts about history, government, and societal functions that may have little meaning in student's world. Use of texts that limit the scope of historical or societal events, for example, omit influence of religion in society, history, or role of particular ethnic groups. Taught through the lecture, fill-in-the-blank or short essay assignment test; then advancing to next chapter of text.	Engage with and experience the world. Explore real world issues where facts of history, government, and society must be discovered and used. Use opportunities to be a responsible member of a community. Develop basic participatory understanding and skills. Engage in structured controversy around real-world issues.

	Art[n]	Used as a time filler or recreational activity, often reserved for Friday afternoons. Little concern for continuity, consistency, and content. Arts and crafts activities which may be cut and paste or color within the lines without a concern for developing students' understanding of and appreciation for the world of art.	Discipline-based art education treats art as a subject for study. Art content derived from four disciplines: art production, art history, art criticism, and aesthetics. Art studied from the perspectives of artist, art historian, art critic, and aesthetician.

[a]Based on Palmer, 1983; pp. 33–46; Glasser, 1990, pp. 89–103.

[b]Based on O'Neil, 1992b, pp. 1–4; Langer, 1989, pp. 61–79; Gardner, 1991, pp. 200–224; Leinhardt, 1992, pp. 20–25; Caine & Caine, 1991, pp. 79–88.

[c]Based on O'Neil, 1992a, pp. 1–3; Smith, 1986, pp. 169–203; Barell, 1991.

[d]Based on Sergiovanni, 1990, pp. 23–27; Leithwood, 1992, pp. 8–12.

[e]Based on O'Neil, 1992a, pp. 1–3; Brophy, 1992, pp. 4–8.

[f]Based on Strategic Planning Commission, 1988; Samples, 1987, pp. 25–56.

[g]Based on Sergiovanni, 1992.

[h]Based on Johnson, 1990, pp. 249–287.

[i]Based on Wiggins, 1992, pp. 26–33.

[j]Based on The Holmes Group, 1990, pp. 55–56.

[k]Based on Kearns & Doyle, 1991, pp. 20–24.

[l]Based on Leiberman, 1988, pp. 4–8.

[m]Based on Berman, 1990, pp. 75–80.

[n]Based on Greer & Silverman, 1988, pp. 10–14.

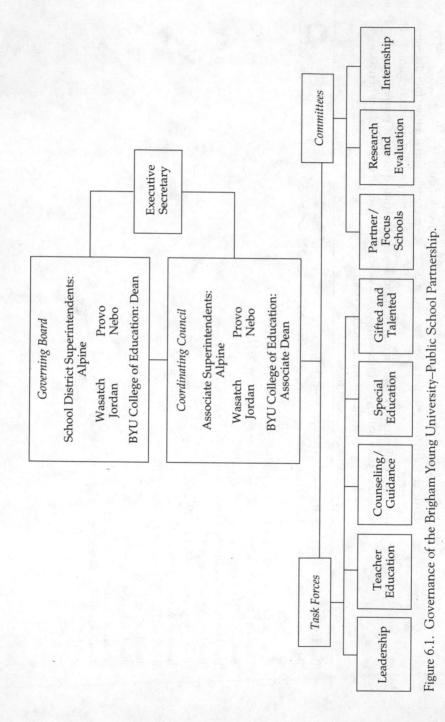

Figure 6.1. Governance of the Brigham Young University–Public School Partnership.

Governing Boards

The governing board is the validating organization for our school-university partnership. Most governing boards for such partnerships comprise the superintendents from the participating school districts, the dean from the college or school of education, and an executive director. The latter is employed by the partnership and salaried by the partners in accordance with their ability to pay. All board members have equal voting rights with the exception of the executive director, who functions only as an advisor. The board selects one of the superintendents to act as chair. The executive director may furnish the agendas for the regular meetings, allowing time for presentations from partner school faculty and university educators working on the partner school level.

On the journey to renewal, the governing board functions in a policy-setting role. For example, its members foster and nurture the vision and goals of the entire partnership. To give guidance and direction to the journey of our partner schools, our governing board ratified the following mission, created by the board and other school, district, and university representatives in a strategic planning session: "The mission of partner schools and the partnership is to improve teaching and learning by merging theory and practice through preservice and inservice education, curriculum development and research. In an atmosphere of collaboration and trust, partnership educators will provide leadership in assuring a quality education to empower all students to function effectively in society as competent, productive, caring, and responsible citizens" (BYU-Public School Partnership, 1989).

Partner School Sites

Once the governing board has established the mission and clarified the functions of the partnership, it is time for principals, teachers, and university professors to work together in designating sites to function as partner schools. Faculty and principals from schools interested in becoming sites are invited by district and department administration to attend presentations of partnership principles and goals. If faculty members and their principal at an invited school are sufficiently interested in joining with the university in efforts to promote educational renewal in the designated areas, both parties commit to collaborate under the mission and purposes of the partnership (Harris & Harris, 1993a).

Partner School Committees

When partner school sites have been selected and agreement and commitment have been reached, a partner school committee is formed to empower personnel in the schools and bring decision making closer to those who will be implementing the decisions. Generally, this committee will comprise the school principal, one teacher from every grade level, and the university professor who supervises the student teachers and coordinates university activities at the school. The committee is encouraged to select one of the teachers as chair and to have the university professor act as executive secretary. It should meet regularly to discuss ideas and to make decisions for implementing plans. Initially, much of its work may focus on building trust among the members and establishing ownership in the school-university collaboration effort. Later, planning and implementation will become more specific, and volunteer teachers will assume responsibility for preservice, inservice, curriculum development, and research duties.

People in the Trenches

The official work of the partner school committees should be supported and supplemented by a continual flow of informal discussion among teachers, principal, professors, and parents. New ideas, researched ideas, and ideas that have been cherished for years—all are appropriate subjects of discussion, and all can contribute constructively to the function of partner schools. Many parents, for example, have workable suggestions about ways that the school might be run or material that might be taught in classrooms, but they have never thought they would be able to present these ideas successfully and change old practices. Many teachers have realized that they exercise some power and autonomy in their own class-rooms, but they have also thought their influence ended at the classroom door; they have never considered opening the door and making suggestions in the larger context of affecting the curriculum of others' classes. They have not thought of adding their experience and observations to the knowledge of others to affect the ways new teachers are prepared (M. F. Harris & R. C. Harris, 1992). For exam-ple, a group of teachers at one of our partner schools saw a need for professional development in an area important to their school. Rather than wait for the slim chance that someone on the district staff would decide to put on an inservice presentation on the topic, these teachers requested and gained permission to organize a series of professional development experiences entirely on their own ini-tiative. Veteran teachers of twenty-five years had never participated in anything like this before; younger, less experienced colleagues found it an exhilarating experience.

Cross-School and Cross-District Linking

By the second year of partner school operation, partner school com-mittees should begin holding cross-school and cross-district coun-cil meetings in order to share successes and challenges beyond their single schools. Traditionally, educators in the schools have been iso-lated not only from educators at the university, but from educators in different schools and in different districts (see, for example, John-son, 1990, p. 148). Just as isolation can be detrimental, sharing can be extremely constructive. In our partnership, we refer to these meetings as *linking workshops*, because they are designed to link edu-cators from schools and university and to link educators across and between districts (Harris & Harris, 1991). In our partnership, edu-cators found it useful and stimulating to bring together principals, faculty, and professors from two partner schools in two different dis-tricts—individuals who had not had any opportunity to get acquainted in the past. Much of the meeting time was profitably spent in participants' getting to know each other and sharing chal-lenges, insights, and dreams. With this relationship as a foundation, participants were then able to collaborate on new curriculum strategies. On other occasions our partnership arranged for teachers from four or more partner schools to meet for up to three hours to share ideas and experiences. Their classes were covered by student teachers who were sufficiently competent to take over for them.

Partner Committees Across Districts

When limited instances of cross-school and cross-district collaboration have been successful, partner school committees often find it useful to establish a more regular and official linkage. For example, the chair of each partner school committee and the principals of all the schools might meet in a forum to coordinate efforts for joint ventures. Their collaborative efforts might include new models for mentoring student teachers, inservice programs that could be presented in several settings, or curriculum or research projects that might be implemented in schools in a variety of ethnic or socioeconomic areas.

In our partnership, the cross-school–cross-district group, which became known as the partner schools committee, was cochaired by a university professor and a teacher. This committee sponsored a series of linking workshops centered around a local need for critical thinking in the curriculum (Gardner, 1983). At these gatherings, teachers, principals, and professors came together for strategic planning, in-depth sharing, and mutual support. Eventually they sponsored a conference which included educators throughout the partnership area. As a final follow-through, subcommittees were formed from the partner schools committee to initiate and organize partnership-sponsored professional development work and future linking workshops, and to promote further external and internal communication.

District Partnership Council

When each school district has only two or three partner schools, one partner schools committee can adequately promote cross-site correlation and collaboration. However, our partnership found that as the number of partner schools per district reached five or six, cross-district correlation meetings became large enough to be unwieldy. When this occurs, district-wide partnership councils should be formed, with each school sending its principal and one teacher, augmented by university professors and district administrators. Chaired by a principal or teacher, the council should meet regularly to facilitate interdistrict sharing and collaboration.

Identifying Roles

A partnership has a mission and goals charted by the leaders, paradigms that enable participants to understand where they are going (and how and why), and a superstructure of boards and committees that give basic support and encouragement. But these components cannot produce lasting renewal without the commitment, cooperation, and hard work of the people who staff the university and the schools. It is people, not structures and theories, that produce change. Describing the "human face of reform," Robert Evens (1993, p. 19) says, "Whether the nation's classrooms will be restructured depends on whether educators will make the changes asked of them—a vast process of adaptation that must be accomplished teacher by teacher, school by school." The history of education contains many initiatives that received momentary frenzied attention, then fell into obscurity, denigrated as bandwagon or hobbyhorse activities when people on the grass-roots level lacked the commitment or concern to follow through on them.

A group of educators personally committed to change through partner schools has compiled the following roster of responsibilities for the various participants in the journey to renewal (BYU-Public School Partnership, 1993):

Partner Schools
1. Collaborate with the university to simultaneously renew teacher education and public schooling.
2. Organize renewal work around the four functions

of partner schools: preservice preparation, inservice education, curriculum development, and research/inquiry.

3. Provide a full-time partner school facilitator.

4. Establish a partner school committee to implement the four partner school functions.

5. Manage funds received from the partnership.

Partner School Principals

1. Collaborate with the university in helping the school faculty to model exemplary education and pilot innovative practice.

2. Appoint a full-time facilitator to implement four functions of partner schools: preservice preparation, inservice education, curriculum development, and research/inquiry.

3. Establish and serve on a partner school committee to coordinate and implement the four partnership functions.

4. Assist in selecting cooperating teachers.

5. Observe preservice teachers as requested by the facilitator, cooperating teachers, or the university coordinator.

6. Participate in the summative evaluation of preservice teachers.

7. Participate in school, cluster, district, university, and general partnership councils, conferences, and workshops.

8. Initiate inservice training as faculty needs become apparent.

Partner School Facilitators

1. Organize and coordinate practices and activities that will facilitate the four functions of the part-

nership: preservice preparation, inservice education, curriculum development, and research/inquiry.

2. Assist the principal in establishing the partner schools committee; work actively with the committee to facilitate the four partnership functions.

3. Assume major responsibility for mentoring and evaluating interns.

4. Support the university coordinator in mentoring and evaluating preservice teachers.

5. Support the cooperating teachers in mentoring and evaluating preservice teachers.

6. Participate in team evaluation of preservice teachers and provide written formative and summative evaluations.

7. Provide a review of policies, procedures, and expectations to be presented to preservice teachers at district and school orientation sessions; assist with the orientation sessions as needed.

8. Collaborate with other school facilitators, district personnel, and university coordinators to provide ongoing workshops and classroom visits for preservice students.

9. Facilitate staff support in improving preservice preparation, inservice education, curriculum development, and research/inquiry.

10. Communicate partnership information and business to those in the school.

11. Inform school community—including parents, PTA and community groups—regarding partnership activities.

12. Participate in school cluster, district, university, and general partnership councils, conferences, and workshops.

13. Document partnership activities that contribute to improving teacher education and renewing schools.

University Coordinator

1. Supervise and evaluate the performance of preservice teachers.

2. Instruct cooperating teachers in methods and procedures for mentoring and evaluating preservice teachers' performance.

3. Assist schools in setting up inservice education opportunities.

4. Encourage school teachers to explore ways to strengthen and upgrade curriculum.

5. Encourage teachers and university professors to use the partner school as a setting for inquiry and research.

6. Participate in partner school committees when possible.

7. Collaborate with school facilitators to provide ongoing workshops and site visits for preservice teachers.

8. Conduct seminars concurrent with field experiences for preservice teachers.

9. Assist in selection of cooperating teachers to participate in preservice training.

10. Coordinate classroom placement of preservice teachers.

11. Participate in school cluster, district, university, and general partnership councils, conferences, and workshops.

12. Demonstrate leadership in promoting all aspects of the partnership.

13. Document partnership activities that contribute to

improving teacher education and renewing schools.

14.   Present the teacher preparation program to partner school faculty.

Collaborating Teachers

1.   Model current best teaching practices.
2.   Support the four functions of a partner school: preservice preparation, inservice education, curriculum development, and research/inquiry and serve as a leader in one of the areas.
3.   Become familiar with the university teacher preparation program, including relevant syllabi and assignments.
4.   Mentor, supervise, and evaluate preservice teachers.
5.   Share personal, school, and district teaching resources.
6.   Schedule a regular planning and evaluation time with preservice teachers.
7.   Review preservice teachers' lesson plans and provide appropriate feedback.
8.   Participate in team evaluation of preservice teachers and provide written formative and summative evaluations.
9.   Be flexible in allowing preservice teachers to implement various teaching methods and classroom management techniques.
10.   Encourage preservice teachers to observe in other classrooms.
11.   Mentor other preservice teachers within the school.
12.   Attend partnership events: inservice sessions, conferences, workshops, council meetings.
13.   Teach for other faculty who are attending inservice and other partnership activities.

Sustaining the Progress

To sustain the work of partner schools, a number of school and university components must be created, reassigned, and redesigned (Fullan, 1993). Within the clearly designated but flexible partnership structure, all participants in the educational setting must be open to new channels of thought, communication and decision making.

Participants in each partner school must understand the partnership's goals in order to maximize the potential of partner school activity. Although partnerships may use different terminology to describe their goals, most of them, as described in Chapter One, focus on four goal areas, simultaneously striving to renew preparation of prospective teachers, strengthen practicing teachers, develop improved curricula for public school classrooms, and conduct research and inquiry that strengthens all participants (see Figure 1.1).

Preservice Preparation

"Honey, you can forget all that stuff they taught you over on the hill. Now you're here, we will show you how it is done in the real world." Prior to our partnership, these or similar words often greeted preservice teachers as they arrived for their practicum training. Although schools "cooperated" with the university by allowing the preservice teachers to practice in classrooms, they felt little if any ownership or responsibility for training them, and classroom teachers placed little value on the theories and ideas that preservice teachers had learned during their university experience and were anxious to try. Though school and university educators were usually cordial to each other, school educators considered university professors to be arrogant and out of touch with the realities of everyday schooling, and university educators viewed teachers and principals as preoccupied with survival and oblivious to the issues of meaningful learning. Talk to each other as equals? Join in professional meetings to exchange ideas? Explore their interdependency on each other for the success of the overall education profession? "Not likely!"

But as the partnership began to take shape, both groups realized that they would have to learn to serve together as they could not serve effectively apart. First of all, together they found that expectations had to be aligned: student teachers could not effectively serve two masters. After informal interchanges with school educators, supervising professors drew up rough drafts of their expectations, then submitted them to the principals and teachers for collaborative revisions and extensions. Seminars that had previously been taught to preservice teachers exclusively by professors were now team taught by teachers, principals, and professors working together. Cooperating teachers learned new techniques, presented them in the seminars to the preservice teachers, then observed as the preservice teachers tried them out in the classroom. Professors took their turn on the "hot seat," teaching in real classrooms, while the preservice and cooperating teachers observed and evaluated. The professors got burned a few times and improved their teaching in the process.

New models of supervision were developed as collaboration increased. One cluster of partner schools developed a technique in which each evaluation of a preservice teacher involved two observers: a *mentor*, who focused on the strengths of the lesson, and an *evaluator*, who looked for ways that the teacher could improve. This method ensured that both strengths and needs were brought out and discussed during the reflection time after the lesson. Partners found that there was never a lesson that had no good aspects, and conversely, there was never a lesson that did not have aspects that could be improved (Harris, Huff, McDougal, and Gull, 1990).

Inservice Education

Traditionally, professional development for practicing teachers had been imposed from the top down: teachers and principals had little say in which workshops or conferences they would attend or what material would be presented. Tight administrative budgets usually limited the number and the effectiveness of such inservice experiences.

If university professors were involved, they were brought in as outside experts, chosen by top-level district administrators who were as far removed from the everyday classrooms as the professors were. Fortunately, when our partner schools began to be established, collaborative models of professional development brought improvements in frequency, choice, relevancy, impact, and follow up of inservice education.

More frequent inservice training experiences were made possible in two ways. Limited inservice sessions could easily be attended by cooperating teachers when they could leave their classes in the care of their own preservice teachers. Full-school inservice sessions were facilitated by cooperating teachers from other partner schools who left their classes with their student teachers to swarm on the school needing inservice training, covering all classes so that the entire school could attend the sessions for the specified time period. Not one dollar of school funds needed to be spent for substitutes; thus the number of inservice sessions was not limited by expense or by substitute availability.

Varied and interesting inservice activities have emerged from this process. For example, faculty and principals from two partner schools, in two separate districts, had a common interest in learning more about the writing process, so they invited a writing specialist from a third partnership district to meet with them for a day of instruction at the university's conference center. After hearing the district specialist's ideas on writing, they met in small, grade-level discussion groups, with mixtures of teachers from the two schools, and shared insights about their own experiences in teaching writing and other topics of concern. In another partner school, all the teachers who had student teachers traveled together in a van to visit a partner school in the district where an innovative Math Their Way program was underway. They had an opportunity to observe the program in action and to question the teachers who were experimenting with it. In another approach to inservice training, teachers in partner schools were surveyed as to their interests and needs. In response to the teachers' indicated preferences, the university offered a series of classes on art education, music education, counseling, and social activism in social studies learning. These classes were held on campus during school hours.

Curriculum Development

A striking example of curriculum change in our partnership occurred in response to teachers' discontent with existing methods of reading instruction. Research revealing the detrimental effects of the three-homogeneous-reading-groups model had been published prior to 1986, when partner schools were initiated into our partnership. Some teachers in the partnership district had been concerned with what they had read but had not felt sufficient incentive to go through the effort of changing their practices. District guidelines, the pull of tradition, normative thinking, and the behavior of their peers all seemed to support the status quo. But when teachers and principals volunteered to become participants in partner schools, they took on the challenges of improving their curriculum through critical self-examination and of providing excellent models for the new teachers who were practice teaching in their classrooms. As they opened their classrooms to a steady flow of observers—including university professors, preservice teachers, and visitors from other schools and districts—these teachers began actively seeking specific kinds of professional knowledge that would make their schools the exemplary sites they had been charged to become. For example, one partner school faculty member invited people with particular expertise in teaching the writing process to come to the school to present. Following these presentations, the teachers made site visits to a few classrooms in which teachers were moving away from the reading groups and beginning to integrate reading and writing, without ability-based grouping. The visiting teachers began making changes in their own classrooms, allowing their preservice teachers to see some aspects of a holistic reading and writing curriculum in everyday practice. They even reported their attempts to their peers, frankly discussing the problems they were having and the directions they were moving for future application. Similar changes occurred across the curriculum in math, science, and social studies (Anderson and Harris, 1993).

As trust has increased between public school teachers and professors, both groups have become more willing to recognize and respect the insights and critical contributions of the other. Professors have shown greater sympathy for the challenges practitioners face in dealing with thirty-plus students in a classroom, including numerous demands to nurture children whose home life does not support learning. In turn, practitioners have loosened their defensiveness, becoming more willing to allow preservice teachers to try new ideas learned at the university; many cooperating teachers have been so impressed with a new practice introduced by a preservice teacher that they have incorporated the new method into their own teaching repertoire. Some studies that have been done in the partner schools (Anderson, 1992; Roberts et al., 1992) have indicated that though similar gradual changes are occurring in most schools, these changes are faster and more pervasive in partner schools.

Research and Inquiry

Traditionally, university researchers have conducted research on learning and teaching with school faculty cooperating but not actually participating in generating questions, gathering and analyzing data, reporting results, and eventually applying insights to changing practice in school and university classrooms. In contrast, the partner school model includes both school and university personnel in all aspects of the action research process.

The results of this inquiry and research have been valuable to both school and university educators; many have changed their classroom practice because of what they learned (Harris & Harris, 1991). But of more significance to both groups in our partnership has been the realization that teaching can be enormously fulfilling as an experience in thinking as well as in serving. When school and university educators have engaged in collaborative inquiry and become immersed in the importance of asking questions and seeking answers, they have become conscious of the importance of reporting their insights and of making changes in their practice in accordance with what they have learned through their inquiry processes.

As part of the research and inquiry activity, school and university educators attend conferences and meetings of organizations such as the Association of Teacher Educators, National Association for Gifted Children, Association for Supervision and Curriculum Development, National Association of Elementary School Principals, and others, to make presentations and gain new ideas. Cost sharing enables school and university educators to attend and present together. Transportation is economical when participants can travel together in large vans, and usually, district offices cover the hotel and conference registration costs of their teachers. One participant's comment illustrates the value of such experiences for classroom teachers: "I am only a first-grade teacher who never expected to do anything but work with young children in my own classroom. Here I am in St. Louis presenting to other educators from around the country. I am coming to feel like I really have something to offer these people" (Karen Anderson, personal communication, 1989).

Allocating Resources

Organizing the necessary partnership and partner school structures, as well as enabling the necessary personnel to function in their new roles, does require resources. At first, the demands may seem prohibitive. However, partner school participants have found that creative and resourceful management can stretch, adapt, and otherwise expand existing time and finances to meet many partner school needs.

Time

Partner school operation does place a strain on teachers', principals', and professors' time. If inservice training is to be effective, cooperating teachers must have time to participate in instruction, observation, and professional development experiences. In many areas of the country, no professional development time is allotted to teachers; thus any activity beyond maintaining current traditional programs must come out of personal time, unless the partner school can somehow make time available. In addition, partner school work places heavy time demands on the teachers, principals, and professors who must meet in planning sessions and participate in mentoring the preservice teachers who will determine the quality of education in the future (Harris, 1991).

A pattern that has been successful in many partner schools is to provide careful preparation and orientation for preservice teachers so that they are capable of taking over classrooms soon after their practicum experience begins. When cooperating teachers are confident that the preservice teachers understand the programs being used in their classes and have been well prepared with classroom management practices, they are comfortable with leaving their classes in preservice teachers' care while they attend inservice sessions, visit exemplary sites where new methods are being practiced, or meet with principals, professors, or others to make plans both for mentoring and supervising the preservice teachers and for conducting inquiry and research projects in their classrooms (R. C. Harris & M. F. Harris, 1992).

Funding

Partner schools have found a number of ways to increase operations without increasing budget (Harris & Harris, 1994). Often such adjustments simply require reallocation of existing resources and personnel. For example, during one school year the university participating in a partnership had too many preservice teachers for the number of clinical faculty able to supervise them. Examining their resources, university faculty found that a number of their preservice teachers had outstanding talents and preparation and were already capable of taking over their own classes. These preservice teachers were invited to become interns in the classrooms of cooperating teachers who had previously demonstrated strong capabilities in mentoring and supervising preservice teachers. The interns taught the classes independently for twenty hours per week, for which they were paid half a regular teacher's salary. With the classes covered half time, the outstanding cooperating teachers were able to devote twenty hours a week to supervising preservice teachers in other schools, in place of the unavailable university faculty. The half salaries for the interns were paid by the university with money that would ordinarily have been spent to hire part-time supervisors, most of whom would have been retired educators who were not acquainted with current programs and practices in the partnership. Both university and schools benefited from having clinical supervisors who knew the current programs and were up-to-date on child needs and educational practices. In addition, working in other partner schools enabled the cooperating teachers to observe methods and practices not in use in their own schools, which contributed to their own professional development and to the repertoire of ideas that they could implement in their own schools.

Another way of creatively manipulating funds is to use mentor or cooperating teachers in classrooms other than those in which they currently teach. When these mentor teachers have sufficiently capable preservice teachers, the mentor teachers can cover for another teacher who does not have a preservice teacher but would like to attend a professional development session. Using this technique, our partner schools have enabled most teachers to participate in three to five professional development experiences each year, without deduction from the teacher's pay or extra outlay from the school or university to pay for substitutes. Because some state boards of education provide a temporary certificate for any person who is participating in an official university teacher-preparation program in the school, legal and liability considerations are covered. In states where a certified teacher must always be in the room, policy revision efforts should be mounted. Policymakers may enact such changes as a way of supporting educational renewal.

Sometimes funding can be stretched by creative use of personnel, particularly in exchanges between school and university faculty that benefit both groups. In one of our partner schools, a university reading specialist taught first grade, while a district gifted-and-talented program specialist taught a specialized methods course at the university. The university and district continued to pay the instructors' respective salaries, as both positions were ably covered. Both individuals and institutions benefited by the exchange, and no additional funds were consumed.

The spirit of collaboration in the common cause of renewal seems to create miracles where the cost of partner school operation is concerned. A recent study in our partnership revealed that when resources such as parking, copying, telephone service, space, professor time, teacher time, and similar items are given a dollar value, the partnership activities in each partner school cost $32,502 for one year (Harris & Harris, 1994). Of this, the school contributes $20,212 (62 percent) and the university $12,290 (38 percent). However, if costs are figured on a per-student basis, the school pays $68.86 (11 percent), while the university spends $565.32 (89 percent). The large difference in school and university expenditures occurs because the school serves many times more students than the college of education does. Neither institution could afford to increase its budget by even a fraction of these per-student costs. At the time of this study, our partnership was operating twenty-three partner schools, at an overall estimated cost of $747,523—three-quarters of a million dollars! Yet during that school year not a single dollar was transferred between the two institutions, nor were any external funds brought into the partnership for the purpose of supporting partner schools.

Conclusion

One of the major purposes for the partner schools that function as the professional development school envisioned by the Holmes Group in *Tomorrow's Schools* is to promote inquiry into critical questions about teaching and learning. The researchers said:

We do not mean professional development schools to be just laboratory schools for university research, nor a demonstration school. Nor do we mean just a clinical setting for preparing student and intern teachers [and administrators]. Rather, we mean all of these together: a school for the development of novice professionals, for continuing development of experienced professionals, and for the research and development of the teaching profession.

We mean these schools to help the teaching profession in six ways:

By promoting much more ambitious conceptions of teaching and learning on the part of prospective teachers in universities and students in schools.

By adding to and reorganizing the collections of knowledge we have about teaching and learning.

By ensuring that enterprising, relevant, responsible research and development is done in schools.

By linking experienced teachers' efforts to renew their knowledge and advance their status with efforts to improve their schools and prepare new teachers.

By creating incentives for faculties in the public schools and faculties in education schools to work mutually.

By strengthening the relationship between schools and the broader political, social, and economic communities in which they reside [1990, p. 1].

The Holmes Group has been one of the master cartographers affecting the journey of our partnership toward educational renewal. We find that our partner school operation is summarized and given meaning and direction through the Holmes Group's list.

Our partnership was launched when many educators at the

university and in the public schools were dissatisfied with existing programs and practices. Both groups realized that renewal was needed—both in the preparation of new teachers and in the upgrading of teaching in the schools. As they met together, both groups realized that these two needs are interdependent: renewal in the schools depends on the skills of teachers—those currently in the field, and those being prepared at the university; renewal of the teacher preparation program depends on strong classrooms for practicum coursework and ultimately on strong students graduating from public school and entering teacher-training programs (Green & Harris, 1990). Though they had traditionally been formally cooperative but not close, the two groups decided that renewal must be a joint, interactive venture. Guided by a new paradigm that recognized the contribution of each group and the importance of collaboration, they began asking questions and exploring solutions together. An organizational structure was established, roles were assigned, resources were allocated, and the launch was successful.

Our partner schools have sustained their momentum for almost a decade (Harris and Harris, 1993b). Four functions have carried them forward: preservice preparation of new teachers, inservice education of current teachers, continual development of improved curricula, and ongoing collaboration in inquiry and research. Renewal is not a fixed point; the journey will be ongoing. We do not regret our launch, and we have every hope for a continuation of our productive adventure.

References

Anderson, K.J. (1992). The partner-school effect in curriculum and instruction reform. Unpublished master's thesis, Brigham Young University, Provo, UT.

Anderson, K. J., & Harris, R. C. (1993, October). *The partner school effect in curriculum and instruction reform.* Paper presented at the annual meeting of the Northern Rocky Mountain Educational Research Association, Jackson, WY.

Barell, J. (1991). *Teaching for thoughtfulness.* New York: Longman.

Berman, S. (1990). Educating for social responsibility. *Educational Leadership, 48*(3), 75–80.

Bracey, W. B. (1993). The third Bracey report on the condition of public education. *Phi Delta Kappan, 75*(2), 104–118.

Brophy, J. (1992). Probing the subtleties of subject-matter teaching. *Educational Leadership, 49*(7), 4–8.

BYU-Public School Partnership (1989). Partnership strategic planning report. Provo, UT.

BYU-Public School Partnership (1993). *Proceedings: Elementary Schools Linking Workshop.* Unpublished report to the partnership.

Caine, R. N., & Caine, G. (1991). *Making connections: Teaching and the human brain.* Alexandria, VA: Association for Supervision and Curriculum Development.

Darling-Hammond, L. (Ed.). (1994). *Professional development schools: Schools for developing a profession.* New York: Teachers College Press.

Deming, W. E. (1986). *Out of the crisis.* Cambridge, MA: MIT Center for Advanced Engineering Study.

Evens, R. (1993). The human face of reform. *Educational Leadership, 51*(1), 19–23.

Fullan, M. C. (1993). Why teachers must become change agents. *Educational Leadership, 50*(6), 12–17.

Gardner, H. (1983). *Frames of mind: The theory of multiple intelligences.* New York: Basic Books.

Gardner, H. (1991). *The unschooled mind: How children think and how schools should teach.* New York: Basic Books,.

Glasser, W. (1990). *Quality school: Managing students without coercion.* New York: HarperCollins.

Goodlad, J. I. (1984). *A place called school.* New York: McGraw-Hill.

Goodlad, J. I. (1990). *Teachers for our nation's schools.* San Francisco: Jossey-Bass.

Green, E. E., & Harris, R. C. (1990). Creating long-term collaboration: The BYU/Public School Partnership experience. *Tech Trends, 35*(1), 12–16.

Greer, D., & Silverman, R. H. (1988). Making art important for every child. *Educational Leadership, 45*(4), 10–14.

Harris, R. C. (1991). Educational renewal: Not by remote control. *Metropolitan Universities, 2*(1), 61–71.

Harris, R. C., & Harris, M. F. (1991). Symbiosis on trial in educational renewal. *Researcher, 7*(2), 15–27.

Harris, M. F., & Harris, R. C. (1992). Glasser comes to a rural school. *Educational Leadership, 50*(3), 18–21.

Harris, R. C., & Harris, M. F. (1992). Preparing teachers for literacy education: University/school collaboration. *Journal of Reading, 35*(7), 572–579.

Harris, R. C., & Harris, M. F. (1993a). Partner schools: Places to solve teacher preparation problems. *Action in Teacher Education, 14*(4), 1–8.

Harris, R. C., & Harris, M. F. (1993b). Renewing teacher education and public schooling via university/school collaboration: A decade-long case study. *Contemporary Education*, 64(4), 234–238.

Harris, R. C., & Harris, M. F. (1994). Exploring costs & benefits of partner schools: Tangibles & intangibles in a university/school partnership. In M. J. O'Hair & S. J. Odell (Eds.), *Partnerships in education yearbook II* (pp. 45–62). Ft. Worth: Harcourt Brace.

Harris, R.C., Huff, S., McDougal, B., & Gull, G. (1990). *Supervisors into the water with new teachers: In triangulation mentoring all risk and all grow*. Paper presented at the annual meeting of the Association of Teacher Educators, 1990, Las Vegas, NV.

The Holmes Group. (1990). *Tomorrow's schools: Principles for the design of professional development schools*. East Lansing, MI: The Holmes Group.

Johnson, S. M. (1990). *Teachers at work*. New York: Basic Books.

Kearns, D. T., & Doyle, D. (1991). *Winning the brain race* (Rev. ed.). San Francisco: ICS Press.

Kuhn, T. (1963). *The structure of scientific revolutions*. Chicago: University of Chicago Press.

Langer, E. J. (1989). *Mindfulness*. Reading, MA: Addison-Wesley.

Leiberman, A. (1988). Expanding the leadership team. *Educational Leadership*, 45(5), 4–8.

Leinhardt, G. (1992). What research on learning tells us about teaching. *Educational Leadership*, 49(7), 20–25.

Leithwood, K. A. (1992). The move toward transformational leadership. *Educational Leadership*, 49(5), 8–12.

Levine, M. (Ed.). (1992). *Professional practice schools: Linking teacher education and school reform*. New York: Teachers College Press.

O'Neil, J. (1992a). Rx for better thinkers: Problem-based learning. *Update*, 34(6), 1–3.

O'Neil, J. (1992b). Wanted: Deep understanding—"Constructivism" posits new conception of teaching. *Update*, 34(3), 1–4.

Palmer, P. (1983). *To know as we are known: The spirituality of education*. San Francisco: Harper San Francisco.

Palmer, P. (1992, March/April). Divided no more: A movement approach to educational reform. *Change*, pp. 10–17.

Roberts, C., Ingram, C., & Harris, R. C. (1992). The effects of special versus regular classroom programming on higher cognitive processes of intermediate elementary aged gifted and average ability students. *Journal for the Education of the Gifted*. 15(4), 332–343.

Samples, B. (1987). *Open mind, whole mind: Parenting and teaching tomorrow's children today*. Rolling Hills Estates, CA: Jalmar Press.

Sergiovanni, T. J. (1990) Adding value to leadership gets extraordinary results. *Educational Leadership, 47*(8), 23–27.

Sergiovanni, T. J. (1992). Moral authority and the regeneration of supervision. In C. D. Glickman (Ed.), *Supervision in transition*. Washington, DC: Association for Supervision and Curriculum Development

Smith, F. (1986). *Insult to intelligence: The bureaucratic invasion of our classrooms*. Portsmouth, NH: Heinemann.

Smith, F. (1990). *To think*. New York: Teachers College Press.

Strategic Planning Commission. (1988). *A shift in focus: To empower Utah's children to function effectively in the society in which they will live*. Salt Lake City, UT: Utah State Board of Education.

Wiggins, G. (1992). Creating tests worth taking. *Educational Leadership, 49*(8) 26–33.

Wheatley, M. J. (1992). *Leadership and the new science*. San Francisco: Berrett-Koehler.

7

Initiating District-Wide Change

Monica M. Beglau and Kolene F. Granger

In J.R.R. Tolkien's fantasy *Lord of the Rings*, Frodo the Hobbit has a ring that makes the wearer invisible by a single turn. Teachers and administrators in universities and public schools could make good use of such a ring. Some of the conversations that reveal the most about problems and needs in a school-university partnership seem to change abruptly when participants see a partnership person rounding the bend in the hall.

If we could travel invisibly, like Frodo, through a number of partner school sites, we would see some sites at a stage in their progress in which classrooms and hallways seem filled with university students. In one classroom, a preservice teacher is conducting a math lesson, while her cooperating teacher is visiting another school to observe an exemplary new reading method that she would like to consider implementing in her class. In another class, the children are at recess and a preservice teacher, his cooperating teacher, and a university professor are discussing what did and did not go well with a new classroom process they have been trying out. They plan to present the results of their research at a convention in a few weeks. The school and the university are indeed partners in these projects.

Scenes like this have recurred often in this book. They are part of the basic context of partner schools. But not all schools in a district can be partner schools. Does the affiliation of some schools with a university cause problems in the other schools in the district?

In a school about two-and-one-half miles across town from the partner school, there are no professors and only two preservice teachers, neither of whom seems prepared to take over a class. If, still invisible, we slip into the teacher's room, we might overhear the following conversation:

> TEACHER A: I don't see the fairness in this partnership thing. Why do those partner schools always get the student teachers? I'm just as capable of trying out that new reading program as Ruth. But there's no chance for me to go over and see it happen.
> TEACHER B: How come partner school faculty are the only ones going to the partnership workshops? Ruth told me she gets a flyer announcing the partnership workshop series. Why doesn't our school get them?
> TEACHER C: Did you hear about that van load of teachers and professors that went to the National Council of Teachers of Mathematics conference? Where do they get the money to pay for a trip like that? Who covered their classes while they were gone? I've been in this district for ten years, and I've never gone to a national conference. I've always had great results with math, but nobody asked me to be part of a study.

But teachers always seem to be a little sensitive when it comes to resources and opportunities. Before we return Frodo's ring, let's eavesdrop on three district administrators:

> ADMINISTRATOR A: The university professors are spending a lot of time with their students in a couple of schools. Those student teachers are getting a rich experience, and the kids get the advantage of some new methods and ideas—not so much of the same recycled lesson plans and bulletin boards.
> ADMINISTRATOR B: You're right. Not only do the schools get site visits, the professors furnish inservice [training] and supply enough student teachers to take the classes so the teachers can go to the sessions. The teachers and principals team with the

professors in evaluating the student teachers, so everyone learns more. I wish more of our personnel could have these advantages. ADMINISTRATOR C: But we don't have the luxury that those professors do. We have to worry about all the schools in the district, not just a special few.

Because the work of change must usually begin on a small front, a disproportionate amount of attention and resources must be focused on a few sites. This sometimes creates ambivalent feelings among those charged with caring for the growth and development of all professionals and all learners. They must consider the needs of those schools that are not the recipients of the extra attention and resources necessary for experimentation and inquiry. And they must be aware that professional jealousies arise as some educators receive opportunities for development and assistance while others do not—and that those feelings are often justified.

Once the participants in a partnership know the difficulties that can attend partner school arrangements, there are steps that they can take to avoid such problems. Let's become visible again to see what equally visible things are being done in some partnerships to make partner schools not isolated, privileged sites but change agents, positively affecting all schools in a partnership district. Indeed, to promote effective teacher preparation and significant school renewal, the work of partner schools must eventually touch all. But how can the initial concentration of limited resources for critical changes at a few isolated sites eventually come to influence and benefit an entire district or several districts? After a number of years of struggling with this question, we have developed some tentative solutions. Our purpose in this chapter is to elaborate on some of those solutions and point to results that have emerged so far.

Administrative Patterns, Committees, and Councils

Providing access to the resources, inquiry and influence of the partner schools for schools throughout a district can proceed according to either a top-down or bottom-up pattern. Both have been tried and have shown promise (Woolf and Harris, 1993).

Top-Down Steering Committees

People who function in the highest administrative levels in state departments of education, school districts, and colleges of education have a broad perspective as a result of their training and experience. In some partnerships, a committee of individuals from university colleges of education and the state department of education, with administrative representatives from all participating partnership districts, has been formed to consider ways of sharing partner school advantages with nonpartner schools.

These committees have tried to anticipate problems that might arise from the necessary inequity between partner and nonpartner schools and have worked to inform all schools in all participating districts of the function and capabilities of the school-university partnership model. They have created brochures, videotapes, and other communication mechanisms to enable all schools in all partnership districts to understand the processes carried out in the partner schools and the goals to be achieved. In addition, they have sponsored annual conferences to which they have invited representatives from all schools, regardless of partner or nonpartner status.

Top-Down District Councils

Once partnershipwide steering committees have created and disseminated a vision of educational renewal through the partner schools model, they generally give way to district councils that adapt the designs and procedures to the circumstances and needs of their own districts. Again the planning and communication are top-down: once partner school sites are designated, the district council takes the responsibility for sharing with nonpartner schools what is learned and accomplished at the partner schools. District councils have implemented a number of strategies to facilitate greater involvement:

- They have encouraged educators in partner schools to host visitors from other schools in their district or in other districts.

- They have sent invitations to administrators and teachers at nonpartner schools to attend professional development workshops conducted by partner school personnel.

- They have designed three- to five-year partnership rotation patterns so that the opportunities and obligations of partner school status can be shared throughout the district.

- They have sent district newsletters with reports and updates on partnership function to all educators.

Bottom-Up Partner School Committees

In contrast to partnerships that develop and function largely in a top-down pattern, other school-university collaboratives employ a bottom-up model. Though the governing boards of such partnerships may include high-level district and university administrators, these boards have kept guidelines and policies simple and have focused on empowering educators at school and department levels. Their goal is for collaborative ingenuity to be generated by teachers, principals, and professors. In bottom-up partnerships, the district council is charged specifically with promoting equity among the schools.

Bottom-Up District Councils

When most districts had only one to three partner schools, cross-school linking was accomplished through a committee consisting of principal, teacher, and professor representatives from all partner schools. These committees were able to offer mutual support, share problem-solving strategies, initiate partnershipwide projects, sponsor linking workshops, organize partnership annual conferences, and set up professional development activities.

But when districts began to have larger numbers of partner schools, partner school committees became too large to conduct business efficiently. To meet the need for a more efficient representative group, district councils were formed from the bottom up, with representatives from each partner school in the district, following the same general pattern as the partner schools committee. At their monthly meetings, these councils conduct the business of the partnership for their district, including making decisions for the dissemination of information and workshop and conference agendas.

Questions Committees and Councils Face

As Sirotnik and Goodlad (1988) have suggested, the goals of partnering emerged as questions raised by educators were discussed and answered. When the right questions were asked, the best answers were framed. Some questions commonly asked by district committees can give districts insights into what they must do to maximize the effects of partner schools on schooling throughout the district.

When Should More Partner Schools Be Established?

If educators in any part of a district, especially administrators or teachers in the nonpartner schools, feel that any of the purposes of partner schools are not being met, such needs should be brought first to the district's coordinating council. Along with the feasibility of creating a new partner school in the district, possible ways of meeting the needs within existing partner schools can be explored by the council. For example, if requested inservice education has been repeatedly turned down because of logistical problems in covering classes and scheduling workshops, the problem might be that partner school people and resources are spread too thin. When informed of the nonpartner schoolteachers' desire for inservice development, the district council can examine allocations of personnel and space within the existing partner schools to determine whether hiring one or two more interns would free the necessary personnel. If the partner schools are already stretched to capacity, the council might find it necessary to take steps to create either a new partner or an associate school.

If study of the partner schools throughout the district reveals that capacity is stretched in all four areas of partnership function—educator preparation, professional development, curriculum development, and research and inquiry—then a new partner school might be considered. However, if the problem that has been identified centers mostly around providing supervision and training to preservice teachers, the council will probably elect to set up an associate school, which will specialize in preservice preparation, linking in with a full-fledged partner school for the other functions already covered adequately in the district.

What Are the Procedures to Select a New Partner School Capable of District-Wide Impact?

If a school has sufficient staff commitment it may be encouraged to apply for partner school status. School and staff characteristics can be matched most effectively to district-wide needs if the district council has diverse representation so that varying perspectives can be considered during the selection process.

When a school applies to be a partner school, the district council generally sends a team to explain the partnership to school staff, describing the obligations, showing a video giving further insight into partnerships, and answering staff questions. Applicant schools should then be initially screened by questioning related to the partnership mission statement, purpose, principles, and outcomes. The school's philosophy, needs, and goals should be assessed, along with the support of the faculty and the strength and resources of the school in the areas of the four partnership goals. Some schools reveal during questioning that they are primarily interested in having preservice teachers and less concerned with strengthening staff knowledge or curriculum; many have little interest in participating in research. Though training preservice teachers is an important part of partnership function, a school can contribute more toward school renewal if it is continually upgrading staff skills and researching curriculum innovations that can be shared.

Although district councils designate a procedure for screening applications, council members have discovered that schools are usually self-selecting. During screening, some schools realize that their faculty are not fully able to support the partnership principles, to accept the obligations for focus and growth, or to commit the time required for complete partner school function. Some request another year to prepare.

What Are the Responsibilities, Obligations, and Opportunities of a New Partner School?

From the beginning, a partner school that is expected to contribute constructively to district-wide renewal should expect to provide supervision and training to preservice teachers. The initial preparation for this responsibility will probably be intense, as the preservice teachers need to be readied to take over classrooms as soon as possible in order to experience the full range of responsibilities as a teacher and to free cooperating teachers to participate in partnership functions throughout the district. In many partner schools, preservice teachers are given training in specific programs and methodology prior to the actual student teaching practicum so that they are prepared to participate in experimentation and research, which can be more efficiently disseminated if it is initiated early in the school year.

A new partner school may participate jointly at first with an established partner school. Collaboration between partner schools can be particularly valuable in establishing the preservice program, as teacher preparation patterns and practices that have worked well in one school can often be profitably implemented in another. Frequently new partner schools are asked to participate in research with more experienced partner schools. The new school provides an additional site for experiments and the established schools model research processes and structures for the less experienced participants. Participation in established research projects allows neophyte researchers to see potentials of research and helps to generate questions. Moreover, the questions raised in new partner schools may be more relevant to nonpartner schools in the district than the questions raised in established partner schools which may have become atypical through long association with innovative programs. New partner schools are expected to collaborate frequently with nonpartner schools in implementing promising new programs and practices and in disseminating results of their experiences. Participation in partnership-sponsored activities such as conferences and linking workshops is, of course, mandatory; it is through these activities that what partner schools learn can be most directly shared throughout the district and beyond.

How Does the District Council Support New Partner and Associate Schools?

To support new partner schools in their roles as participants in district-wide change, district councils should urge personnel from new partner schools to attend any of the partnership meetings and conferences that are appropriate to their operation. Grant money received for inservice education in other partner schools can be shared with new schools by planning joint inservice sessions. What is learned in this inservice education can generate research into new programs and methods and subsequent implementation techniques in new partner schools, and this learning can eventually be shared with other schools. District partnership action plans should try to allow new partner schools time to plan and receive feedback as they develop their initiatives.

Organization of Secondary School Partnership Projects

Elementary teachers seem to more readily accept the premises of partnering. In districts with an active partnership, elementary schools often seem to work more easily within the structure than secondary schools. Through the liaison efforts of the district council, they contribute effectively to the development and growth of schools throughout the district.

Secondary teachers, however, have been more reserved in their interest and involvement. Many districts have found that secondary teachers participate more readily in partnerships that are based on projects. In this approach, no one school is designated as a partner school. Instead, any teacher, principal, or district administrator with an idea for a project is encouraged to go directly to university officials. The project approach to partnership is built on the following strategic planning beliefs:

- The greater the participation on every level, the greater the success of the partnership.

- In addition to seeking individual and organizational benefits, participants have an obligation to improve the entire system of education.

- Partners must clearly define needs and goals, set priorities, and review projects accordingly if resources are to be effectively focused and progress is to occur.

- By collaborating as professionals, teachers in the partnership can provide a dynamic program to improve teaching and learning.

Secondary school partner departments evolve through a very delicate process. If a secondary partner school or partner department task force operates from the assumption that the advantages of partnering should be available at any level in the partnership, this belief will shape the secondary education functions of the partnership in directions different from those followed by the elementary schools.

Even though the secondary and elementary school partnership groups may share a common mission statement and the charge to develop preservice, inservice, curriculum, and research projects, their approaches will be very different.

Working from the belief that form must follow function, one secondary school task force recommended a partnershipwide cross-district coordinating committee, but designated that its form would be molded by the functions carefully described by the task force. Members of the task force believed that the committee should not take on a life of its own but should develop according to beliefs, goals, and strategies shared by the group members and should be frequently monitored to ensure its responsiveness. The task force was confident that an effective structure would evolve as projects developed and that a school-level organization might emerge in schools where multiple projects were under way. The task force was convinced that the structure of a secondary school partnership needed to be different from that of an elementary school collaborative; thus the governing groups and structures that had been successful in the local elementary partnership were not in any way imposed on the secondary schools.

Preservice Teachers as an Asset

Universities and schools have long collaborated on the placement and supervision of preservice teachers and on other practicum courses that take prospective teachers into classrooms. Unique to the partnership effort, however, is the perspective that the time these university students spend in the schools is an asset to those schools, giving existing faculty added time for their own training. Many of the college students who student teach at the secondary level not only receive mentoring but can become a significant resource to a school. Several examples drawn from secondary school partnerships illustrate how both the preservice teachers and the

school can benefit from a collaborative student-teaching arrangement based on a dual agenda of simultaneously restructuring teacher
education and renewing public schools throughout the district.

At one junior high, preservice teachers are facilitating a schoolwide study skills project. The preservice teachers are taking over the
classrooms to provide time for the cooperating teachers to work on
developing a study skills curriculum. The teachers then return to
their classrooms and provide instruction in this new curriculum to
the student teachers.

At a high school, teachers prepared their preservice teachers
with sufficient mentoring and experience so that they were capable
of teaching classes entirely on their own while classroom teachers
attended a five-day staff development course called Essential Elements of Instruction. After completing the course, the teachers
returned to their classrooms to model the training they had just
received for the benefit of their preservice teachers. In addition,
they modeled and explained new clinical supervision skills. Both
groups gained important benefits from the experience. The supervising teachers learned concepts as they participated in the course
and then increased their retention of the concepts by teaching and
applying them almost immediately. The preservice teachers were
exposed to both the theory and practice of methods and procedures
they would probably not have otherwise learned.

At a large high school, a number of teachers used the time freed
by their preservice teachers to develop many different projects,
including a unified studies project and an integrated algebra/tech-
nology project writing lab. Because there is a close partnership
between the partnering university and the school, the school was
able to indicate areas where project development was occurring and
to request student teacher support in the classroom so that supervising teacher time and effort could go to support the developing
project.

These projects were not limited by a requirement to gain permission at the district or coordinating council level. In fact, the

schools were encouraged to promote more such events by working with faculty in the various secondary education fields and in the secondary education department at the university.

These examples illustrate how focusing resources on the teachers or schools involved in active restructuring, inservice education, research, and evaluation has benefited the individual schools but still promoted knowledge, instruction, and programs that have benefits that can be disseminated district-wide. Seeing what has worked well for others is always an impetus for a person or an institution to try something new.

Frequently, secondary schools are so diverse and so large that partnership efforts have not yet achieved the capability of working simultaneously with the entire school. But partnerships can work well with various school departments and with the energized and enthused individuals who recognize the partnership's potential and are ready to work with partnership projects. Often the model set by a group of dedicated individuals will extend throughout an entire school. When this occurs, it may be possible to reorganize the partnership and refocus it at a school and district level.

Personal Sense of Purpose and Organizational Change

While the vision that generates change may begin at the personal level, it rapidly becomes integrated into an individual's occupation. Professionals progress through stages of commitment, each stage resulting in wider ranging change, and Fullan (1993) has noted that "paradoxically, personal purpose is the route to organizational change" (p. 13).

In school-university partnership districts, personal purpose often results in organizational change. When elementary teachers in a K–3 partner school believed there was a better way to use the resources that had been committed to first-grade reading, they demonstrated the strength of their personal purpose. Aided by university faculty with expertise in reading, they investigated new and innovative methods, made decisions, and forwarded recommendations for action—procedures that would have been initiated only by administrators in prepartnership days. As partner school teachers, they took advantage of the resources represented by college students completing practicum experiences and the supervising university professor. They incorporated the students and professor into their teaching team, so that children in their classrooms continued to receive quality instruction while the teachers devoted precious time to their research project. They are planning to share the results of their research not only with schools in their district but with school districts statewide via a compressed video communication system and partnership meetings that are being held to further change efforts across the state. Thus, what began as personal purpose became shared purpose, then partner purpose, and finally the route to constructive change throughout the district and the state.

Even a district with just one partner school can use inquiry from that school constructively to promote district-wide change. In one district's sole partner school, the teachers and principal were "commissioned" by the school board to research alternative forms of assessing and reporting student progress. Along with that responsibility, they were given the resources and the opportunities to conduct various forms of action research. As they worked, teachers from other elementary schools in the district were involved with them, so that the eventual recommendations would be applicable to additional contexts and could be adopted by the school board for use across the district. One of the university faculty assigned to the partner school had extensive expertise in assessment; she consulted and participated in designing the research and in collecting and analyzing the data. As this professor became more and more involved, a new dimension was added to the school-university district collaboration. She conducted graduate-level coursework in assessment for teachers in the community and nurtured their fledgling research projects. Through her participation and guidance, their results were more reliable and the subsequent changes in practice were easier to implement across the district.

Inquiry and Lifelong Learning

Plans and decisions developed in district and partnership councils focus on the importance of both inquiry and lifelong learning. Programs and probes are designed to help public school educators focus on aspects of their everyday classroom work that stimulate them to be continuous learners. As the designs are shared within the district councils, the relationship between inquiry and renewal is strengthened and reinforced. Teachers in many partnership districts report that they are personally energized and reinforced by their work in linking teacher education programs with renewal in the classroom.

Often district councils focus on incorporating inquiry into renewal through research. In one district, a partnership research initiator (referred to as a *worrier*) is selected from each partner school to learn research methods (in particular, action research) through extensive inservice education. In conjunction with this group training, each team of one research initiator and one collaborating university faculty member identifies at least one research project for the initiator's school for the year. These projects are discussed with the other research initiators and exposed to the guidance and suggestions of university faculty assigned to support the efforts.

When research has been completed, descriptions and results of the projects are copied and shared with schools throughout the district to widen the change effect.

The following research questions have generated constructive research and change in this partnership district:

- How does the inclusion resource program affect students, parents, and teachers?

- How does using computer graphics and HyperCard affect students' writing?

- What changes occur in student work when the Don Delay method of focusing on the middle group of students is used?

- How do parents react when teachers use performance assessments in reading instead of letter grades?

- Is the "less is more" concept applicable to upper-elementary reading instruction?

- What effects do alternative assessments and reporting have on parent conferences?

- What effect does an instructional program designed to increase the self-reliance of children have on their perceptions of their capabilities?

A year after this partnership program was put into practice, the teams of research initiators and university faculty identified inquiry and research projects not only at the partner school level, but at district and partnership levels as well. At meetings of school leaders from partnership districts throughout the state, one district shared in detail the varying approaches it had developed through its research in preservice education. Collaboration within and among districts has resulted in innovations in curriculum, new models for methodology, and a number of helpful activities and frameworks. An important message has emerged from what is often the chaos of reform: "Sharing is survival."

Communicating Reform

When collaboration has been established and inquiry has been successful, change can be diffused across a school district through the process of communicating reform. An account of a district coordinating council meeting in one partnership district shows how such communication can be practiced.

The meeting was conducted and organized by an elementary partner school teacher, who had been released to supervise university interns and to work as a teacher on special assignment, or modified assistant principal, in addition to her duties as the district coordinating council chair. Her planning committee consisted of a chair-elect and a past chair, who were both elementary principals, and the assistant superintendent of instructional services. The assistant superintendent had formerly managed all of the chairing and most of the planning, but he had stepped back to provide opportunities for others to become empowered in leadership roles. The planning committee regularly met before the monthly meeting.

At this session of the district coordinating council, participants were organized into six partnership teams—one of principals, one of coordinators, and four of initiators—for educator preparation, professional development, curriculum development, and research respectively. Each team had worked previously on defining roles in its schools and within the partnership. This session was devoted to further refining roles, sharing ideas, and setting district-wide partnership goals in each area. The topics were related to the strategic planning done in the past.

The teams were animated and excited and showed that sharing between university and district educators was prolific. Comments like "That's a good idea, I think I will follow up with . . ." and "Let's set a time to learn more about . . ." were frequently heard. The groups often specified a particular focus, with members participating equally. Thoughts such as "I think we can help the most in these areas" reflected the positive, cooperative tone. In addition to sharing input on student teacher placements, joint university-district support of a museum exhibit, and reminders of upcoming mentor teacher training, each group shared the goals it had developed with the entire council.

This partnership had evolved slowly to this high level of ownership, involvement, sharing, and commitment. Through this meeting, the importance of providing opportunities, resources, and responsibility was once again reinforced. The district coordinating council meeting demonstrated that there seem to be no shortcuts for *communicating* reform.

Successful Projects

When structures have been adopted that promote maximum participation on all levels and effective channels of communication are in place, partnerships have been able to initiate exciting programs that have affected schools throughout their districts.

Long-Range Professional Development

Fullan (1993) considered mastery a crucial ingredient in successful change. He argued that one-shot workshops and disconnected sessions of training contribute little to the mastery public school teachers need in order to effect change. However, in partner districts with a heavy emphasis on long-range staff development, mastery begins to be a reachable goal.

One partnership district found itself with an unfilled university coordinator position when the professor assigned to that responsibility was on sabbatical. The university suggested that the money allotted as salary to that position could flow to the partner schools if they would be willing to meet the additional supervision and evaluation demands. Educators in the partner schools were eager for the funds and for the opportunity. They agreed that funds would be used for inservice education to promote district-wide school improvement, and that other schools in the district, not just partner schools, would be invited to attend. Each partner school suggested specific uses for its share of the one-time funds. The faculties were so appreciative and careful with the money that many managed to make it useful for two years. Although the partner schools took on the extra work that made the funding available, an opportunity to master skills in a wide variety of areas was created for many other teachers in other schools in the partnership district.

Demonstrating Mastery

A district enrolling approximately 8,000 students has an energy-rich tax base that provides ample district resources for staff development. Before teachers can be assigned to a partner school and permitted to work with preservice teachers, they are required to demonstrate mastery in such critical teaching skills as cooperative learning or individualization. A modest financial premium is offered as an inducement for completing the inservice coursework. In addition, master teachers offer peer courses in coaching and mentoring skills, which teachers must complete before a student teacher will be assigned. With this strong tradition in staff development, it is not surprising that this district is a leader in implementing distance learning technologies. Through a special project funded by a communications foundation, teachers in this district, along with educators from other partnership districts around the state, have formed teams with university faculty members to develop preservice and inservice training modules on a variety of topics related to educational change. Module topics have included integrating technology into education, developing research skills in students of all ability levels, implementing cooperative learning techniques, and developing coaching and mentoring skills. The modules are taught by collaborative teams of university and public school educators over a statewide interactive compressed video network.

Character Education

In another partnership district, participants expressed a desire for a district-wide goal in character development. One of the elementary partner schools was especially interested in this goal and offered to work on curriculum development in the area. An administrative intern from the university coordinated the work of a team of teachers in developing a literature-based approach to studying basic principles of character. The teachers on the team were released from their classrooms without cost to the district through the assignment of preservice teachers. The results of the project will be disseminated across the district and state.

Conclusion

In each of the cases we have described, commitment by teachers, administrators, and professors; trust among participants; and communication within the partnership and with schools throughout the district have enabled partner schools to become effective agents for district-wide change.

At a state partnership conference, Roger Soder (1992) discussed the "creative tensions" that can result from the establishment of partner schools, describing these tensions as analogous to the necessary tensions between the walls, ceiling, and floor of any structure. He explained that if one group's interests "won," the likely result would be the collapse of the structure. He proposed that there is a morality to teaching that gives educators a professional responsibility to reflect upon and question the value of partner school relationships. Partnerships are changing the lives of students, teachers, administrators, professors, and all those involved in the business of education.

Kleinsasser and Paradis (1993) summarize what the faculty at one state university learned about legitimizing the change process and revising their teacher education program to include closer ties to partnership districts: "Changes in the undergraduate program legitimized by vote, administrative action, and the almost unexplainable but powerful momentum created by implementing the program will have far-reaching, long-term effects on the personal and professional lives of faculty in the College of Education" (p. 8). At a time of stressful change and intense discomfort the faculty members of the state university's college of education turned to the public school administrators with whom they had served on clinical teams and to public school teachers to help solve logistical problems for preservice college students. "During the changes and arrangements, cohort faculty leaders drew energy from the public school faculty, especially during the most difficult moments concerning housing and scheduling. We found that other members of the university community may approve a program, but it is not until the program is implemented that they begin to understand the ramifications of the change strategies" (p. 13). Partner school participants learn, often through trying and frustrating circumstances, that they can trust each other, learn from each other, and draw strength from their association.

If the work of partner schools is demanding and often frustrating, are the benefits worth the price? As participants on all levels agree, the benefits are unpredictable, unstable, and abstract—but they are strong. Perhaps Pirsig (1974), in *Zen and the Art of Motorcycle Maintenance*, captured the essence of what partnership educators are trying to do when he suggested that "value, the leading edge of reality, is no longer an irrelevant offshoot of structure. Value is the predecessor of structure. It is the pre-intellectual awareness that gives rise to it. . . . Reality is made up, in part, of ideas that are expected to grow as you grow, and as we all know, century after century. . . . It has forms, but the forms are capable of change. . . . You have to have some feeling for the quality of work. You have to have a sense of what's good" (p. 255).

Partner schools are built on the dual agenda of simultaneously restructuring teacher education and renewing public schools. As districts have discovered ways to improve the quality of education within single districts and across districts, they have come to recognize that the source of renewal and the source of energy for improvement on a district-wide level lies within the individuals in the classrooms and in the schools.

References

Fullan, M. C. (1993). Why teachers must become change agents. *Educational Leadership, 50*(6), 12–17.

Kleinsasser, A., & Paradis, E. (1993, April). Goodlad's re-structuring model in Wyoming: Fragile partnership or social disruption? Paper presented in the symposium *Strategies for teacher education reform: Six cases and analysis*, annual meeting of the American Educational Research Association, Atlanta, GA.

Pirsig, R. (1974). *Zen and the art of motorcycle maintenance*. New York: Bantam Books.

Sirotnik, K., & Goodlad, J. I. (Eds.). (1988). *School-university partnership in action: Concepts, cases, concerns*. New York: Teachers College Press.

Soder, R. (1992, October). Recalling the national dual agenda and Wyoming's response. Paper presented at the Wyoming School-University Partnership conference, Casper, WY.

Woolf, T. & Harris, R.C. (1993, October). Organizational dynamics of the BYU-Public School Partnership. Paper presented at the annual meeting of the Northern Rocky Mountain Educational Research Association, Jackson, WY.

8

Promoting Statewide Collaboration

Barbara Little-Gottesman, Patricia Graham, and Carol Nogy

The scene has the appearance of the usual statewide meeting of agency administrators and college personnel. Five deans of colleges of education, representatives from university arts and sciences departments as well as the education colleges, and many people from partner schools statewide are present. Representatives from the state department of education have also joined the group. But instead of debating the usual agenda of mandates and policy exceptions, these administrators and teachers are silent and attentive. They are watching a demonstration of peer coaching, modeled by three restructuring consultants who have been asked to aid the statewide educational collaborative in some of its efforts for renewal.

The three consultants assume the roles of student intern, college supervisor, and classroom teacher. The "supervisor" teaches a new technique, while the "intern" and "classroom teacher" act as coaches, following a structured five-step process of peer coaching. Then the intern teaches, coached by the teacher and the supervisor. They rotate roles until each has taught and been coached and has participated twice on the coaching team.

As the demonstration concludes, everyone joins in questioning the participants and critiquing the process.

PROFESSOR: I wonder about having the intern critique the college supervisor. There should be a professional distance, you know. What about the professor's credibility if things don't go as well. . .

TEACHER A: The professor should be able to do herself what she's telling the intern to do. If *she* can't make something work, she shouldn't be judging a teacher or grading an intern on it.

SCIENCE PROFESSOR: Judging really shouldn't be an issue here, for any of them. What the three of them are looking at is a teaching act—a process that is or is not working. The professor's personality or credibility isn't being critiqued—or the teacher's or the intern's for that matter. They're looking at a phenomenon—that's all.

TEACHER B: We've been using peer coaching at our school for years. We strip off our plumage, admit we're all human, and ask for each other's help. You say we're all peers—professors, principals, teachers, interns. If we are, then we should teach together, talk about what we do, demonstrate what we think will work, and receive feedback from peers who are in a position to see what we can't see and understand what we may be too narrow or too conceited to understand.

Collaboration for Change

Although this meeting and frank exchange might be a little unusual in any partnership, it does illustrate what can happen when isolated partnerships join together in a statewide collaborative. If positive change is to occur in education, those involved in all aspects of education must become a part of that change. This meeting demonstrates how a broad collaborative can bring together those with diverse interests, experiences, and viewpoints, ultimately helping to accumulate a critical mass for change.

Levels of Innovation

For an innovation to result in significant educational renewal, it must advance sequentially through levels of use: orientation, preparation, mechanical use, and finally routine use (Hord, Rutherford, Huling-Austin, & Hall, 1987, p. 55). The peer coaching demonstration could have been repeated on staff development days in a number of districts and at faculty meetings at universities, and discussion at each demonstration would probably have brought out at least some of the major points generated at the meeting. But presenting the demonstration and inviting input with the major players at five colleges and thirty representative partner schools at once saved much time and energy. The ins and outs of preparation and mechanical implementation were streamlined as educators throughout the state pooled experience and frankly compared and contrasted what had and had not been effective. Thus, broad participation can advance the agenda for change much more quickly and efficiently.

Relationships

Many kinds of relationships form when various groups with overlapping interests come together to work on mutual concerns. A *cooperative* relationship occurs when participants are willing and able to work with and accommodate others for mutual benefit. Most colleges of education have a cooperative relationship with schools that accept their preservice teachers for practicum training. They meet together when necessary and accommodate each other. *Consortium*, which comes from a Latin word meaning *fellowship* or *agreement*, refers to a group formed to pool resources in an enterprise that would be beyond the strength or resources of any one member. Many school districts and universities form consortia in which they share personnel, facilities, equipment, research, and other resources—each accessing the other's expertise and materials when beneficial. A *collaborative* goes a step beyond a consortium to share resources and at the same time work jointly with those resources. A collaborative involves mutual effort focused interactively toward goals that overlap the interests of all parties, even though those parties, like those at the statewide meeting, might be varied and occasionally at odds.

Historically, colleges of education and public schools have often competed for resources and renown. Over the years, however, more and more of them have formed cooperatives and consortia to reduce competition and take advantage of the other's strengths. Now colleges and school districts in many states are forming collaboratives in which they work purposefully and mutually to strengthen teacher education and renew education in the schools—two goals that they now recognize as overlapping and symbiotic. The meeting that witnessed the peer coaching demonstration is typical of the interactions of the collaboratives formed in one state, where collaborative relationships among colleges of education and public schools have extended statewide. Recognizing collaboration's benefits, Calvin M. Frazier (1993) has recommended that state legislatures promote such collaboratives by clearly designating the entity responsible for the "simultaneous renewal" of school restructuring and teacher education (p. 10).

Components of a Statewide Collaborative

A statewide collaborative includes a wide expanse of territory and a wide variety of participants. For administration to be efficient and productive, the collaborative's organizational structure must be carefully established. In one of the earliest statewide collaboratives, the following organization has been effective.

Neutral Center or Coordinating Mini-Agency

When school-university partnerships throughout one of the southern states decided to collaborate statewide, their first step was to establish a neutral center, a mini-agency to coordinate efforts for restructuring, renewal, and innovation throughout the state. The advisory board charged this center with the mission to promote successful change in schools by serving as a catalyst for school restructuring and by developing model school sites through training and continuing cross-functional teams" (cited in Gottesman, 1993, p. 2). The cross-functional teams are made up of schoolteachers and administrators working with college and business partners, all concerned with educational renewal. The governing board for the center has mandated active participation from the deans of the colleges of teacher education, all state agencies involved in education, all associations of teachers and administrators, the state legislature, and a variety of business interests.

Education reform bills written by the state legislature provide for twenty-eight approved programs of teacher education, both public and private. As the collaborative requires that the teacher education programs form partnerships with the public schools to advance the agenda for simultaneous reform of teacher education and school restructuring, in effect state money goes to support collaboration between schools and teacher education in order to improve public K-12 schools and teacher education, whether the college partner is a public or a private institution. The neutral mini-agency requires strict accountability for the funds; thus, the money cannot be diverted by the colleges to another agenda.

The statewide collaboration coordinated by the neutral agency helps the school districts avoid what Seymour Sarason (1990) calls "the predictable failure" of educational reform, a failure that occurs when "the symbiotic relationship between schools and the university is marked by strong ambivalence. School personnel often derogate the quality and relevance of their professional education, and university faculty look upon the poor quality of our schools as in large measure due to the poor intellectual and personal qualities of school personnel. The expression of this ambivalence is kept in check by the power of each to alter the other adversely" (p. 66). School and university personnel cannot be constantly devaluing each other's work when they are committed to a collaborative partnership in which they must work together to upgrade each other's programs and advance each other's goals. By funding school/university partnerships, a center can support partnership work with public or private institutions. The neutral mini-agency facilitates administration of partnerships and distribution of funds.

The neutral agency must be formed by direct mandate from the legislature for the express purpose of restructuring, renewing, and otherwise reforming public education throughout the state. Partnerships also may be officially mandated by legislative act. All participants or potential participants in the renewal of K–12 education or teacher education should be involved in partnership governance; these participants may include business and legislative representatives if appropriate. The representatives of all areas should be included in collaborative training programs and in distribution and utilization of funds.

If the collaborative agency is truly neutral, no one university will dominate the reform process. Instead, that process can be explored within each partnership, with colleges and schools collaborating on training and resources, exploring together the research and national trends, and ultimately pursuing their own applications. As inquiry is an important aspect of partnership function, participants should reach a collaborative agreement to allow for experimental programs in which the neutral center, the universities, and the public schools will be involved. Each partnership should be accountable for progress in its experimental programs, with the neutral coordinating center facilitating the reporting and communicating responsibilities. The neutral center should have the power to reward partnership work and in turn have the accountability for the use of state funds.

Advisory Board

In addition to assistance from a neutral collaborative agency, the successful statewide collaborative for simultaneous renewal of K-12 and teacher education should have support from a smaller advisory board representing the policymakers who are directly responsible for reform (Frazier, 1993). This board is responsible for tracking the progress of the experimental partnerships and programs. It might include as members the state superintendent of education, the state commissioner for higher education, the senate education chair, the house education chair, a governor's office representative, a university representative (dean), a public school representative (superintendent), a business representative, and the head of the neutral miniagency. Even if this board met twice a year, it could be instrumental in evaluating the results of the experimental programs statewide and in advocating changes in state education policy in light of persuasive results from pilot programs.

Critical Issues

Many of the critical issues involved in forming and maintaining a statewide collaborative are discussed by John Jones and Brian Hall (1986), who suggest a model that has the vision of goals and values at its center, surrounded by structure, working climate, and community environment as wider circles developing from this central vision. In a statewide collaborative, it is essential that the vision of goals and values is shared by all participants, and that this vision is central to all organizational, motivational, and interpersonal involvements.

Central Vision

The central vision of a statewide collaboration is to improve both the education of K–12 students and the preparation of the teachers who will be teaching them. Since both colleges and schools will need to surrender some of their traditional territory and break down traditional barriers that exist between them, they must be *internally* committed to both the moral and political agenda of restructuring and renewal. Both colleges and schools must be intrinsically committed to renewal, and that commitment to the postulates of renewal that have been chosen and adopted by the collaborative should be in writing as well as in a felt philosophy.

Participatory Decision Making

In a partnership, participatory decision making equalizes all partners: college people, school people, arts and sciences people, and coordinating agency people. Participatory decision making should occur on all levels: among faculty and administrators within each school or college; among college and school personnel within each collaborative; and among all entity representatives in the neutral agency, on the advisory board, and or in other groups that coordinate relationships and activities between collaboratives within the statewide linkage.

For participatory decision making to function effectively, participants on all levels must adopt a collegial relationship, as described by Peter Senge (1990): "First, everyone involved must truly *want* the benefits of dialogue more than he wants to hold onto his privileges of rank. If one person is used to having his view prevail because he is the most senior person, then that privilege must be surrendered in dialogue. If one person is used to withholding his views because he is more junior, then that security of nondisclosure must also be surrendered" (p. 245).

Risk Taking

A natural outgrowth of participatory decision making is a willingness by partnership members to take the risks associated with innovation. Despite research and test results that may support a new policy, method, or approach, many educators find it almost impossible to relinquish some of their traditional practices. One of the primary functions of the collaborative is to provide the support that enables partners to leave the safety of what is established and to risk undertaking a possible improvement. In one statewide collaborative with a neutral restructuring center, the center furnishes resources for risk-related training sessions, such as a retreat focused on managing change and a seminar on conflict resolution. These sessions provide change agendas for innovators throughout the collaborative, without taxing the resources or curriculum of any one college or school.

Teaming

The teaming that begins within the college or school must extend to teaming between the school and college. Whether efforts are focused on decision making or on planning and teaching new curricula, school and college teachers and practitioners must be equally represented in those efforts. Team members must be considered equal, and there must be trust between them; if equality and trust are present, change agendas will be more beneficial for the students.

Clarity

When the partnership is statewide, clarity on two aspects of partnership is particularly necessary. Individual issues and goals must be spelled out, and the overall vision and perspective—the big picture that gives purpose and direction to everything involved with partnership function—must be carefully defined. Since small issues, such as schedules and meeting times, can cloud the greater issues of vision, goals, and significant aspects of renewal, a facilitator or the neutral coordinating center should be charged with ensuring that subordinate issues support overall goals without distorting or diminishing them. Even in successful partnerships, visitors may be so dazzled by innovative programs within a school that they lose sight of how the school-university partnership functions collaboratively to produce and promote the innovations that excite them. Partnership participants must be sure that they do not become similarly distracted and lose sight of the process that makes the product possible.

Larger Community

A partnership's influence extends beyond universities and public schools. The larger community affected by the partnership may include state agencies, professional associations or unions, accrediting bodies, cooperating agencies, and even competing organizations. If representatives from the collaborative are also major players in these additional community entities, they can extend the influence of renewal into agencies beyond the schools. One of the advantages of the statewide collaborative is that a united voice representing many facets of innovation is much stronger than individual voices or solitary innovators.

Such critical issues as central vision, participative decision making, risk taking, teaming, clarity, and community require in-depth discussion as partnerships are formed, along with regular consideration by all parties as the programs progress. Classroom teachers, college professors, superintendents, interns, and legislators should address how well the partnership is functioning in these areas with the same frequency as they address finances and budgets.

Advantages

When a collaborative is organized statewide, with a neutral coordinating agency and a functioning advisory board, collaborative members can take the power of their learning and expertise to other ventures within the state. They can use their collaborative skills to establish other groups and to distribute and redistribute power within the collaborative organization and outside the collaborative as desirable. The advantages of a statewide collaborative can be summed up under four headings: the ability to pool resources, the capacity to accumulate a critical mass, the strength to directly influence other colleges and schools, and the position to exert some long-term influence on state education policy.

Pooling Resources

A statewide collaborative has the obvious advantage of enabling participants to pool resources and expertise to accomplish projects and innovations that none of them has the capability to accomplish individually. In this era of severe budget cuts, pooling of financial resources is particularly desirable. An educational collaborative can be compared to a food cooperative: together, the members can purchase more materials and services than they could individually; by sharing, they increase the variety and quality that each is able to enjoy.

Less obvious, but significant, are two additional advantages of pooling financial resources. First, funding that comes from the state can flow through the neutral agency or center; thus the state legislature does not have to take a stand on funding the pilot program of one university over another. When appropriating funding for renewal programs, state legislators are often prevented from putting money where experimentation is most active due to such issues as equity, fairness in geographic distribution of funding, and similar political concerns. The agency, however, can channel funds to the partnerships that can be most productive with them. Second, federal and private grants are now frequently awarded to collaborative organizations. Indeed, many federal grants *require* that proposals demonstrate evidence of collaboration between schools and colleges. For example, in recent years National Science Foundation (NSF) grants have included a collaboration requirement, emphasizing collaboration and wide dissemination of results as program traits that the NSF values and desires to fund. Collaboratives that involve multiple schools and colleges, of course, have a distinct advantage.

Moving More Learners

The advantage of being able to move a critical mass of learners more quickly and efficiently through processes of renewal is no less important than the resource advantage. Traditionally, school renewal has occurred one school at a time. Many state and local districts have advocated systemic organizational reform. One statewide collaboration, which consists of five colleges and thirty fully functioning partner schools, has found that the common structural unity and the sense of common purpose that unite the sites have greatly facilitated efforts toward this systemic renewal. Experimental successes and barriers experienced throughout the state can be shared more efficiently through the communication channels of the neutral coordinating center than through the sporadic and often unpredictable communication that typically occurs among teacher education programs in a state. Seminars, retreats, and sharing conferences coordinated by a center allow all participants to learn of the advances and innovations that others are finding to be successful. With common money channeled through the center by the state, nationally renowned trainers can be brought in to conduct seminars and conferences, an advantage many sites could not afford on their own.

Experimentation and research projects conducted at multiple sites in the partnerships in a statewide collaborative are often more capable of being generalized than inquiry at one-college collaboratives. More variables can be represented during experimentation at multiple sites, as demographics will vary greatly. A collaborative that reaches throughout a state will usually include both rural and urban districts, both schools with homogeneous populations and schools with populations that are ethnically and culturally diverse. When successes and failures can be rapidly shared, replication occurs more quickly and easily as well.

Disseminating and Influencing

Another significant advantage of a statewide collaborative is the influence it can have on colleges and schools in the state that have not yet established partnership relations. These other colleges and schools can be invited to send teams to the retreats, seminars, and planning sessions coordinated by a neutral center and financed by the state. Thus other schools benefit from new ideas presented by experts brought in by the collaborative or generated by partnership inquiry. They also benefit from seeing how partnerships function and noting the advantages that partnerships bring to universities and schools.

An example of this extended influence occurred when a state with a statewide collaborative received a Carnegie grant to experiment with curricula for preparing middle school teachers. Under the funding from this grant, partnerships to contribute both curricula and recommendations were formed by middle schools and colleges that were not at that time participating in collaboratives in order to contribute both curricula and recommendations.

Those who participate in statewide collaboratives hope that, as Cal Frazier (1993) advised, approved teacher education programs in all states will eventually include partnerships as the essential ingredient in teacher preparation.

Influencing State Policy

The collective voice of a statewide collaborative is, of course, stronger than the single voice of any one entity, whether it be a state research university or a small private liberal arts college. On some occasions, a large collaborative can influence approval or funding that might not otherwise be obtainable.

Steps in Establishing a Statewide Collaborative

Although each state will face different requirements, needs, and frustrations, a few basic preparatory steps are recommended for those interested in establishing a statewide collaborative to unite school-college partnerships for educational renewal. Initially, all parties must be prepared with an awareness of each other's needs and an understanding of the potential of a partnership to meet those needs. Next, agreements must be reached and specific plans formulated. Finally, long-range goals and plans for the collaborative should be projected by its participants.

Preparation

For the purpose of discussion we will assume that the body originating the statewide collaborative is a college or university. This body must first be prepared, so that its faculty will clearly understand the purpose and vision for the renewal agenda. Intensive awareness sessions can provide this understanding; they should begin more than a year before the actual organization of the collaborative is to take effect. When the institutional faculty have internalized the purpose and vision, awareness training and preliminary planning should extend to the leaders of K–12 education and to other university people in teacher education and in arts and sciences in all the potential collaborating groups. Finally, awareness meetings should be held to present persuasive data to all legislative committees involved with educational policies and funding.

Proposals and Plans

After approximately a year of awareness and preliminary planning meetings, it is time to prepare a written plan or proposal for collaboration. A specific plan for the neutral center to facilitate the collaboration should be included with the initial agreements and prospectus to be presented to the sponsoring legislative committee. The legislature should be requested to establish and support this agency as the entity to which funding can be directed and through which funding can be channeled to benefit educational renewal throughout the state.

Long-Range Planning

In addition to meeting the immediate requirements of organizing and setting up the statewide collaborative, participants should engage in long-range planning as well. Such planning should allow for frequent and intensive sharing of local successes and partnershipwide agendas among all participants within the collaborative. Also provisions should be made so that the results of experimentation and inquiry conducted in the collaborative can be systematically shared with colleges and schools in the state that do not choose to participate in committed partnerships. If results are disseminated widely, the research conducted in and by the collaborative will be seen to benefit the entire state rather than just a few partnership institutions.

Conclusion

Partners pay a price for forming a statewide collaborative. Many struggles are involved in initiating and maintaining it. Institutions that have formerly competed for recognition and funding need to overcome traditional rivalries and mistrust. Even when basic trust has been attained, participants need to forge a common vision and keep that vision central to the function of the collaborative. Subordinate issues such as meeting times, institutional requirements, or separate research agendas—and of course impediments such as partner school favoritism, district equity, and personal rivalry—must not be allowed to distort or diminish the vision that is the overall purpose for which the collaborative was formed. Institutional agendas must be kept in proper perspective to collaborative agendas, a difficult requirement for many partners. Finding time to devote to the partnership is often a hardship, and collaborative meetings and activities may be difficult to schedule; but the power of the united voice that represents the concerns of educational renewal balances the inconveniences and demands.

To those now participating in statewide collaboratives, the advantages outweigh the inconveniences and demands. The vision of simultaneous renewal of teacher preparation and public education is clearer for those who share it over a broad swath of geographic space and demographic situations. A collaborative voice is a strong voice: legislators listen with more attention; so do members of the profession and the public. The collaborative gives innovators a support group: experiments, research, successes, and frustrations can easily be shared with empathetic collaborators through the telephone or electronic mail. Funds are more easily obtained and more efficiently used, as money can be pooled to buy training, services, and other resources and as legislators are more willing to allocate funds that will be efficiently used. But overall, the statewide collaborative works because its goals are to improve teacher preparation and renew schooling throughout the state; and those within and without the collaborative realize that these goals are paramount if students in the state are to be prepared to live and work as literate, productive citizens in the American democracy of the twenty-first century.

References

Frazier, C. M. (1993). *A shared vision: Policy recommendations for linking teacher education to school reform.* Denver, CO: Education Commission of the States.

Goodlad, J. I. (1990). *Teachers for our nation's schools*. San Francisco: Jossey-Bass.

Gottesman, B. (1990). *Reinventing schools for the 21st century: It's how change is done in South Carolina*. Rock Hill, SC: South Carolina Center for the Advancement of Teaching and School Leadership.

Hord, S., Rutherford, W., Huling-Austin, L., & Hall, G. (1987). *Taking charge of change*. Alexandria, VA: Association for Supervision and Curriculum Development.

Jones, J., & Hall, B. (1986). *The Genesis effect: Personal and organizational transformation*. Mahwah, NJ: Paulist Press.

Sarason, S. B. (1990). *The predictable failure of educational reform: Can we change course before it's too late?* San Francisco: Jossey-Bass.

Senge, P. (1990). *The fifth discipline: The art and practice of the learning organization*. New York: Doubleday.

9

Building Links with Families and Communities

Hal Lawson, Randy Flora, Sally Lloyd, Katharine Briar, James Ziegler, and Jan Kettlewell

In *There Are No Children Here*, Kotlowitz (1992) tells the true story of nine-year-old Pharaoh and his eleven-year-old brother Lafayette, two boys growing up in the housing projects in inner-city Chicago, a neighborhood that "hungrily devoured its children" (p. 10), in an apartment in which "nothing . . . the children would tell you, was as it should be" (p. 8).

Kotlowitz graphically portrays the challenging environments that children in poverty, like Pharaoh and Lafayette, face every day. He shows how schools, law enforcement agencies, and organizations such as welfare units and the housing authority, which were created to help solve the problems of families living in poverty, can unintentionally and ironically intensify the problems they were intended to solve.

A New Perspective on Services

Changes are occurring in a growing number of public schools and health and human service agencies. These changes are intended to help children like Pharaoh and Lafayette. Because children spend a significant number of their formative years in public schools, and because the primary purpose of schools is to promote the learning, growth, and development of students, school personnel are beginning to accept expanded responsibility for the well-being of children

(Adler & Gardner, 1994; Dryfoos, 1994; Sizer, 1992) and, in some cases, their families. School personnel are also beginning to realize that they cannot do it alone. For example, one psychologist cannot deal with the pervasive needs of hundreds of students in four large urban schools, and professionals in schools and in health and human service agencies must have help from parents. At the same time, public agencies are recognizing the complexity and interdependence of children's needs, especially the "nesting" of these needs in their family contexts. Family-centered practices are gaining currency as a result. Public agencies are joining with school personnel in viewing the local school as one focal point for providing service to persons in need, as a place where the needs and wants of children and families can be identified and addressed through interagency and interprofessional collaboration. This necessary collaboration and these integrated services can occur, however, only if the school itself becomes a different kind of organization than it has been in the past.

Experiences in some urban settings reveal that the school partnership can extend beyond its function as a cooperative venture between a local school and a nearby college or university to engage in collaborative relationships with all the other agencies (such as health, child welfare, and juvenile justice) that have the purpose of serving the children and families in the community. Proposals for such interagency and interprofessional collaboration are founded upon a new mode of analysis and planning known as relational or ecological analysis.

A *relational analysis* of schools, universities, and community organizations requires us to begin with the lives of children and families and to consider how each institution may "wrap around" them. For instance, if a school-university partnership were to expand into a multi-agency community partnership, how might this partnership make a difference for Pharaoh and Lafayette? For these children and others, school might become a quasi-neutral ground that may provide temporary relief from hunger, fear, and violence. Keeping in mind the needs children bring with them to school, and given what is known about family dynamics and community characteristics in areas where people live predominantly at or near poverty levels, it becomes clear that schools must join with the entire spectrum of community services if they are to address the needs, problems, and aspirations not only of individual children but of their families. A child like Lafayette, who has recently watched some of his closest friends die at ages thirteen and fifteen, is not highly motivated to improve his reading so that he can finish school, let alone go to college.

Educators, particularly teachers and principals, are often blamed for the effects of conditions they did not create and cannot ameliorate alone. Help from social workers and other service providers often comes only after a crisis has been reached and a child has been labeled "at risk" or "a problem." For these children, life in school is part of a never-ending catch-up game, in which they are stigmatized and categorized as second-team players that teachers really would like to trade to special educators. For Lafayette, who had a deficiency in reading, help did not come until after he had been arrested along with several other boys for breaking into a truck.

Traditional school-university partnerships are unable to meet the multidimensional needs of such children, let alone the needs of their families. The needs that manifest themselves in what teachers may see as learning problems—as in Lafayette's case—have their roots in school-family-home-neighborhood relationships. In this relational frame of reference, Lafayette's "reading problem" will be reframed; clearly, the solution is not the university's reading methodology workshop, or the schoolteacher's experience with Reading Recovery. If the roots of such learning problems are in a child's home or neighborhood, solutions must be found there. School-university-community-family partnerships, which can use the resources and learning of a wide variety of concerned participants, are formed to frame, identify, and solve these problems. This concept of partnership includes families, their homes and neighborhoods, and the agencies and institutions that serve them. When children have multifaceted and interdependent needs, partnerships attempting to meet those needs must become multidimensional as well.

Just as schools need to become more nurturing, ready to meet the developmental, learning, and health needs of all children and their families, the health and human service professions also need to become more educative and promotive, to prevent crises in children and their families. New partnerships, in short, may begin with schools but, by including families and community agencies, proceed beyond them. Thus, these partnerships involve *educational* renewal, not just *school* renewal.

Exploring New Partnerships

Several approaches to these broader partnerships and to educational renewal are possible (Hooper-Briar & Lawson, 1994; Lawson & Hooper-Briar, 1994). Because relational analysis and planning cause us to ask new kinds of questions as we meet each successive challenge, and because we are exploring new issues, the work involved is inventive, pioneering, and self-corrective. Hence, the following thoughts represent the views of *some* members of an emerging cross-system partnership and serve as a developmental marker. We begin by describing the group's relational analysis, discussing the types of renewal that seem most basic to an expanded school-university-family-community partnership. We conclude by describing current issues in our systems change agenda, examining the implications of those issues for the future of the partnership.

As the comparison in Table 9.1 demonstrates (Lawson & Hooper-Briar, 1994), a relational approach to partnerships requires an expanded conceptual vision. This vision begins with the familiar school-university partnership but extends to the school-university-family-community partnership.

In the broader concept of the partner school, the child and the child's family are at the center of the partnership. Schools, families, and communities must become mutually supportive, educative, and interdependent, as planning for the care and education of children by families, neighborhoods, agencies, and schools requires many kinds of services and supports, together with synchronized strategies

Table 9.1. Two Approaches to Partnership.

	Professional development school	Family empowerment and integrated services model
Purpose	Simultaneous improvements in schools and programs for the education of educators	Synchronized changes in the organizations serving children and families
Theory of change	1) School reform and renewal as a stand-alone strategy (categorical)	1) School renewal as one part of community development (relational)
	2) Reformist bias: improving existing systems	2) Transformational bias: within and across systems change
University's orientation	Research, Development, and Diffusion (R, D, & D)	Design, Development, and Research (D, D, & R)
Kinds of collaboration	Primarily two-way: university-school	Multiple ways: universities, agencies, schools, businesses and corporations, families
Role of families	Clients	Partners

for change. The traditional school-university partnership differs significantly from these extended partnerships. Traditional partnerships center on reforming schools, focusing on individual children, and improving the preparation of educators. The new concept of educational renewal involves all of the organizations serving children *and families*. The partner school becomes one of several organizations; as such, it must coordinate its efforts with those of multiple agencies, not just with the function of the partner university. Families in the traditional partner school are often seen as clients to be served, but in the new concept they are seen as fully participating partners in change. Families are empowered to help themselves and other families—including the preparation of family members to serve as paraprofessionals in schools and community agencies.

Figure 9.1 presents a graphic model of the relationship of families to all of the community agencies and organizations. In this model, family support and empowerment are at the center of partnership efforts at renewal, and parents are viewed as the most significant partners in the learning and development of children. Though traditionally blamed for the problems and needs their children bring to school, parents become, according to this model, an important part of the solution, supported by educators and other human service professionals. To make this model function, local determination of community needs and local autonomy over school organization and assessment must be maintained.

To illustrate how the school-university-family-community partnership can affect educational renewal, we will describe how our own expanded partnership, which included university, schools, and community service groups, approached a specific national educational goal: that all children will come to school ready to learn. We had always considered this goal overly simplistic, feeling that it seems to "blame the victim." Among its implications are that families are solely responsible for preparing their children to attend school, that families operate in a vacuum unaffected by other influences in the community, that family efforts to ensure readiness

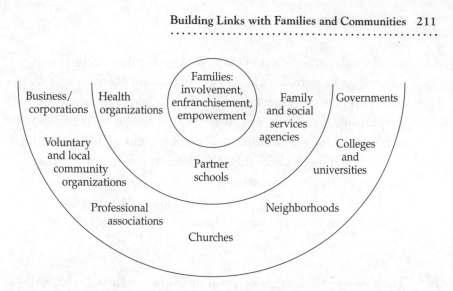

Figure 9.1. Family Relationships with Community Resources.

require no support from the community, and that schools and communities need not be held accountable for the parts they play in denying some students appropriate opportunities for learning, development, and health.

We chose to reframe this national educational goal from a relational perspective. We decided that school communities will work as partners to ensure that both the schools and the key community organizations are ready to promote the learning, development, and well-being of all children and their families. Inherent within this reframed goal are four core assumptions: all children can learn; children have more likelihood of learning when schools and communities work together; schools must accommodate the diversity of student learning needs; and family-centered strategies and supports need to be added to child-focused initiatives.

Communities

We have coined the term school community to describe family-school-community ecologies. This term designates both the internal community of the school, the equivalent of the school's culture, and the external community, the school's outside environments, including the stresses and forces that shape families' abilities to nurture and protect children as well as the relevant agencies that serve families. These two communities are not, of course, mutually exclusive. Ideally, the two communities enjoy a symbiotic relationship, jointly nurturing the learning, development, and well-being of children and families and contributing simultaneously to the development of neighborhoods, towns, and cities. Such joint efforts are born from shared visions, as is implied in an African proverb: "It takes a whole village to raise a child."

Villages

The above proverb suggests new dimensions for shared responsibility for children. Families, broadly defined, are the central social units in a village; as such, they provide primary health promotion and care, social services, and education. In fact, families provide some 90 percent of the teaching, counseling, and health care of children. In this perspective, it is impossible to consider the needs, wants, problems, and dreams of children without placing them in the contexts of families. Hence, we and others endorse family-centered services and supports.

The image of a village also includes extended families, mutual-aid networks, healthy workgroups, local control by stakeholders, a manageable scale, and overall conviviality. It implies common commitments to inform, nurture, protect, and empower children and families. When the proverb holds true, the child and the family are a shared focal point for all those in the village.

In a village, everyone is a stakeholder. Organizational structures are horizontal, emphasizing democratic processes and encouraging civic engagement. Many learning barriers that children manifest can be traced to the ways in which the community allocates resources, jobs, and income. Child and family issues are village issues.

To ensure the greatest possible opportunities for children and their families, everyone in a village needs to be deputized to participate in the solutions to the developmental needs of the children. Schools cannot educate and nurture children without all systems, stakeholders, and village members working together. These and other images associated with a village broaden the vision of what a partner school could be. People need to think of themselves as members of families and villages, conceiving of themselves, their roles, and their behaviors in both schools and universities from this perspective.

Expanded Partnerships

Like all school-university partnerships, the new expanded partnerships involve school reform and improvement, including preservice and inservice teacher education. But this is only the beginning. After all, reform implies tinkering with existing delivery systems to meet emergent needs. Reform of schools and of teacher education alone, though making important strides in many areas, does not go far enough in serving children in areas where poverty, crime, and other societal problems are located in school communities.

Instead of being considered school system challenges, children's needs, problems, and aspirations may be recast as family support/ empowerment and community development issues. Using relational analysis and planning, educators can be important links in the support network that involves parents or caregivers working with professionals from health and human service agencies, corporations, and governmental and civic leaders.

Expanded partnerships cultivate support and empowerment networks for children and families. They mobilize parents, agencies, and services to address constraints and barriers to children's learning, development, and health. The partners band together on partner school sites (school-based services) or near these sites (school-linked services). They invite professionals from education and human services into the community to discuss and plan for educational renewal. The agenda that began with school reform is thus expanded to include organizational restructuring, cross-system collaboration, family support, and community development. The intended result is the *transformation* of the organizations and systems that serve children and families.

School-linked and school-based services depend on educators' commitments to the learning, development, and well-being of children and families and to the ability of collaborative units to meet the multiple facets of those needs. Similarly, these same commitments to children and families and receptivity to collaboration must be present in health and human services agencies. These commitments stem from shared visions, which are central to expanded partnerships.

A third group that must be committed to meeting needs and to collaborating in order to do so consists of the children and families themselves. Not only must family members make their voices heard by the professionals in schools and community agencies, but parents and youth also must be organized, deputized, and mobilized to assist with the work in these areas.

Experiences

Recently a school in a district served by a school-university-family-community partnership was facing closure due to a problem with head lice that educators and agency personnel had been unable to solve. Absenteeism was high, children were falling further and further behind, and closing the school was a possibility. When the help of parents was solicited, they became full participating partners with the school and the social service agencies. They solved the head lice problem when professionals could not. Parents also formed and staffed homework clubs for children to help them keep up with the work they had missed. Older students became full partners as they helped transport young children safely to and from school. Others formed a helping group for "misunderstood students," whose rejection by teachers and principals was interfering with their attendance and their learning. Parents who had never before participated in the school noticed other parents working to protect their children's health and well-being and involving themselves in their children's education. The nonparticipating parents then offered their involvement and support. In short, children and families became genuine contributors toward solving what might at an earlier time have been regarded as just a school problem—but this time it was considered a family and a community problem.

The intent of the extended partnership is to empower families and community members to address their own concerns and renewal. In the following case, a composite of several school communities that have built successful school-university-family-community partnerships, a more complex and serious situation needed to be addressed.

Teachers in an elementary school with many children of immigrant families began noticing signs of disabling levels of stress among a number of students when parents were laid off from their jobs with the closing of a local industry. In the wake of the closure, health and human service agencies, recreation programs, the police, and other helping organizations suffered cutbacks in staff, causing hardships for consumers of these services as well as for those whose employment was affected. Among the children, absenteeism had been rising, along with stress-related learning barriers. As many kinds of services were needed to help the children and their families, the principal, teachers, caseworkers, and parents felt the school would be a good central place to coordinate helping activities. Knowing that these children and families might make up caseloads for eight or more social workers, they felt justified in asking their local health and human service agencies to consider sending in family counselors, job club developers, and income maintenance workers, along with small business and legal service representatives. Together, these parents and professionals negotiated consensus that children should receive priority among all organizations whose mission touched children and their families. Their goal went beyond children's learning outcomes to address the needs of the larger community, hoping that through an integrated service strategy they could mobilize community leadership to address these problems.

Through a community consortium, more than twenty agencies

agreed to work to reduce the hunger, housing, joblessness, discrimination, and after-school problems being faced by the children and their families. Consortium members obtained small grants from every known source (community development, United Way, and local corporate and other philanthropic funds) for new service strategies by which parents became providers of services through a family resource center. Youths from the upper grades ran their own self-help groups, including outreach for truants. The community consortium and the new services at the school opened up avenues to additional help for specific families and for entire classrooms that were experiencing the heaviest stress. More than ninety parents, representing many of the varying cultures in the community, became actively involved either as paraprofessionals or as volunteers. Two local universities sent their student interns to the school to offer services; in addition, university faculty considered the implications of these new service strategies for curricular change at their universities.

The school took on a very different atmosphere within the next six months as it continued to support families and to work with other systems to build the community. Absenteeism dropped, and the frequency of behavioral problems decreased. Parent-run homework clubs for children and job clubs for parents strengthened school achievement, economic development, and even job placement opportunities.

This example shows how expanded partnerships can meet the needs of each child in the village, and how parents and children as well as schools and agencies play central roles in cross-system change. If the partnership had been limited to the school and the university, the problems faced by students and their families could not have been solved. The problems demanded the involvement of the entire community, of all agencies charged with serving families and children.

A Student Experience

Fifteen-year-old Samantha first approached the public school in her neighborhood when her little sister was sent home because she had scabies. Samantha had been taking care of her four siblings and her own baby since her mother had disappeared a month before. The six of them were living in a building fifteen miles from the school; it was in such poor condition that it was about to be torn down. Samantha was anxious that her brothers and sister finish school, as it seemed that she would not be able to finish herself.

Samantha was referred to the Health-Wellness Program, a division of the Community Services Action Committee, one of the agencies that is part of an active partnership of schools, universities, community agencies, and parents. The Health-Wellness Program works one-on-one with students and their families; if families cannot or will not come to the school, caseworkers from the program go to the families. In this case, they had to go looking for Samantha's mother, while working with Samantha to come up with the best situation they could for the children. Samantha's mother was finally located. She is a drug addict. She genuinely loves and cares for her children—when she is not on drugs. She has been in and out of rehabilitation; but she always goes back to drugs within a few weeks of her release. The best way to help the family, therefore, seemed to be to begin with Samantha herself.

The counselors helped Samantha obtain financial aid to support the children. They located a good sitter for Samantha's baby so that Samantha would be able to finish high school. Unfortunately, the distance between the home, the sitter, and the school requires a long bus ride, but Samantha does not want to change schools. So she gets on the bus at 5:57 A.M. each day to take her baby to the sitter, travels two and one-half hours, then calls her counselor from the baby-sitter's home. The counselor picks her up and drives her to school. She is an hour late for school on this schedule, but her classes have been arranged to accommodate this timing. Her teachers have been supportive. Because she has not missed a day of school, she is able to obtain funds from LEAP, a local program of financial assistance. The counselor comments, "This is the kind of help that she needs. The complexity is overwhelming with the kind of problems the family has." Life is not easy for Samantha, but with the supports provided by the partnership, both educational and human services help have been extended to her—and Samantha is going to graduate.

A Partnership Experience

The school-university-family-community partnership that has helped Samantha is extending its aid to many students in its service area. Parent support groups have been formed for troubled families, and funds are being sought to develop parent centers in some neighborhoods. A work project developed through the partnership is helping unemployed parents to find jobs. The university in the partnership is developing a wellness class in which university students from allied health fields will participate. In addition, university students are planning an in-school suspension class for students who have been removed from regular classes because of behavior problems. The nursing department at the college is working with the school and with the social agencies to establish a site-based health clinic at the school so that nursing help will be more readily available to the students. Although this program had two hundred officially referred medical problems during the past year, they estimate that they actually handled nine hundred health-related situations that required medical intervention.

A nurse-teacher participating in the program described what she had seen that explained why schools and agencies need close cooperation:

> [Most people] do not realize the complexity of the problems these students have. I made a home visit to a student who is in the top 20 percent of the senior class. Quite literally there was no ceiling in the house. Conditions under which these students live are monumentally bad. We have students who have to run light cords from one apartment to another in order to be able to get dressed in the morning. And teachers are trying to teach.

But when students have problems like these, they are not ready to learn. The teachers are totally frustrated with these problems getting in their way, and the students are acting out. They do not realize the complexity of their problems. You have to help meet those basic needs before they can learn.

Promoting this necessary understanding and cooperation is one of the purposes of the partnership. As the nurse-teacher said, "We try our best to keep the teachers in our corners; they are our greatest allies, and they are the students' best allies." The partnership is providing instruction for both inservice and preservice teachers in dealing with the problems of students in the school's geographic area. As the area is urban, particular emphasis is given to racial tensions and needs.

When the partnership began its extended services, most referrals came from teachers at the school; but in the second year, the students realized the help that was available and about half the referrals came from students themselves. By the third year, most of the referrals were from students. In one year, there were more than two hundred referrals.

Voices

A number of students who have been helped through the partnership have been interviewed about their experience, and their voices offer ample evidence of its effectiveness.

"I really like it. It really helps you to get things together. If you have problems, they come through and help you. . . . If they can help you, they do, if not they recommend you to someone who can. What if you need tutoring. . . . What if your girlfriend quits you. . . . I can talk to them. I've encouraged my friends about it. Some might come in. They know my mother. She comes."

"I have this problem. I have a little girl, and I have a real hard problem with child care. Mrs. H. took me all around . . . called around for me, talked with my counselor trying to find a way I could stay in school so I could graduate this spring. . . . I'm doing fine in school. I'm going to the community college for surgical tech after I graduate. They even have child care at the community college."

"The main thing I like about it is that they listen to me, any-thing I have to say, and look me in the face, and I know they are paying attention to me. In my surroundings it is unusual for adults to do that. . . . Sometimes in the morning I don't feel like coming [to school]. [But] I had a group. When I knew I would see them I would get up and come and see them. I also like the hugs they give me. And they tell us they love us and everything."

Students were also asked what the program had done for them.

"I was in a state where I couldn't concentrate on anything, they helped me get over it."

"I was real depressed at the beginning of the year. I talk with Ms. B and Ms. H. It's helped me a lot."

"Helped me with my illness [sickle cell anemia] especially with my crimes."

"Helped me have confidence."

"Made me worthwhile."

Then students who had participated in the program were asked what would have happened if they had not had it.

"I probably would still be in a shell and afraid to talk to someone."

"Always unhappy. Always scared."

"I would probably skip a lot and be failing extremely bad."

"I probably would commit suicide."

"I would be in a lot of trouble."

"I would be dead."

Challenges

The experiences of the school-university-family-community part-nerships have demonstrated their potential for success. But what are the challenges associated with such cross-system change? What action steps are necessary to create a school-community village? We suggest the following:

• Improve preservice and continuing education of both school and human service personnel, emphasizing their shared commitments; pro-vide interprofessional education to increase the sensitivity of all par-ticipants to cultural diversity, sharing values and knowledge that lead to family-friendly organizations and environments.

• Develop school curricula, from preschool through college, with an emphasis on equal access to knowledge for all children, ped-agogical nurturing, school stewardship, and democratic education (Goodlad, 1990).

• Create structures for community collaboration (school-uni-versity-family-community relationships), with schools becoming the hubs of family support villages that foster the learning, devel-opment, and well being of all children and families.

• Strengthen and develop all participating organizations—uni-versities, schools, and human service agencies—paying particular attention to the continuing education of professionals, to collabo-rations among professionals and parents, and to multicultural needs and issues.

• Include families with diversity in race, class, gender, and exceptionality in shaping, delivering, and receiving education and human services.

- Develop fresh approaches to assessment, evaluation, and research, designing these approaches for multiple purposes and audiences.

Conclusion

We began this chapter by referencing a story about two young boys in inner-city Chicago. Because the efforts of the school, welfare agencies, the housing authority, law enforcement, and psychiatric and social service agencies were fragmented and separate, neither the children's nor the family's needs could be met. Children with the potential to be excellent students were caught in a downward spiral of poverty, deprivation, violence, addiction, lawlessness, and abuse. But partnerships are changing the pattern for many children.

Many of the needs of expanded partnerships are now known, yet many questions about their evolution and functioning remain.

Needs

If a network of partnerships is organized to advance a common agenda, participation by all families, children, educators, and human service personnel must be ensured. To strengthen participation, appropriate preservice education and continuing professional development of educational and human service personnel must be provided. But such education and development should go beyond the typical school reform agenda. If the vision of school-university-family-community partnerships is to be realized, then the preparation of educational personnel must emphasize the teacher as a leader in the classroom, the school, and the community. Teachers should be prepared to inspire vision and support internally motivated learning and collaborative work among their students and peers. They should learn to become leaders of learning in a school in which everybody teaches, everybody learns. Because they focus on the whole child within a family context, teachers also need to be advocates for support in the community for children and families, particularly those conditions and relationships that pertain to learning.

Teachers must be prepared to detect risk factors in children. Though they should not attempt to do social work and psychological counseling, teachers must know enough about the health and well-being of children and families to be able to communicate effectively with parents and other human service professionals, to reduce barriers to learning, and to refer a troubled child and family to appropriate community and family services. To function effectively in their new roles, principals will require preparation that helps them promote productive relationships among professionals working in school sites and with parents and other community representatives.

In addition to strengthened and refocused teacher preparation, some measure of interprofessional education should also be required for participants from the various collaborating units, providing them with a common denominator of vision(s), mission(s), norms, values, knowledge, and language. Visits to innovative school sites can provide insights into the ways the roles of principals, teachers, school social workers, health care professionals, and others change as these individuals are involved in collaborative partnership work.

In turn, social workers and health care professionals need to know more about the schools and the broader concept of education. Acquiring this knowledge is one part of a larger shift that must occur in social service philosophy and delivery, a shift from operating with deep-end crisis systems to operating with front-end promotion and prevention strategies that rely upon the education and empowerment of children and families. In brief, the human services must become more educative at the same time that educators become more service oriented (Lawson, in press).

Because the aspirations and problems of children and families are many and diverse, partnership participants must establish the trust that will enable them to work together across organizational boundaries in support of the chronically vulnerable family as well as the family in a temporary crisis caused by divorce, illness, or death. All groups should seek to restructure services in ways that encourage children and families to help themselves and each other. For example, professionals must learn to trust family members to help frame problems and solutions. Professionals must also learn to trust each other and to work together across organizations.

Educational renewal, as approached through school-university-family-community partnerships, needs to renew not only preservice and continuing education, but also the school's organizational systems. For example, if teachers are to help in solving student problems rooted in family-community ecologies, then they will need to take on new perspectives, develop new skills, and be open to working with a variety of daily and annual schedules. The typical 8:00 A.M. to 3:30 P.M. teaching day and ten-month calendar with a predictable routine may not be appropriate. Flexible scheduling for students and teachers, including year-round calendars, might be necessary within developing family-community ecologies. Of course, such flexibility has many implications for contract, salary, recognition, promotion, and other employment issues.

Similarly, if university professors are expected to teach and engage in scholarly inquiry in collaboration with school and/or agency personnel, then they too will have learning needs. The current structure of their calendar and workday might also be inconsistent with the new demands, work roles will need to be reconfigured, and promotion and tenure criteria will need to honor collaborative work.

Questions

Learning our way through such a large and ambitious systems change agenda has involved us in asking new questions as well as in seeking answers to questions already proposed. The following questions may serve as useful points of departure for colleagues involved in structuring school-university-family-community partnerships:

- Should the need to improve outcomes for children and families be a priority for universities?

- What roles might partner schools and universities have

in developing visions for school-based and school-
linked services?

- How and in what ways might universities, partner
schools, and delivery systems be changed, both separately and jointly?

- What roles might partner schools and universities play
in influencing state and national policy?

These questions and the preceding discussion suggest implicit
challenges. We believe that the following challenges, which one
partnership has faced, are also representative of those faced by many
other school-university-family-community partnerships:

- This partnership currently involves eleven partner school
communities, all at different stages of developmental readiness. How
can all of them be assisted without promising more than the partnership can deliver and while remaining faithful to the partnership's
core values about local control and determination?
- Not all university faculty and students are enthusiastic about
the vision and values associated with new expanded partnerships.
How many participants are necessary to maintain the momentum
for cross-system change? What are the rewards and costs of such participation? How can the vision become more widely shared?
- A collaborative involves not only shared visions, values, and
goals but also shared resources. How can the partner organizations
develop and implement resource sharing during a time of fiscal con-
straint and decline?
- The kinds of change envisioned affect university faculty greatly.
How will the professional development of faculty be facilitated?
- Schools are not universally recognized as family-friendly or as
culturally responsive; many community members are suspicious
about whether the schools will welcome human service professionals. How can the schools help parents and service providers feel

wanted, honored, and enfranchised? What kinds of assistance are required to facilitate shared discussion and creation of a shared vision?

To move from school reform to educational renewal by reforming the several systems that serve children and families represents a revolutionary change. The present and future challenges are formidable, perhaps overwhelming. But to take the easier option of continuing present ineffective reform measures within the schools alone is, we believe, unacceptable.

John Goodlad and his colleagues (Goodlad, Soder, & Sirotnik, 1990) offer a vision and accompanying rationale for the moral dimensions of teaching. By extension, we might argue that education and the human services are ethical-moral and value-driven professions. If the educational and human service professions are ethical-moral callings, then problems in this society's organizations and delivery systems that adversely affect the well-being, learning opportunities, and living conditions of children and families must concern all educators and human service personnel. If educators stop at partial reform, tinkering with existing systems rather than attempting first steps toward cross-system change, they might jeopardize the democratic virtues on which schooling and the U.S. Constitution are premised. Against this backdrop, the present and future challenges presented by this cross-systems change agenda may be formidable, but they are ones we willingly accept.

References

Adler, L., & Gardner, S. (Eds.). (1994). *The politics of linking schools and social services*. London: Taylor & Francis.

Dryfoos, J. (1994). *Full-service schools*. San Francisco: Jossey-Bass.

Goodlad, J. I. (1990). *Teachers for our nation's schools*. San Francisco: Jossey-Bass.

Goodlad, J. I., Soder, R., & Sirotnik, K. A. (Eds.). (1990). *The moral dimensions of teaching*. San Francisco: Jossey-Bass.

Hooper-Briar, K., & Lawson, H. (1994). *Serving children, youth, and families through interprofessional collaboration and service integration: A framework for action*. Oxford, OH: The Danforth Foundation and The Institute for Educational Renewal at Miami University.

Kotlowitz, A. (1992). *There are no children here*. New York: Anchor Books.

Lawson, H. (in press). Schools and educational communities in a new vision for child welfare. *Journal for a Just and Caring Education, 1* (1).

Lawson, H., & Hooper-Briar, K. (1994). *Expanding partnerships: Involving colleges and universities in interprofessional collaboration and service integration*. Oxford, OH: The Danforth Foundation & The Institute for Educational Renewal at Miami University.

Sizer, T. (1992). *Horace's school: Redesigning the American high school*. Boston: Houghton-Mifflin.

10

Evaluating Partner Schools

Richard W. Clark

Partner schools are being created because people believe that these partnerships can make an important contribution to educational renewal. However, those who are creating partner schools have not come to complete agreement about how to evaluate this contribution. In this chapter, I raise a significant question: How should one determine whether partner schools are achieving what they are intended to achieve?

Based on their survey of legislators and other state officials on behalf of the Education Commission of the States, Frazier (1993) and Finney (1992) report that these policymakers agree that professional development schools, partner schools focused on teacher education, could be created. They report that this is one of the few educational issues about which there appears to be universal agreement among policymakers. And many organizations are seeking to promote the development of school-university partnership sites, including the Holmes Group; National Network for Educational Renewal (NNER); American Association of Colleges for Teacher Education (AACTE), with support from AT&T and the Ford Foundation; various states, including Texas and Massachusetts; the American Federation of Teachers (AFT); the National Education Association (NEA); and the National Center for Restructuring Education, Schools, and Teaching (NCREST).

The materials shared in the preceding chapters demonstrate the complexity and difficulty of creating and operating partner schools. But for all this commitment to create something that will improve present practice, and for all the considerable good faith efforts focused toward making such places successful, evaluation of the efforts is often an afterthought. Frequently, sites developing such schools lament the lack of money to provide for thorough evaluations. ("We would really like to evaluate our partner school if only we had the money to hire someone to do it.") When evaluation activities are conducted, they are carried out gingerly, so as not to offend the parties engaged in these fragile new collaborations.

After examining some theoretical issues related to evaluating such undertakings as partner schools, I briefly discuss the values that seem to be shared among those advocating these new educational settings, and I conclude by offering suggestions about the processes that should be used to evaluate partner schools.

Theoretical Evaluation Design

Sirotnik's chapter, "The Meaning and Conduct of Inquiry in School-University Partnerships," in *School-University Partnerships in Action* (1988) should be read by anyone interested in the question of evaluating partner schools. In this chapter and elsewhere, Sirotnik argues persuasively that the paradigm for evaluating educational programs (and for conducting much of what passes as research in education) is not useful for evaluating the progress of school-university partnerships. If these traditional, linear, positivist approaches, rooted in what Sirotnik calls "classical scientific methodology" (p. 171), were appropriate, one would expect evaluation of partner schools to be designed through a procedure like the following.

• Determine what the desired end is. For example, a goal might be stated as follows: students in schools and teacher educators need to improve their learning. (Traditionally, K–12 student learning might be measured by an established instrument such as the Iowa Test of Basic Skills, while prospective teacher learning might be measured by the National Teacher's Exam. Improvement might be measured in terms of comparisons with previous school and college results on the same tests. Whether scores are significantly higher would be measured by statistical procedures).

• Create an experimental design. The evaluator would seek to design the experiment so the effects of the partner school on student learning could be isolated from other activities that might be influencing learning. Partner schools would thus become the independent variable in the experiment. Statistical techniques would produce comparisons that would show not only whether students were learning more in partner schools, but also whether comparable students in nonpartner schools and teacher preparation programs were *not making similar progress*. Like an agricultural expert studying the potential of a new corn hybrid or a medical researcher testing a new drug, the researcher would focus on making certain that it was the independent variable (partner school) that was the source of any improved learning, not something else. In the case of corn, for example, a new fertilizer or more favorable weather conditions could cause improvement, so the researcher attempts to hold such variables constant. In the case of partner schools, new admission standards for college students, who may be potential student teachers and inservice teachers, a change in school leadership, or changes in the district's curriculum are among the additional factors that could influence outcomes.

• Implement the design, using an outside expert to ensure objectivity. Because outsiders are assumed to be the only unbiased observers, and because expertise is required to perform various research functions including data analysis, experts with no prior connection to the experiment are usually enlisted.

• Report results to an external agency, frequently the funding source for the independent variable (partner school). Unfortunately, the report may not be seen by anyone in the partner school, or it may arrive months or even years after critical decisions have been made that could have benefited from the study results.

This approach has been highly successful in identifying improved corn hybrids and in finding drugs that effectively prevent or treat diseases. However, Sirotnik is one of many who have pointed out its inability to provide answers to social policy questions. More than two decades ago, Cronbach (1975) argued for research that would make continual adjustments on the basis of individual, context-specific responses. More recently, Fullan and Miles (1992) stressed that using the traditional linear approach in the study of change simply does not work. Generally speaking, the linear model does not seem useful in dealing with the messiness of such real-world social experiences as the creation of partner schools. (See also Sarason, 1972 and 1982.)

While researchers continue to argue the applicability of the positivist model of research, perhaps the most telling indictment of it in educational policymaking is that (at least in my experience) there is no significant instance of such research having determined major policy. Consider the following two examples. First, reasonably well controlled experiments demonstrate that grade retention has a negative effect on students; however, this research seems to have little influence on whether states, school districts, schools, and/or teachers retain students as a means of teaching them that they have to meet high standards. Second, studies that show time to be a significant variable in learning have had little effect in altering the regularities of schooling that provide the same length of period and number of days for all students in all subjects.

If the classical scientific model is unlikely to evaluate partner schools accurately, does this mean that there is no alternative evaluation process? If policymakers frequently seem to ignore the results of evaluations of various educational activities, does this mean there is no use in evaluating partner schools? The answer to both questions is *no*. There is an evaluation approach that should be taken, and people making decisions regarding partner schools do make judgments about the form and continuation of these schools based on values that this approach can address.

Basic Considerations: Stakeholders, Common Values, and Satisfactory Processes

Evaluators of partner schools need to start by identifying all the stakeholders—all the parties whose support is necessary to the successful functioning of the school. Evaluators need to know not only who these parties are but what questions are critical to each of them. Answering questions raised by university-based participants in partner schools and ignoring questions critical to school-based people is likely to lead to dismissal of the evaluation as irrelevant by the individuals whose work is being evaluated. Similarly, tending only to the questions of professional stakeholders and ignoring those raised by parents and community members can also lead to rejection of the evaluation by people whose support is critical to continuation of the school.

Goodlad (1988) posits the need for a symbiotic relationship between schools and universities, with each institution succeeding in satisfying its needs, and Hampel (1993) has recently reminded us of lessons from the history of relationships between higher education and public schools that suggest the need for these symbiotic partners to sustain their self-interests. Schlechty and Whitford (1988) suggest that symbiosis is insufficient; instead, we need a truly organic relationship in which the partners join to become a common system and satisfy new common needs. Such notions advocate a relationship among stakeholders that is substantially more advanced than the relationship currently achieved by most school-university partnerships (Wilson, Clark, & Heckman, 1989; Goodlad & Soder, 1992). Evaluators need to be able to describe the nuances of the relationships among all the stakeholders: those relationships that have been achieved and those still being sought.

Different groups generate partner schools, and variations in these groups encourage the participation of varied stakeholders. For instance, sites involved with the NNER emphasize that the partnership should include participants from public and/or private schools; one or more school, college, or department of education (SCDE); and one or more school, college, or department of arts and sciences (SCDAS). But the stakeholders whose questions must be answered by evaluation activities are broader than this partnership: they include, at least, students, parents, and business leaders; the state and its various legislative and regulatory bodies; and interested faculty, professional associations, and welfare organizations.

Sirotnik (1988) observes that "given the root meaning of the term, it seems rather redundant to point out that evaluation is a *valuing* activity" (p. 174). As such, it requires that participants clarify the values that are under consideration. Evaluators and stakeholders must be explicit about the values they expect of partner schools. Moreover, the extent to which stakeholders support values in common becomes one of the most critical questions in evaluation. Any assessment of the progress or accomplishments of partner schools should be couched in terms of the expectations of all stakeholders. If there are significant differences in stakeholder expectations, evaluation is likely to be difficult. For example, inconsistencies in evaluation can be anticipated when school-based educators expect partner schools to produce teachers who are trained to follow rules and college-based educators expect to produce teachers who are change agents. The persistence of different views of the teacher's role in the classroom and different goals in promoting educational renewal also have an impact (Darling-Hammond, 1993).

The process used for evaluation should engage the stakeholders in valuing activities. Sirotnik (1988, p. 175) has pointed out that such valuing "rests on the notion of evaluation as the process of generating knowledge, by and for people who use it, enlightened by experiential data (both quantitative and qualitative), so long as critical perspective is maintained throughout the process." He calls this process "collaborative inquiry." I suggest that urging stakeholders to engage in collaborative critical inquiry is not enough. From the beginning, the evaluation process must include the participation of external parties—critical friends—who have the dual responsibility of goading the stakeholders to look carefully at themselves and of providing a mirror for the insiders to use in examining their own efforts. But before considering this more complex process in depth, we need to give further consideration to the values associated with the movement toward partner schools, the values on which most evaluation criteria and procedures will be based.

Values, Common and Otherwise

Sirotnik (1988) observes that "the 'teeth' of collaborative inquiry are the act of making it critical—that is, the act of people confronting descriptive information and the knowledge they derive from it with the values base driving their programmatic efforts. It is for this reason that the assumptions, beliefs, and agenda forming the foundation of the [partner school] must, at every opportunity, be made as explicit as possible. This reservoir of values forms the basis for critique; moreover, the values are themselves subject to critique" (p. 175).

In the literature, there is no shortage of value statements concerning partner or professional development schools. The Holmes Group (1990) and the National Center for Restructuring Education, Schools, and Teaching (NCREST) (1993) have developed useful examples. Also, Appendix A at the end of this chapter contains examples of recent statements of values for partner and professional development schools. The one I have chosen to use as an example here is from the National Network for Educational Renewal (NNER). In March 1993, representatives from NNER sites began identifying their expectations for partner schools by compiling a list of thirty statements. This list was subsequently converted to the following description of the network's expectations of partner schools. Many NNER sites had previously contributed to value statements, including those prepared by NCREST and the Holmes Group. As might be expected, the NNER description incorporates many of the ideas stated by these other groups. And, as do the members of other groups, site representatives continue to struggle with the practicality and feasibility of generating a common list of expectations, given the perceived variety of conditions across the member sites. The document that follows is the latest version of the NNER statement (Clark, 1994), reproduced in a slightly altered format.

NNER *Compact for Partner Schools*

(Revised May, 1994)

Partner schools in the National Network for Educational Renewal (NNER) share a commitment to the 19 postulates enumerated by John I. Goodlad in *Teachers for Our Nation's Schools*. Each of these postulates has a bearing on the way in which partner schools are created and operated with the 15th speaking most directly to the subject:

Programs for the education of educators must assure for each candidate the availability of a wide array of laboratory settings for simulation, observation, hands-on experiences, and exemplary schools for internships and residencies; they must admit no more students to their programs than can be assured these quality experiences.

In addition to the 19 postulates, NNER settings share common values which influence the way in which they approach their overall mission of simultaneous renewal of schools and the education of educators. These shared beliefs include the following:

1. Partner schools of the NNER assure that all learners have equitable access to knowledge.
2. Partner schools recognize and honor diversity, commit to multicultural curricula and culturally responsive practice, prepare individuals for active

participation in a democratic society and promote social justice.

3. Partner schools accept their moral responsibility to contribute to the growth of students as citizens in a democratic society, contributors to a healthy economy, and fully human individuals versed in the arts and ideas that help them take advantage of their talents. In short, they are schools prepared to enculturate learners for participation in a democratic society.

4. Partner schools enable teachers and other educators to make educational decisions with their students and other stakeholders.

5. Partners should create educative communities which seek to develop a more just and sustainable society.

Thus, partner schools give direct attention to four moral dimensions: enculturating the young in a social and political democracy, providing access to knowledge for all children and youths, practicing pedagogical nurturing (the art and science of teaching), and ensuring responsible stewardship of the schools.

Whether called professional development schools, centers for teaching and learning, or by some other name, NNER partner schools are not an end but a means by which schools and universities seek to accomplish four purposes:

1. Creating and sustaining a learning community which enables P–12 learners and partners to construct meaningful knowledge.

2. Preparing educators.

3. Providing professional development.

4. Conducting inquiry.

Representatives of the NNER sites met on three occasions and helped develop the following general expectations and associated examples. These general expectations are arranged in relation to the four major purposes of partner schools. (References to university-based educators are intended to include representatives from the arts and sciences as well as from colleges, schools, or departments of education.) Each NNER setting is unique. Consequently, during the next five years no two settings are likely to make the same amount of progress. Nevertheless, the settings have agreed to use the guidelines in the NNER document as a compact to assist them in assessing growth. They expect to renegotiate the contents of this compact from time to time so it can serve as a guide to a difficult work.

NNER Expectations of Partner Schools

As NNER settings develop and perfect their partner schools, they may use the following expectations, or guidelines, to help them determine how well they are accomplishing each of the four major purposes, how consistent their work is with the nineteen postulates, and whether their work is really guided by the set of shared values. There are fourteen expectations in all.

Expectations of Partner Schools

Purpose 1: Create and sustain a learning community which enables P-12 learners and partners to construct meaningful knowledge.

1. Learning Community
All members of the partner school community communicate in such a way as to create a learning community.
Example:

Parents, community members, and partners join with preservice educators and students to support each others' commitment to life-long learning.

2.   *Equity and Excellence*

Partners work to provide equity and excellence for all enrolled
P-12 students and other members of the learning community.

Examples:

> Partners need to assure that the curriculum and instruction of
> the partner school seeks to have all students achieve common,
> high expectations.

> Students will be expected to develop a variety of learning
> strategies such as problem framing and questioning in order to
> construct meaning.

> Partners need to assure that the school varies instructional
> practices to meet the needs of all students.

> Partners need to assure access to learning by all students.

> Partners need to work to achieve the goal that differences in
> student achievement not be associated with factors such as
> race, gender or social class.

> Written descriptions of curriculum in partner schools will
> reveal high expectations in keeping with local, state and
> national standards.

> Classroom observations in partner schools will reveal that edu-
> cators are making effective use of a variety of instructional
> techniques.

> All NNER settings will be able to demonstrate progress in
> implementing alternatives to tracking of students in partner
> schools. This will include appropriate uses of cooperative
> learning.

> Assessments of student performance will demonstrate that the
> partner school is succeeding in having all students meet high
> expectations.

Purpose 2: Preparing Educators

3. *Collaboration*
Educator preparation programs in partner schools are based on continuous collaboration among partners to assure that the partner school is an integral part of the total preparation programs.
    Examples:

> Partners communicate a common vision of the goals and purposes of the partner school in written and oral communications about the school.

> Regular meetings of partners deal authentically with essential linkages between what happens at the partner school and the campus-based segments of the education preparation program.

> Each NNER setting will be able to share meeting minutes which demonstrate growing collaboration concerning partner schools.

> Each NNER setting will be able to demonstrate through testimony of preservice candidates and school and university faculty that the work in the partner schools is an extension of work which occurs on campus.

4. *Needs of Diverse Students*
Educator preparation in partner schools assures that prospective teachers and other educators understand the learning needs of all students and are committed to helping all students learn.
    Examples:

> Preservice teachers and those being prepared for other educator roles will be provided experiences with diverse student populations which enable them to develop understanding,

sensitivity, and respect for ethnic, linguistic, social and cultural differences.

Prospective educators will be helped to develop a repertoire of strategies for meeting the needs of students with diverse learning needs. This repertoire will include the problem solving skills needed to assess student needs and select appropriate instructional strategies.

Observations and written programs will indicate that preservice candidates at each NNER setting have guided experiences working with diverse populations of students.

Observations will reveal that preservice teachers at each setting use mechanisms such as portfolios, videotapes, case studies, interviews, and logs to learn from their experiences in analyzing student needs.

5. *Pedagogy, Curriculum and Attitudes*
Partner schools will seek to have preservice teachers construct the pedagogical skills, curriculum knowledge, and attitudes necessary to educate all learners.
   Examples:

Preservice teachers will have a variety of experiences which are based on a shared understanding between school and university based educators of current best practices in classroom teaching and learning.

Preservice teachers will be expected to integrate theory and practice as they plan and carry out classroom instruction which is consistent with contemporary theories of how children learn.

Preservice teachers will be skilled at applying the wide variety of instructional techniques and strategies required to help students with differing learning styles and backgrounds.

Evidence from interviews and observations of preservice teachers and from interviews of partners will reveal that preservice teachers are mastering a wide variety of instructional skills.

Observations in partner schools will reveal that contemporary learning theories and best practices are being integrated into the everyday life of the students.

Observations, interviews and course descriptions will reveal that campus-based courses and partner school learning activities for preservice teachers incorporate consistent instruction in professional skills.

6. *Academic Knowledge*

Partners will collaborate in a continuous renewal that reflects contemporary knowledge of all relevant academic disciplines from the arts and sciences.

Examples:

Preservice teachers in partner schools will have participated in a general education that enables them to enter into the human conversation.

The curriculum in the partner school will reflect contemporary knowledge in the major disciplines of the arts and sciences.

Preservice teachers will have the pedagogical-content knowledge needed to link student learning to the key elements of the major disciplines.

University faculty in arts and sciences will be engaged with faculty from education and from the schools in reworking the substance of the curriculum in partner schools.

Preservice teachers will be able to demonstrate appropriate proficiency in those disciplines they are expected to teach.

Purpose 3: Provide Professional Development

7. Collaboration and Student Needs Driven

Professional development for educators is collaboratively defined and is based on the diverse needs of students to be served by the educators.

Example:

> Observations of school and university based educators who work with partner schools will reveal instructional practices that are consistent with professional development collaboratively derived from analysis of the needs of students in the partner school.

8. Linkages

Professional development should link theory, research, and practice.

9. Special Needs

Professional development to help professionals work with special needs students should be provided.

10. Inter-professional

Professional development should help educators understand how professionals from various fields can best work together as part of an "educative community."

Purpose 4: Inquiry

11. Critical Social Inquiry

Partners should engage in critical social inquiry concerning school and teacher practices.

Examples:

Partners engage in collaborative action research groups using such social categories as race, class, gender, and/or ethnicity as frameworks for analysis of school curriculum and instructional practices.

Partners will be able to share examples of critical social inquiry regarding their school and the broader community of which it is a part.

12. Critical Inquiry in Reflective Practice

Partners should engage in critical inquiry as a means of generating continuous improvement of education in the partner school.
    Examples:

Adults and children in the partner school generate questions about teaching and learning, gather information, develop practices, and assess the consequences of those practices on student learning.

Preservice teachers (as others at the setting) reflect upon classroom experiences with other preservice teachers and their university and campus-based teachers and mentors.

School- and university-based educators use reflective practice in order to grow professionally.

Observations will indicate that members of the partner school community spend time reflecting together in groups.

Evidence is available that the results of such inquiry are used to inform school practice and educator preparation.

13. Inquiry as Scholarship

Partners should use the partner school as a setting for scholarly examination of professional practices.

Examples:

Partners conduct in accordance with norms of scholarly research including review by and discussion with colleagues.

The results of scholarly inquiry at the partner school are disseminated through such vehicles as conference presentations, scholarly journals, videotapes, professional development workshops, and infusion into college curricula.

Representatives from each setting within the NNER will publish scholarly examinations of professional practice conducted by school- and university-based educators at partner schools.

Across All Purposes

14. *Resources*
Partner schools are supported by sufficient people, time, and money.
  Examples:

University and school faculty responsible for conducting teacher preparation programs are allocated sufficient time for planning, conducting and assessing such programs.

Sufficient numbers of well-qualified school- and university-based educators are retained to enable the partner school to accomplish its responsibilities related to teacher preparation, professional development, inquiry, and the education of P-12 students.

Necessary and sufficient support is provided for professional development, including time, peer support, and opportunity for reflection.

The collaborative work engaged in by all partners will be equitably weighted in connection with all personnel decisions including compensation.

Sufficient supplies and equipment are made available to support the learning of P-12 students and preservice teachers at the partner school.

Comparisons of partner schools with non-partner schools at NNER settings will reveal that the partners have the time, staff, and money required by the multiple purposes they are expected to accomplish.

Even when their various value statements overlap, stakeholders are often reluctant to accept any statement as a standard for evaluating their progress—even if they are to do the evaluating. To some extent, this reluctance reflects the general hesitancy of educators to accept external standards. Such concerns may be reflected in criticism of the value statements as "too linear" or "atomistic."

Other concerns may have their roots in differences in the ecologies of various partner schools. For example, schools set in rural areas and perceiving a need to prepare educators for rural settings may find they have different values from urban schools. Institutions in geographic areas with a marked religious orientation may seek to develop graduates with different qualities from those who pass through other schools.

Whatever the reason for resistance to a common value base, such a base must be identified to some extent within any set of partner schools to be evaluated, or the evaluation will be meaningless. While individual value statements may be appropriate in conducting internal assessments of partner schools associated with separate institutions of higher education, comparisons across sites cannot be conducted without agreement on the criteria to be used for the assessment. The introductory section of the NNER statement and its fourteen general expectations with accompanying indicators may serve partnerships as the starting point for constructing a value statement that will be generally accepted.

Process: Formative and Summative

The processes used to evaluate partner schools should be similar whether the purpose of the evaluation is to help shape the development of the school (formative) or to assess how well the school has accomplished its intended purposes so far (summative). In either event, as I suggested earlier, evaluators should engage in collaborative critical inquiry.

Sirotnik (1988) provides the following functional definition of critical inquiry:

> The process of making inquiry critical can be conveniently represented by a set of interdependent generic questions that guide the discourse between the stakeholders of a collaborative inquiry. These questions are as follows:
> - What is going on in the name of [the issue in question]?
> - How did it come to be that way?
> - Whose interests are (and are not) being served by the way things are?
> - What information and knowledge do we have—or need to get—that bear upon the issues? (Get it and continue the discourse.)
> - Is this the way we want things to be?
> - What are we going to do about all this? (Get on with it.) [p. 175].

To answer these questions, stakeholders must possess well-developed communication and observation skills. They must be prepared to gather thick descriptions of the ongoing activities of the partner school. It is not possible to answer questions about what is going on

by waiting until the partner school is several years old and then trying to remember what happened at the beginning.

Recently, I was involved in creating four partner schools. While
we attempted to identify an evaluation design at the beginning of
the project and knew we should be documenting progress, we discovered two years later that we had very different ideas of how to
evaluate the schools. Unfortunately, because our files were incom-
plete, we could not agree on which commitments we had made at
the beginning of the project. This lack of common commitment
made it difficult to accomplish the formative evaluation goal of
determining the degree to which the partner schools were measuring up to our original intentions. It also made it difficult to answer
some stakeholders' summative questions, such as whether we were
getting what we wanted from the partner schools.

The failure to plan for and collect a complete set of records chart-
ing the progress of partner schools becomes particularly problematic
when leadership changes within a partner school or the university.
At such a time, summative evaluations are frequently needed, yet
lack of information often makes such analyses superficial.

Minutes of meetings of collaborative groups, calendars of major
events, descriptions of courses, records of student performance on
various kinds of assessments, portfolios, videotapes, operating budgets, newspaper clippings, and journal articles are among the items
that should be included in information collections. However,
records of deliberately planned inquiry are also essential. Materials
such as pre- and postexperience interviews of preservice teachers,
periodic interviews of school and university administrators and faculty, and interviews and surveys of students and parents in the partner school need to be included. Focus groups of people who play
different roles (for example, teachers, preservice teachers, students,
and parents) can provide multiple perspectives on what is happening in the partner school.

Beyond such sources, specific data concerning the classroom life
in the school need to be obtained. While teacher and student

reports (from surveys or interviews) can be helpful, ultimately there is no substitute for extended critical observation of the classrooms. Shen (1993) provides an example of what can be learned from a relatively simple inquiry into the opinions of participants in partner schools. Observations of classrooms can take a variety of forms. Members of the partner school community may engage in collegial observations of each other's teaching. In one setting within the Brigham Young University–Public School Partnership, school and university faculty observe preservice teachers and are in turn observed by these prospective teachers. Classroom observation can include single sessions, but the more extended the observation period, the more productive the information. Observers may also choose to shadow particular students for a day (or some other period of time) in order to experience the partner school through student eyes. These observations should be carefully documented, including review by the observer with the person(s) observed to negotiate meaning from the observations.

It is essential that the stakeholders in the partner school gather their own information and communicate with each other about the basic questions identified earlier. Such work enables them to understand where they are making progress and to modify their work as appropriate. However, this work is unlikely to occur unless the stakeholders identify what Sirotnik (1988) calls a "chief worrier" (p. 183) to oversee the design of the work and the actual gathering and analysis of the information.

The University of Texas at El Paso (UTEP), one of the NNER sites, secured funding in the summer of 1993 for work related to its new Center for Professional Development and Technology. Its proposal included a commitment to collaborate in the design and management of the center by public school personnel, university faculty, education service center staff, and community members. While clearly identifying these parties as stakeholders, it unambiguously placed responsibility for evaluation of the effort in the hands of the project director, who determined that "the evaluation approach followed will be holistic and humanistic. It will examine a range of abilities in pre-service and inservice teachers, and it will verify the degree to which these abilities are integrated and employed. Individualizing the evaluation tools in accordance with the culturally diverse nature of the program will be a priority and will provide an equitable process. In order to validate this approach, evaluation will be both ongoing as well as internal and external in character" (Descamps, 1993, p. 13.22).

The basic design of the UTEP proposal (reproduced in Appendix B at the end of this chapter) calls for three types of evaluation approaches: first, internal evaluation by an evaluation specialist, a full-time staff person; second, informal, case study examination of each of the five partner school sites involved in the proposal; and third, external evaluation by a consultant retained to provide information to UTEP and the funding agency. Forty-two outcomes are identified and listed in relation to the objectives of the project. These outcomes will be reflected in numerous documents. Such advance planning should assure the thick descriptions that will allow the participants to use the evaluation activities to refine or redirect their efforts.

The planners at UTEP also recognized that it is essential that stakeholders encourage outsiders to examine the partnership's work and share the results of these observations with the stakeholders. Negotiating meaning with outside observers can be one of the most useful ways of understanding the progress that is being made at a partner school. Such observers need to fully understand the values and beliefs that are driving the partner school, and they have to clearly recognize the questions that are of value to the stakeholders. Given such understandings, they can play an effective role as critical friends.

Too much of educators' experience with evaluation is associated with assessment by outsiders who report to third-party funding sources and share little or none of their information with the participants in the effort being evaluated. While reports to funding sources (a significant group of stakeholders) are inevitable—documentation should be designed to be useful to as many of the varied stakeholder groups as possible. In order for this to be accomplished, provisions for sharing information must be made from the beginning of the venture.

Not only do many external evaluations fail to contribute to the critical examination of practice by insiders, but many insiders also fail to critically examine their own work. Such internal inquiry needs an external priming—whether from a funding source or from a party such as a university scholar who is interested in understanding more about partner schools. Designs such as the one from UTEP try to correct the failures of both internal and external evaluations.

The final question Sirotnik proposes calls for action. Too often assessment becomes an end rather than a basis for action. By integrating the action step with the inquiry steps, Sirotnik follows a line of scholars, including Dewey, who urge that reflection and action be combined (Fine, 1994; Lieberman, 1992). Without this final step, asking all the other questions has little effect on the partner school.

Conclusion

In summary, when stakeholders gather to design their approach to evaluation, they should heed the following guidelines:

- Be clear about values and beliefs as they will be represented in the partner school.

- Be clear about the purpose of assessment and the questions that need to be answered to satisfy that purpose.

- Be in agreement regarding which information developed in the normal course of the partner school efforts needs to be preserved as evaluation data.

- Be in agreement regarding what new information needs to be acquired.

- Be in agreement regarding who should collect and analyze information; assign someone to take the lead in the assessment effort.

- Be specific about how the assessment will culminate in action.

People who create partner schools, convinced as they are about the efficacy of their new settings, still owe it to themselves and to the people who populate those settings to examine their progress and use this examination to renew their efforts continually. Traditional forms of evaluation are unlikely to satisfy the needs of these settings, but by using collaborative critical inquiry, partner school stakeholders can use evaluation to enhance the quality of their efforts.

Appendix A: Examples of Value Statements

In *Tomorrow's Schools,* the Holmes Group (1990) became one of the first to offer a set of values for professional development schools. These values focused on teaching and learning for understanding for everybody's children; creating a learning community; continuing learning by teachers, teacher educators, and administrators; engaging in thoughtful long-term inquiry into teaching and learning; and inventing new institutions. Preparing for their seventh annual meeting in January of 1993, Holmes Group leaders stressed that "the professional development school as conceptualized in . . . *Tomorrow's Schools* is the key to carrying out innovation in educator preparation that is simultaneous with public schools reform" (The Holmes Group, 1993, p. 16). They then offered eight additional value statements for discussion purposes among their constituents. The first of these suggested that there is no single model of the professional development school (PDS) but that "a PDS should be a public school whose student population exemplifies the diversity and the teaching challenges of the community" (p. 16). The second statement spoke to the need for coherence of purpose and design among various local examples of PDSs within the Holmes Group, while the third emphasized the need for a public contract among the partners in the creation and maintenance of the PDS. These partners were identified as the university (represented by its president), the college of education, the school district, the school, and the teachers association. Fourth, each school of education was to have a published plan to guide the development of the number of PDSs required. Fifth, all educators in the SCDE program of preparation and development were to be expected to carry on field assignments in one or more PDSs. Sixth, becoming quite explicit, the discussion guide suggested that teacher leaders in PDSs will have completed their certification by the National Board for Professional Teaching Standards. Seventh, the PDS will be the base for professional training and the locus of much of the research conducted by the SCDE. Finally, the guide proposed for consideration the requirement that each PDS work frequently with others in order to provide sufficient diversity of experience for participants in educator preparation programs.

Behind such statements lie more general values: the importance of consistency within groups without giving up the autonomy of individual members, the importance of formal inquiry, the value of approval of a group from the top (university president), the value of the National Board for Professional Teaching Standards (or any such national certification process), the importance of university faculty conducting much of their research in and with schools, the importance of engaging in research, and the primacy of the university SCDE among the partners responsible for the PDS.

One Holmes Group dean, Frank Murray (1993), has suggested ten necessary features of PDSs. They can be summarized briefly as follows:

1. The primary and overriding goal of the school is to have *all* its pupils use their minds well.

2. All members of the school must make a commitment to teaching and learning important and essential knowledge.

3. The school must have high expectations for all its pupils.

4. The mode of instruction in the school should be personal and fully responsive to the individual needs of all students.

5. The pupil must be actively engaged; his or her intellectual cooperation is a precondition of acquiring understanding.

6. Understanding should be exhibited by pupils in as direct and immediate fashion as possible, unlike the indirect means employed by most school tests.

7. The school must be a model of the values of decency, honesty, integrity, democracy, and altruism that it hopes its pupils will acquire.

8. The teacher in the school demonstrates professionalism by continually learning and continually inventing and discovering

the means needed to respond to the diverse needs of students.

9. The PDS must be organized and financed in a manner allowing the foregoing necessities. It must provide support for teachers to engage in reflection and planning.

10. The school will team with other support services in the community to provide a coordinated plan for the welfare of the children enrolled.

This list of ten overlaps considerably with the nine Common Principles that serve as the core value statements for the Coalition of Essential Schools and of other reform efforts of the late 1980s (Sizer, 1984, 1992).

Representatives of several groups interested in professional development schools have been convened by NCREST partially for the purpose of developing a common values statement. As of the spring of 1993, the vision statement generated by that group began with this preamble, which identified underlying values:

> The primary goal of a professional development school is to develop knowledge and practices that will lead to success for all students. A professional development school celebrates diversity, is committed to multiracial and multicultural education, to appreciation for the varied talents, interests, ways of knowing, and circumstances of all children, and to preparing educators who appreciate and build on the special benefits of diversity in human experience and learning. A professional development school supports and enables diversity in teaching methods that complement the variety of student learning styles.
>
> The PDS recognizes that "it takes a whole village to raise a child" and that a partnership among families, students, community, schools, and universities comprises the foundation that underpins successful education. This

partnership is based on mutual trust, respect, and parity, and is seen as mutually beneficial.

The PDS views education as a transformative process for all—promoting inquiry and extending the horizons of children and adults while transforming educational institutions and social relationships. A major function of a PDS is to create a shared vision among school and college faculty for developing new models of professional education. The PDS also serves as a catalyst for systemic reform, empowering all partners to work more effectively toward shared goals on behalf of children and their families [NCREST, 1993, p. 3].

From this preamble, the NCREST vision statement continues to specify goals and purposes, commitments, and enabling considerations. While the preamble identifies the values on which the vision is built, anyone using this document as a starting place for evaluation needs to look carefully at all its value statements. Darling-Hammond (1994), the codirector of NCREST, has edited a collection of essays that provides additional insights into the values behind the various efforts to create professional development schools.

Appendix B: Evaluation Design, University of Texas, El Paso, Schedule #4C—Program Evaluation Design

This appendix reproduces the evaluation design outline drawn up at the University of Texas, El Paso, for its partner school project.

> Progress toward program objectives will be assessed and documented using three types of evaluation:
>
> *Full-time evaluation specialist.* The project's internal evaluation will be conducted by a full-time staff specialist, who will be housed at the university and will spend a half day per week at each of the PDS sites. The specialist will conduct the following procedures:
>
> 1. Identify outcomes for both field-based and campus-based components of the teacher preparation program.
> 2. Identify teacher preparation outcomes, and develop instruments and processes by which they can be measured.
> 3. Identify student outcomes, and develop instruments to assess the impact of the program on the performance of children from participating PDS classrooms.
> 4. Collect data on the performance of preservice teachers and participating pupils.
> 5. Compare performance data of students from the traditional preservice program and from non-participating PDS classrooms with that of students from the new program.
>
> *Site Councils and Teacher Center Board.* The site councils from each of the PDS sites will meet monthly to review the program and document progress toward the project's objectives. The Teacher Center Board will meet every other month to review the reports of the site councils and to receive recommendations from the evaluation

specialist. The Board will make necessary program adjustments in accordance with this information.

External evaluators. Two experts from outside the Center will be employed to evaluate the project throughout the year and to provide information to the Teacher Center Board and the Texas Education Agency. Project activities will be changed, adapted, improved, or discontinued in accordance with this information.

The following outcomes will verify that program objectives have been attained:

Administration:

Bylaws and minutes of meetings of Teacher Center Board and PDS Site Council

Personnel:

Appointment forms

Recruitment plans to attract candidates to areas of teacher shortage in the region and the state

Commitment letters from school teachers and university faculty

Lists of students enrolled in courses and interns assigned to sites

Log of technology training sessions

Reports on staff development training

Students:

Data documenting the linguistic, cultural, and economic diversity of the PDS sites to which preservice teachers are assigned.

Collaborative research study pilots by the school-university faculty on the learning process of elementary, middle, and high school students.

Report on the involvement of parents and community in the design and implementation of the field-based program.

Program design:

Report describing needs assessment on graduate education

Reports of effective teaching practices and exemplary programs

Reports on school and faculty visits to exemplary classrooms

List of outcomes required of preservice teachers

Redesigned course syllabi

Curriculum plans for summer workshop

List of teaching materials

Report of model for community experience component

Log of staff development sessions

Description of training renewal model for interns, school and university faculty, and administrators

Description of innovative student-centered curriculum pilots at the elementary, middle, and high school levels

Report on program dissemination

Technological support

Reports of ongoing technological assistance

Description of telecommunications and distance learning systems

Assessment portfolios

One sample assessment portfolio for each preservice teacher preparation program: elementary, middle, secondary

One sample assessment portfolio for each classroom category: elementary, middle, secondary

A sample assessment portfolio of a school mentor and a university clinical faculty

References

Clark, R. W. (1994). *Partner schools and the National Network for Educational Renewal: A compact for simultaneous renewal.* Seattle: Center for Educational Renewal, University of Washington.

Cronbach, L. (1975). Beyond the two disciplines of scientific psychology. *American Psychologist, 30*(2), 116–127.

Darling-Hammond, L. (1993). Reframing the school reform agenda: Developing capacity for school transformation. *Phi Delta Kappan, 74* (10), 752–761.

Darling-Hammond, L. (Ed.). (1994). *Professional development schools: Schools for developing a profession.* New York: Teachers College Press.

Descamps, J. (1993). *Phase 4 proposal.* El Paso: Center for Professional Development and Technology, University of Texas, El Paso.

Fine, M. (Ed.). (1994). *Chartering urban school reform: reflections on public high schools in the midst of change.* New York: Teachers College Press.

Finney, J. E. (1992). *At the crossroads: Linking teacher education to school reform.* Denver, CO: Education Commission of the States.

Fullan, M. G., & Miles, M. B. (1992). Getting reform right: What works and what doesn't. *Phi Delta Kappan, 73,* (10), 744–752.

Frazier, C. M. (1993). *A shared vision: Policy recommendations for linking teacher education to school reform.* Denver, CO: Education Commission of the States.

Goodlad, J.I. (1988). School-university partnerships for educational renewal: rationale and concepts. In K.A. Sirotnik and J.I. Goodlad (Eds.), *School-university partnerships in action.* New York: Teachers College Press.

Goodlad, J. I., & Soder, R. (1992). *School-university partnerships: An appraisal of an idea* (Occasional Paper No. 15). Seattle: Center for Educational Renewal, University of Washington.

Hampel, R. L. (1993). Apart-nerships. *Record in Educational Administration and Supervision, 13,* 27–31.

The Holmes Group (1990). *Tomorrow's schools: principles for the design of professional development schools*. East Lansing: The Holmes Group.

The Holmes Group (1993). Discussion guide for "Tomorrow's Schools of Education," annual meeting of the Holmes Group, January 1993. East Lansing: The Holmes Group.

Lieberman, A. (1992). The meaning of scholarly activity and the building of community. *Educational Researcher, 21*(6), 5–12.

Murray, F. B. (1993). All or none: Criteria for professional development schools. *Educational Policy, 7*, 61–73.

National Center for Restructuring Education, Schools, and Teaching. (1993). Vision statement: Professional development schools network. *PDS: Network News, 1*(1), 3.

Sarason, S. B. (1972). *The creation of settings and the future societies*. San Francisco: Jossey-Bass.

Sarason, S. B. (1982). *The culture of the school and the problem of change*. Boston: Allyn & Bacon.

Schlechty, P.C., and Whitford, B.L. (1988). *Shared problems and shared vision: organic collaboration*. In K.A. Sirotnik and J.I. Goodlad (Eds), *School-university partnerships in action*. New York: Teachers College Press.

Shen, J. (1993). *Voices from the field: School-based faculty members' vision of preservice teacher education in the context of a professional development school* (Occasional Paper No. 16). Seattle: Center for Educational Renewal, University of Washington.

Sirotnik, K.A. (1987). Evaluation in the ecology of schooling: the process of school renewal. In J.I. Goodlad (Ed.), *The ecology of school renewal*. Eighty-sixth yearbook of the National Society for the Study of Education, Part One. Chicago: University of Chicago Press.

Sirotnik, K.A. (1988). The meaning and conduct of inquiry in school-university partnerships. In K. A. Sirotnik and J. I. Goodlad (Eds.), *School-university partnerships in action: Concepts, cases, and concerns* (pp. 169–190). New York: Teachers College Press.

Sirotnik, K.A. (1989). The school as the center of change. In T.J. Sergiovanni and J.H. Moore, (Eds.), *Schooling for tomorrow*. Boston: Allyn and Bacon.

Sirotnik, K.A. and Oakes, J. (1986). Critical inquiry for school renewal: liberating theory and practice. In K.A. Sirotnik and J. Oakes (Eds.), *Critical perspectives on the organization and improvement of schooling*. Boston: Kluwer-Nijhoff.

Sizer, T. R. (1984). *Horace's compromise: The dilemma of the American high school*. Boston: Houghton Mifflin.

Sizer, T. R. (1992). *Horace's school: Redesigning the American high school*. Boston: Houghton Mifflin.

Wilson, C., Clark, R. W., & Heckman, P. (1989). Breaking new ground: Reflections on the school-university partnerships in the National Network for Educational Renewal (Occasional Paper No. 8). Seattle: Center for Educational Renewal, University of Washington.

11

Conclusion

The Promise of Partner Schools

Russell T. Osguthorpe, R. Carl Harris, Sharon Black, and Melanie Fox Harris

Today's children and adolescents are growing up in a world of social and economic upheaval, radical changes in traditional patterns of family life, and continually increasing demands to contribute to the democratic society in which they live. Traditional structures and methods of education are not adequate to help them meet today's conditions or tomorrow's challenges. Educators must significantly change the way they teach, and the only way this can occur is for significant changes to be made in the way teachers are prepared. New buildings, more computers, better instructional materials—these will never meet students' needs unless teachers are educated effectively to use these tools to help students learn. Current teachers, as well as those who are preparing to enter the profession, must continually seek to improve in their roles as those who are charged to facilitate learning.

The experiences reported in the previous chapters attest to the fact that partner schools show promise for meeting these needs: more effective preparation of teachers, more effective curricula for students. More time will be necessary to determine if that promise will actually be fulfilled. Because the goals for partner schools are so lofty, the challenges faced in reaching the goals are great. As we consider the examples of partner schools in this book, and others we have observed throughout the nation, we are convinced that the greatest challenge is creating partner schools that are balanced and whole in their approaches to educational renewal. Although one partner school might be conducting superb research, it may not be using the results of the research to produce new curricula that can be used in the school. Another partner school might be producing new curricula but not gathering data on the effectiveness of these curricula with students. These partner schools have agreed to undertake to achieve all four goals we introduced in Chapter One: educator preparation, professional development, curriculum development, and research-inquiry. But they have allowed some goals to take precedence over others. When some goals do not receive appropriate attention, the partner school will not function at its maximum potential; it is not fully complete in its development, and because it is not yet complete, it has not yet fulfilled its promise.

What can educators learn from others' work in teacher education and school renewal that could strengthen partner schools in each of the four goal areas? What would a complete partner school be like? What can educators learn from the preceding chapters that will help partner schools fulfill their promise in the future?

Educator Preparation

The remarkable aspect of teacher education programs nationwide has been their sameness: nearly all programs have three components—general education, methods and specialty courses, and practicum. Chapter Three illustrated how partner schools are changing the nature of all of these components. The roles of university faculty, partner school teachers, and student teachers are all changing. More team teaching of methods courses is occurring, and more integration is coming about between methods and general education courses, resulting in greater involvement of arts and sciences faculty in the preparation of teachers. Teacher supervision is being conducted by teams rather than by one university professor. The entire enterprise of teacher preparation is thus becoming a joint effort among school personnel, teacher educators, and arts and sciences faculty. Without partner schools, this kind of role redefinition would likely not occur.

Even though many partner schools have emphasized teacher education, much remains to be done. Most practicing K–12 teachers, even in partner schools, need more time to devote to teacher preparation. To give them this time, universities need to increase intern programs that free one or two teachers on a rotating basis. Freeing teacher time will also enable teachers to work more closely with university faculty in team teaching practicum students. Both universities and schools need to give more attention to effective means of evaluating student teacher performance, including portfolio assessment and observation techniques. Students completing practicum experiences can cover classes for teachers while the teachers work with university faculty to plan jointly how they will improve the learning of K–12 students, as well as strengthen the program leading to teacher certification. Teachers cannot be given more time for professional development unless roles are significantly changed, but some roles cannot change unless state education agencies modify their existing policies on teacher certification.

Professional Development

Chapter Four described one of the most creative approaches to professional development that we have observed. Like many partner school projects, the partner school described in Chapter Four was created out of necessity: the large urban school district in which the school is located recognized that many of its practicing teachers were inadequately prepared to meet the needs of an increasingly challenging student population. By selecting their strongest teachers to work full-time in the partner school as professional development specialists, partnership directors were able to provide effective inservice education for far more teachers than normally possible. And rather than assigning these professional developers to conduct traditional inservice workshops, this partner school experimented with a new form of inservice education in which practicing teachers became "visiting teachers," released from their regular teaching responsibilities in order to spend sustained time working closely with the professional developers in the partner school.

All partner schools must continue to develop new ways of assisting practicing teachers over the duration of their careers. Like a teacher preparation program, career-long professional development requires that educators at all levels modify their roles. Practicing teachers' chief complaint is that they are not given personal time to reflect and plan. Partner schools must be more creative in finding ways to provide them with this time, whether it be through full-time professional development specialists, practicum students, student interns, or some other yet-to-be-identified method. As practicing teachers are given more time, as they were in the partner school described in Chapter Four, they need to work closely with master teachers rather than merely attend traditional inservice workshops. For example, a teacher who needs to strengthen his or her skills in using technology in the classroom needs to receive personal tutoring on the development and use of new courseware rather than to attend a large workshop where participants hear a lecture but are unable to practice on the equipment and the software.

Research and Inquiry

As the authors of Chapter Five explained, research in partner schools is substantively different from the research that has traditionally been conducted in laboratory schools. Instead of university professors doing research *on* students and *on* teachers, everyone connected with the partner school works together to design the studies, gather the data, and analyze the results. As definitions of what constitutes research expand, all partner school participants come to view themselves as researchers, as people who ask questions and find answers. And as teachers and students come to view themselves as full-fledged contributors to the research process, they not only change the way research is conducted in their partner schools, they change the way learning and teaching are performed. When student-initiated questions drive learning, the basic premises of schooling are changed. This is the role of research in partner schools.

Inquiry in partner schools has benefited from the changing nature of research in general. The movement away from a strict positivist methodology, in which (in the most extreme case) students must be randomly assigned to treatment and control groups, has made research in partner schools less artificial and less intrusive. No longer do university professors supply questions and hypotheses and then tell the teachers how a study will be conducted; instead, the teachers and students participate in inquiry, asking the questions that they most need answered. The professor becomes a collaborator, one who joins the search. Whether the particular methodology used is naturalistic, ethnographic, narrative, or some form of action research, all partner school participants work together to find answers to the questions that bear on the teaching and learning that occur in the school.

Several of the chapters in this book presented cases of inquiry that are taking place in partner schools; all are aimed directly at improving student learning. In each case, the process of conducting the research is as important as the findings, because all participants develop in their ability to pose questions and search for answers. All partner schools that we have observed could benefit from doing more such research. We have never observed a partner school that has been conducting too much collaborative inquiry. Such research must become more a part of the fabric of everything we do in partner schools.

No partner school that we have observed has implemented an adequate evaluation system to assess the degree to which partner school goals are being achieved. While Chapter Ten describes a system applicable to many partnerships, other systems need to be developed that respond to the unique characteristics and needs of other partner school structures. Such evaluation differs from the research that partner schools are conducting. Although the methods can overlap, evaluative activities must eventually come to questions of value and worth. And, as the author of Chapter Ten observes, such questions are a challenge for most who are involved in partner schools. So much energy is required to create a partner school and sustain it that little seems to be left to gather evaluative data and analyze it to determine if the partner school is actually achieving its desired aims. Because most partner schools are relatively new, this is understandable; but as partner schools mature, educators, administrators, parents, and legislators will need more than ethnographic descriptions of what happens in these schools; they will need all stakeholders to participate in determining if the partner school is doing what it was intended to do—improve teaching and learning.

Curriculum Development

The concept of a school's curriculum is deceptive. On the surface, curriculum appears to be the most clearly defined of all aspects of the partner school, but in actuality, it is the most illusive. If it is difficult to decide what constitutes research, it is even more difficulty to decide what constitutes curriculum. As a colleague of ours recently said, "The implementation of curriculum is a fiction" (Terry Carson, personal communication, April 14, 1994). What he meant was that curriculum is *never* implemented precisely as it was intended. And maybe the imprecision is a good thing. Curriculum is developed, after all, for students, not the other way around. Student needs should dictate how any instructional approach is used in the classroom.

Chapter Two showed that student voices, even very young ones, are beginning to affect curriculum in partner schools. If curriculum is defined as everything that happens in a partner school that is intended to facilitate learning, then all chapters have relevance here. The way the school is structured (see Chapters Seven and Eight), the system of governance it uses (see Chapter Six), the methods by which teachers group students, the way the school involves community agency personnel (see Chapter Nine), the school's use of parent volunteers and technology—all these are, in the broad sense, curriculum.

Curriculum goes beyond the tangible instructional materials that may be distributed to teachers or students. Some of the most creative innovations we have seen in partner schools are curricular changes that demonstrate fundamental shifts in the ways learning and teaching are conceived and carried out (see Chapter Six). For example, some partner schools have scheduled their school day creatively to allow large blocks of time for integrated activities or to allow more time for teachers and others to help students with special needs. Other schools have experimented with open classrooms or multi-age groupings to encourage students of different grades and ages to appreciate each other and to work together so that everybody can progress. Integrated curriculum units, a variety of forms of cooperative learning, innovative uses of technology, and service learning projects that involve students in solving community problems are all curriculum innovations that are occurring in partner schools—not exclusive to, but certainly facilitated by the partnership participation. Research and evaluation activities should inform curriculum; educator preparation and professional development activities should also result in new curricular approaches that are tested in the school. If this integration does not occur, the circle is not complete; the partner school is fragmented and will not reach its primary goals.

A Glimpse of the Ideal

The current fragmentation and uneven development of partner school goals raises a question: What would a complete partner school be like? We have seen scores of partner schools in the United States and Canada and have been impressed with their creative approaches to educational renewal. They are each contributing in unique ways to the renewal efforts that are occurring throughout the continent. But because most are still in the beginning stages of development, participants in these schools would agree that they are still working to become complete partner schools, schools that fully embrace all four goal areas.

In order to present a picture of a fully functioning partner school, we would like to present Patterson Partner School, a school that is a composite of excellent programs we have seen throughout the country. While Patterson Partner School does not presently exist in one building, everything in it exists in some partner school now in operation. We like to think of Patterson Partner School not as a fantasy, but as a promise. Perhaps no school will or *should* contain all of the specific programs or approaches we describe. However, we offer the description to raise the sights of those presently engaged in partner school work or those who wish to begin such a project. As visitors, let's meet the principal and enjoy a tour of the school.

PRINCIPAL: Welcome to Patterson. You caught me at a good time. I just finished meeting with our partner school committee. We've finally been able to arrange things so that teachers could meet with us during regular school hours. Our practicum students take over all of the classes for an hour every two weeks when we meet.

VISITOR: I realize that this a junior high school, but you don't seem to change class periods every hour.

PRINCIPAL: We are a junior high. But all of our classes include seventh-, eighth-, and ninth-grade students. We're also working with one of our feeder elementary schools and with the high school to begin experimenting with a K–12 school in two to three years. In fact, you can see some of the high school teachers sitting over there. They are coming to our school on a regular basis to see how we do multi-age grouping. I always have to say this softly, but we are trying to make our school more like a kindergarten than like a traditional high school.

VISITOR: Why do you have to say it softly?

PRINCIPAL: Oh, some parents misunderstand. They think I'm talking about watering down the curriculum, but what I'm really talking about is caring for each child as an individual, making our school feel more like family. When kids first go to kindergarten, their teacher knows their name, their interests, and some of their fears—and cares about these things. Kids can ask questions and tell the teacher what they want to know and how they feel about it. Then when they get to secondary school, they become part of a group of 175 students a teacher has in six different periods. Most secondary teachers have an impossible task. How can they come to know students—really know them—when they've got 175? We want to make it possible for teachers to know their students—just as they knew them in elementary school. Come and let me introduce you to one of our teachers. Before he came to us he taught preschool, but he has adjusted to junior high just as I'd hoped.

VISITOR [to teacher, after the introductions]: You have a lot of computers in your classroom. How do you use them in your teaching?

TEACHER: I use them when they fit our needs. Just a few minutes ago, we were discussing percentages, and I explained that poll takers usually report their results in percentages. One of the students said, "Why don't we take a survey in our own class?" I asked the other students what they wanted to survey, and one said, "Let's see how many students have different brands of shoes." So that's what we did. We took the survey on our network, and then one student summarized the data on this pie chart that he made with our graphing software. I want you to take a look at the graph yourself. [The teacher, principal, and visitor walk over to Shawn's desk, where he is working on his computer.] Shawn, do you still have that graph on the shoe brands in the class?

SHAWN [*retrieving a piece of paper from inside his desk*]: You mean this one? I did three of 'em, you know. I did the pie chart, then I did the bar graph, and then I did this one—I'm not sure what you call it.

TEACHER: I didn't realize you did a histogram too. You were really ambitious.

SHAWN: Oh, I like this stuff. It helps me understand better when I can see it drawn out like this. [*Pointing to the practicum student from the university*] Ms. Brinkerhoff showed me how to use the graph software the other day. She's going to help me tomorrow learn how to use this software [*pointing to an icon on the screen*] to draw triangles and squares—the kinds of shapes we're doing in math right now.

VISITOR: It looks like you're really into computers. Thanks for letting me see what you're doing. [*To the teacher, as they walk across the room*] Is it different teaching here at Patterson than in your former school?

TEACHER: There is no comparison. In the other school, I was pretty much on my own. It was a good school, mind you, but nothing like this one. We work together in this school, and I know that it makes a difference. I'm working right now on an action research project with two other teachers and Jan Collins at the university. Actually, this project involves two other partner schools in the other district. We're looking at the effects of using E-mail to improve our students' writing ability. I've got students who come in early every day just to write on the computer so they can send messages to their friends in the other schools.

VISITOR: You mean it's like a pen pal project.

TEACHER: Not really. These kids aren't just writing notes to each other. They're each on different "project teams." Everything we do in science is focused around service learning now. We're asking real questions about real needs in our community. My group's project is examining the possibility of creating a new wetlands using water from a nearby river.

[*Pointing to a student sitting at a computer*] Bethany is just finishing a HyperCard stack she's developed on plant growth cycles. We're going to use it in the project. I actually think the software will be publishable—at least as shareware. This is a quality piece of work. [*Walking over to Bethany's desk*] Bethany, will you show us your software on growth cycles?

BETHANY: Oh, it's really not much. All I've done is show how plants grow. If you want to know what a seed looks like when it sprouts, you push this button. I've used the animation software to show the plant as it breaks out of the seed.

TEACHER: Show us how you can control the speed.

BETHANY: You can speed it up by holding your finger on this key, or you can like slow it down by pushing here [*pointing to the space bar*]. I've got three different seeds in the database right now, one that grows fast, one that's kind of average, and one that takes a long time to sprout. Dr. Taylor [*a botany professor from the university*] said that she thinks some company might want to publish the software package.

VISITOR: How do you know Dr. Taylor?

BETHANY: She comes to our school like every couple of weeks. She's working with Ms. Brinkerhoff. I'm not sure what they're doing, but I think it's like teaching science or something. I get to go to Dr. Taylor's lab once in a while. That's where I got the idea for the software. It was when she showed me this experiment she's doing with corn seeds that I got the idea to do the software on how plants grow.

VISITOR: I hope you'll keep working on it; it's a great project. Thanks for letting me see it. [*Turning back to the teacher*] Bethany's an impressive student, but she probably demands a lot of your time.

TEACHER: This is the kind of time I like to spend; it's the reason I went into teaching. I usually get here early and stay late, just so I can help students like Bethany with their projects. But [*smiling at the principal*] I have a principal who gives me all the support I need. I get time during the day to plan these things because we've got student teachers in our school.

PRINCIPAL: I really like the way we're integrating practicum students into our daily routine. Now that they're in our school for a full year, they blend right in with our full-time staff. They get the experience they need, and our teachers get more time to do creative things.

TEACHER: I also get time during the day to visit teachers in the other schools who are working with us. This is the best kind of professional development because we each have different expertise to bring to the project. One teacher is into the questions about animal life in the wetlands, one is writing on the insect life, and I like plants—so we all learn from each other. Then each week we also meet with science faculty from the university who have been helping with the project from the very beginning. They were telling me the other day that they have changed the way they teach science at the university, just as we're changing the way we're teaching science in our school. They've taught us a lot about science, but I think we've taught them something about teaching.

VISITOR: It sounds as if everything is going great. But there must be some problems.

TEACHER: I could talk about problems for a long time. But I think most of our problems came earlier when we were first getting started as a partner school. There was a lot of misunderstanding—especially about roles. People from the university thought we were going to take over teacher education, and we thought they were going to take over our classrooms. But we're more comfortable now with our roles.

VISITOR: Are you saying that you all see things pretty much the same way?

TEACHER: No, I wouldn't say that. We tell the university if we disagree with something they're thinking about in teacher ed., and they feel free to tell us when they're not feeling good about the direction we're taking the school. But because we meet together almost daily in some form or another, the role definition problems aren't causing much difficulty anymore.

VISITOR: Do you feel that you've really had much influence on how the teacher education program is run at the university?

TEACHER: We don't think of the teacher ed. program as only the university's. Everyone at Patterson feels ownership of the program because we have all helped to design it from the ground up. We were the ones who suggested that the methods courses and general ed. courses be combined and taught here at Patterson.

VISITOR: Are you saying that university professors come here to teach the courses?

TEACHER: This science project is a great example. Preservice teachers are working side by side with Patterson teachers and students in integrated math, science, and language arts courses. And on a regular basis, scientists and mathematicians from the university join us for our project work. They've allowed us to use some of their equipment to measure pollution out at the wetlands site, and they've helped us analyze the data.

VISITOR: So where do you see this project going?

TEACHER: I was talking with one of the university faculty the other day, and she is convinced that we will be able to publish the results of our project in a science journal. All of this makes learning real for our students. They're not learning science so they can perform on a test. They're learning science so they can solve real problems that are just ten miles away from where they live.

VISITOR: So you feel that you've influenced the curriculum in teacher education?

TEACHER: Absolutely. The most important contribution I think I've made is getting all preservice teachers to participate in the multimedia cases project. This actually helps all of the teachers at Patterson—not just the preservice teachers. We capture live teaching and learning episodes that occur right here in Patterson on videodisc and compact disk. We also include examples of students' work, teachers' written plans, students' artwork—you name it—all on disk, so that we can view any segment we want.

VISITOR: How do you use these cases once you've recorded them?

TEACHER: We all use them to discuss what we can learn from an episode that will inform our future teaching. Student teachers also use the segments as part of the portfolios they produce documenting their teaching ability. I know our preservice teachers value these sessions, but to tell you the truth, I probably learn more than they do when I go over a multimedia case with them. These sessions always make me think of ways I want to change my teaching.

VISITOR: But isn't it expensive to create your own videodiscs?

PRINCIPAL: It used to be more expensive than it is now. The university has a piece of equipment that records on CD-ROM for a very low price. But you should know that the university is only too happy to help fund this particular project because they are building a library of these multimedia cases that they can use in their teacher education courses and in the research that we have jointly planned here at Patterson. This is how research fits into everything we do. It helps us improve our curriculum, it causes us to change the way we prepare teachers, and it changes the way our teachers teach. It's even part of the wetlands project.

VISITOR: How do you meet state standards while you're doing wetlands research with your students?

TEACHER: That's a tough one, but the state has been quite flexible with us on a number of counts. They want to see if we can really teach more science with service learning projects and integrated units. So for one thing, our school does not issue traditional grades.

VISITOR: You mean there are no report cards at all?

TEACHER: If you mean report cards that have letter grades—no, we discontinued those three years ago. We evaluate student performance using portfolio assessments. All of my students make a videotape to help document their learning. You should see the one that student over there made on the revegetation of a section of the wetlands. It's an impressive piece of work. You probably don't have time to view the tape, but let's go look at the rest of his portfolio [*walking over to a cupboard filled with student materials*]. Here it is, right here.

VISITOR: What are these goal sheets?

TEACHER: Every day, just before school ends, students and teachers take about fifteen minutes to reflect on their day and set goals for the next day. Then, they write down their goals on these sheets. Recording and reflecting on their goals really helps students take responsibility for their own learning.

VISITOR: I guess these are just samples of the student's best work?

TEACHER: The student decides pretty much what goes in the portfolio. [*Pointing to a set of written papers*] You can see how much progress this student has made in writing since the first of the year. It's important that these earlier papers be in here to show the student's improvement.

VISITOR: Who actually sees the portfolio besides you and the student?

TEACHER: When parents come for back-to-school night, I schedule them so that four or five parents come at a time and stay for an hour. I visit with them briefly, but then they sit down with their child and look over the entire portfolio; they watch the videotape the child has made, and discuss the student's progress. They get an in-depth view of how their child is spending time in school; one thing they find out is just how much time we spend outside of school doing problem-based learning projects. I've had some parents volunteer to come along with us and help in some of these projects. This is the way learning and school should be.

VISITOR: What about the students who aren't making it? What about the ones whose parents don't have the time or don't care?

TEACHER: That's a hard one. I have two students right now who really concern me. Both come from homes that are in some sort of crisis. I suspect that physical abuse is going on in one of the homes—not so much aimed at the child as at the mother. But it's the verbal abuse I worry about with the children. These kids come in here each day and look like they're in another world. Oh, they come out of it from time to time, but you can tell that they don't get the love they need in their homes. I got them into counseling with our school counselor, but that just wasn't enough. These kids needed food on their table in the mornings; they needed someone to care whether they fail history; they needed someone to talk to when they're struggling to resist drugs.

PRINCIPAL: This is when it is so helpful to have ties with our social service agencies in the city. We have a caseworker assigned to our school who meets with me regularly. And in one of those meetings, I discussed these two students. The caseworker got right on it. He met with the families, got them into family counseling, and helped straighten out the financial aid they were receiving from the state. I know that schools cannot and must not replace families. That's not what we're about at Patterson. But we are trying to address the needs of the children who come through our doors, and that means working with families when they aren't able to meet the needs of their own children. This school is their school, and we're just here to serve them.

VISITOR: How about students with disabilities?

PRINCIPAL: We were one of the first schools in the district to move to full inclusion. We have no self-contained classes for children with disabilities. In fact, it was one way we reduced class size. When we combined all our students, the special education teachers began teaching regular classes part-time and also working with other teachers to help them meet the needs of the children who used to be in smaller special ed. units. Let me show you another classroom just down the hall where we have three severely disabled kids integrated all day in a regular classroom.

VISITOR [*looking at essays, poems, and artwork on the walls of the hallway*]: I like the student work all over the walls—and even the ceiling. I don't think I've ever seen so much student work on display.

PRINCIPAL: We believe in showing the work our students do. [*Pointing to shelves in an open assembly area of the school*] We have about 100 plants here that students in different classes are growing. These plants are our students' work too. [*Arriving at the classroom with the disabled students*] The student sitting in the second seat of the third row suffered brain damage when she was about two years old. A horse fell on her and nearly crushed her. She was paralyzed from the waist down at first but gradually got most of her physical movement back. But the learning disabilities linger on.

VISITOR: Does she fit in all right with the other students?

PRINCIPAL: Having a multi-age class helps kids with disabilities. So much of the student work is independent, she never holds anyone back. She just works on her own projects, like everyone else. And the other kids help her when she needs it.

VISITOR: What about the boy with the leg braces?

PRINCIPAL: He's quite a different story. He functions quite well intellectually but requires a lot of assistance to get around. The other kids are great to help him, but it's not always easy. When he falls, a teacher usually has to help get him back on his feet. It's been a real boon to have the special education practicum students in our school for a full year. And now that they all hold dual certification in regular and special education, they work more effectively with the rest of our teaching staff.

VISITOR: You mean special ed. teachers have to go through another certification program on the way to becoming a special ed. teacher?

PRINCIPAL: It's one of the best things we've done in teacher preparation in the partnership. Just two years ago, we decided to move the special ed. program to a graduate program and require that all students get a regular certificate first.

VISITOR: How did you decide to make the switch to a graduate program?

PRINCIPAL: It was a natural part of our work as a partner school. We started talking to the university and suggesting that we hold some planning meetings to look at the future of special education. We had some concerns about how special ed. teachers were being prepared.

VISITOR: So you're saying that after a few planning meetings, you made a major change in the program?

PRINCIPAL: No. It took a full year. But we're all satisfied that special ed. teachers are now getting the kind of program that will prepare them to teach kids with more severe problems and help other teachers more effectively at the same time. It has been a giant leap forward from the old program. The results of our evaluation are pretty convincing.

VISITOR: It doesn't seem to matter what type of program you're talking about—the change in special ed. teacher preparation, the wetlands project, the ways you assess students—all seem to be projects that you're doing as a team. You haven't really described any solo projects, where one teacher does something completely independently.

PRINCIPAL: That's because if a teacher does do something on her own, it eventually finds its way into somebody else's classroom—either at Patterson or at one of the other schools in the district. That is the benefit of partnership work. We all learn from each other.

VISITOR: You've given me a lot to think about. I have a much better idea of what it means to be a partner school. Thanks for spending your time with me. I hope we can get together again when our school gets closer to becoming a partner school.

Conclusion

Any societal shift requires faith and patience from those who bring it to reality. And shifts always move away from something old as they move toward something new. Partner schools are an alternative that avoids the isolation that has characterized teacher education and K–12 schooling from their inception. Partner schools are also an alternative to the laboratory schools of the past that were owned by universities, not by public education. However, we recognize that it is always easier to distance oneself from something that others have abandoned than to replace it with something that others can embrace. There is never a lack of detractors for any educational innovation that emerges. This book has been intentionally positive about the possibilities partner schools present for renewing education at all levels. That does not mean that we do not see the possible pitfalls as well. Some of the pitfalls can already be identified by reviewing the history of the laboratory schools that once dominated teacher education.

All of us in the field of education should learn from our past, but we should not allow ourselves to be paralyzed by it. We must create bold initiatives that will retain the best from the past and apply new knowledge and ideas to build new structures and new programs—initiatives that can lead to better schools for our children and our children's children. We must ignore the cynic sitting on the sideline who mutters, "Reform movements have flashed and fizzled before; why should this one be any different?" Now is the time for schools, universities, parents, and whole communities to sit down together and collaborate to create *complete* partner schools that will give our children what they need. Only in this way will we begin to fulfill the promise of partner schools: excellent education for *all* our children.

Appendix

· ·

National Network for Educational Renewal Site Descriptions

This appendix presents basic descriptions of the fifteen partnerships that currently make up the National Network for Educational Renewal (NNER). Each site's goals and special features are highlighted.

BYU-Public School Partnership

Now in its tenth year of operation, the Brigham Young University (BYU)-Public School Partnership is the oldest continually functioning partnership in the NNER. The BYU College of Education and five surrounding school districts participate as six equal partners, sharing governance, resources, and responsibilities. Since its inception, the BYU-Public School Partnership has grown from four to thirty-eight participating public schools. It focuses on four major concerns: preservice training, inservice training, curriculum development, and research. Each of these areas involves administrators, teachers, and students from both the college and the schools in a collaboration based on mutual trust and respect.

One of the first programs to be developed by the BYU-Public School Partnership was its nationally recognized Leader Preparation Program (LPP) for school principals. The LPP is unique among programs for training potential principals in that it has been jointly designed by the BYU College of Education and the participating districts, and both college and districts participate in all phases of its operation. Principals from the districts select candidates for the program, which is jointly administered and supervised by the university and by mentor principals within the schools. The districts also participate in placement of the graduates, some hiring the individuals they earlier recommended for the program.

Another of the partnership's innovations in preservice preparation is its internship program for preservice teachers. As an alternative to student teaching, a student who has completed the necessary methods program signs a contract with a school district to teach full-time for one school year, receiving half the salary and all the benefits of first-year teachers. Interns are mentored by a master teacher, who has been released from teaching duties to act as intern coordinator, and are supervised by the intern coordinator and a supervisor from BYU.

The partnership also participates in preparing those who did not originally select education as a career to be certified and to succeed as teachers. Individuals holding a bachelor's degree in a liberal arts field—whether they are recent graduates or have worked for many years in another profession—participate with a cohort group in an intensive two-semester field-based training program in the schools. Courses are taught in the schools by school personnel. Courses and practica are carefully interrelated, with a focus on relevance of theory to actual school experiences. Students participating in this program are of a wide variety of ages and experience.

In addition to training teachers, the BYU-Public School Partnership focuses on renewal efforts in the schools. An innovative renewal program that has received wide attention is the Unified Studies Program at Orem High, a secondary partner school. This program involves seventy high school juniors and seniors, two high school teachers, five BYU students, and university faculty advisors in cooperative learning, teaching, service, and scholarly inquiry activities—integrating science, social studies, English, recreation, and fine arts. Emphasis is on experiential and service learning. As the culmination of one year's program, during the summer the group traveled to Romania to perform humanitarian service projects.

One of the most active groups in promoting renewal has been the partnership's Gifted/Talented Task Force. BYU completed its fine arts museum in 1993, and task force members from the college and the schools have collaborated with the BYU College of Fine Arts in designing K-12 curricula to introduce students to a variety of forms of expression in the arts. Public school students participate in experiences in drama, music, dance, painting, sculpture, and design, both in the school and at the museum.

California Polytechnic State University
The Professional Development Center

The California Polytechnic (Cal Poly) Center for Teacher Education is committed to the nineteen postulates stated in Goodlad's *Teachers for Our Nation's Schools* (1990). To achieve the goal of simultaneous renewal of teacher education and public schools, the center has adopted Goodlad's objectives:

1. To promote exemplary performance by universities in their role of educating educators

2. To promote exemplary performance by schools in their role of educating the nation's young people

3. To promote constructive collaboration between schools (and their districts) and universities in assuring exemplary performance of overlapping mutual self-interests (p. 324)

Partner schools (called Pilot Professional Development Schools) are considered full partners with the college in preparing teachers and renewing schools. They are expected to link with other schools in their districts and with community agencies in integrative services participation and to function as part of a school-university evaluation and improvement committee.

Partner schools participating with the Cal Poly development center can expect significant changes and innovations in their student teaching experience. Student teachers are assigned to a school for one quarter before they begin their actual teaching to enable them to become acquainted with their students and cooperating teacher. In addition, the districts conduct workshops and orientation meetings for the student teachers to acquaint them with the philosophy under which the district operates and with the procedures and resources that will form the parameters of their experience. Under a supervision model practiced in the partner schools, the preservice teacher is considered assigned to the school rather than to a specific cooperating teacher, and supervision comes from the school's exemplary teachers in partnership with a supervisor from the university.

Education in the schools is renewed as staff development sessions bring new ideas and instructional strategies to the teachers, and as the cooperating teachers make a conscious effort to model these methods and strategies. Subjects covered include discipline procedures, district curriculum, and safety procedures—including recognizing child abuse. Cal Poly purchases substitute teaching time, a minimum of one full day per quarter, so that cooperating teachers can visit other school sites, work with their supervision team, and attend workshops with their preservice teachers.

A particular area of focus in the Cal Poly program has been multicultural preparation of teachers. The center conducts a special course, Social Studies and Multicultural Education, in an appropriate site in the region and also selects and funds a teacher to serve as adjunct university faculty for multicultural education. All partner schools have sizable populations of students who are English language limited. During the student teaching experience, preservice teachers are expected to create and teach lessons that involve cultural issues and to advance multicultural goals.

The Connecticut School-University Partnership

The reform of teacher education at the University of Connecticut was a response to several factors: the national movement for reform of education, a faculty and administration that were committed to rethinking and reformulating the teacher education process, and the ideas promulgated by the Holmes Group and the National Network for Educational Renewal (NNER).

The teacher education program that was designed and implemented has several key components. Students enrolled in an integrated bachelor's and master's degree program spend the first two years of college in liberal arts and then three years in a combined course of study in the School of Education and the liberal arts. They major in a subject taught in the public schools. The CORE program presents a common knowledge base to all preservice teachers. The CLINIC program places students in a variety of school-based settings throughout their three years in the teacher preparation program. The SEMINAR component provides students with the opportunity to reflect on the theoretical material they are learning in their classes and on the real world of their work in a classroom. In the *subject-specific pedagogy* component, students participate in integrated courses focusing on methodological and pedagogical issues.

One of the cornerstones of the new teacher preparation program is the professional development center (PDC). There are twenty-seven PDCs in eight Connecticut school districts. They are located in rural, suburban, and urban settings. During the three years of the teacher preparation program each student has clinical experiences in all three settings. The PDCs provide more comprehensive support than the traditional university-school district relationship, becoming collaborations of school professionals, university faculty, and preservice teachers dedicated to renewing not only teacher education, but schooling as well.

The PDC also provides an environment in which research-based instructional practices and programs can be observed and experienced by those preparing for professional careers in education. University and school personnel work together to identify educational dilemmas and to work toward meaningful solutions to those dilemmas. Dialogue on all levels, research on current educational practices, and continued questioning and reflection form the basis of the PDC. Within these partnerships, the University of Connecticut is attempting to provide the best possible environment for student academic learning and personal self-fulfillment, to provide opportunities for preservice preparation and career-long professional development, and to conduct collaborative research and development activities that will advance theory and practice in education.

Colorado Partnership for Educational Renewal

The Colorado Partnership for Educational Renewal consists of nine public school districts and eight institutions of higher education in a consortium focused on the following aspects of renewal: exploration and evaluation of current knowledge; equalization of learning opportunities; examination of assumptions, beliefs and practices; encouragement of new directions in educational leadership; and improvement of teacher and administrator preparation. Participants create and apply alternatives to current practices in education.

The partnership's mission is the *simultaneous renewal of school and the education of educators*. This is undertaken through a variety of initiatives, including partner schools and special projects. Serving as vehicles for ongoing renewal, the initiatives are created by the schools and higher education partners.

The *partner schools/professional development schools* initiative is the most comprehensive approach to the partnership's mission of simultaneous renewal. Partner schools are joined with teacher (and other educator) preparation programs to fundamentally change the way teachers are prepared and to promote ongoing renewal in the schools. The four purposes of partner schools are to create and sustain a learning community that enables P-12 learners and partners to construct meaningful knowledge, to prepare educators, to provide professional development, and to conduct inquiry (Richard W. Clark, *Evaluating Partner Schools: Conceptual Frames, Practical Applications* [Occasional Paper No. 18]. Seattle: Center for Educational Renewal, University of Washington Press, 1994).

The American Council of Learned Societies (ACLS) Curriculum Development Project is a teacher-initiated, teacher-directed curriculum development project in the humanities. Teacher fellows receive a year-long leave to study with scholars at the University of Colorado at Boulder (CUB). During this period, they are also creating, disseminating, and implementing innovative curriculum projects in conjunction with teams in their home schools. Additionally, partnership staff work with the teacher fellows and university scholars toward partnership-wide sharing of the projects.

The initiative on *achieving gender equity through collaboration* builds on the progress of eleven schools that have been involved in the partnership's gender equity project. Teams of educators, students, and community members in twenty-two schools across the nine partnership school districts develop deeper understandings of equity issues, engage in collaborative inquiry, and develop action plans to address circumstances in their settings. Equal access to learning is reflected in curriculum materials and teaching practices, adult and student interactions, and the intersection of gender and culture, areas addressed through project work.

The *Curriculum Directors Work Group* provides an avenue for partner districts and higher education institutions to work together on curriculum standards, assessment, materials, resource personnel, and other issues. Additionally, this initiative encourages and facilitates the use of resources developed in partnership projects.

Socratic Seminars explore ideas and issues from readings or artwork chosen for richness in content and their ability to stimulate extended, thoughtful discussion. The seminars strengthen learning by engaging participants in close reading, attentive listening, clear expression, as well as weighing evidence, exploring different views, and analyzing important matters. Partnership projects often use seminars in their work, and special seminar workshops are offered periodically through the partnership.

The DPS/Higher Education Partnership is a pilot project of five Denver schools and four higher education institutions. Facilitated by the Colorado Partnership and the Piton Foundation, the project supports the development of school portfolios that will yield important information on progress in the school and relationships with the community. In process are plans for an Inclusion Network that will connect educators working to address the issue of the rising number of students with special needs. The Inclusion Network is designed to generate new knowledge, share resources, and collaborate for external funding to support finding new alternatives for practice. An overarching goal of the project is linking DPS schools with higher education institutions for their mutual benefit.

The Knight Foundation Science Initiative begins in the 1994–1995 school year. Phase I entails the evaluation and reshaping of existing science courses at the University of Colorado at Boulder through interviews with current teachers who graduated from CUB. Phase II will fund ten science teacher fellows to create science curricula in concert with their school teams and university faculty. These teacher fellows will be released full-time for one year to work on curricula while increasing their own content knowledge.

The El Paso Collaborative for Academic Excellence

The El Paso Collaborative for Academic Excellence is a communitywide endeavor to increase academic achievement among all young people in the El Paso area. Education, business, and civic leaders are combining efforts to improve education on all levels—from elementary schools to the university. Their goal is that all students will gain the skills necessary to succeed at a college or university or to obtain a high-salaried job.

To the El Paso Collaborative, success means that all students will develop competencies needed to keep open all university and career options; gain excellence in reading, writing, and speaking English;

master mathematical computations and complex mathematical thinking; learn about the physical world and comprehend scientific precepts; gain cultural literacy, whether it be artistic, humanistic, social, political and/or economic; and apply their education to identify and solve complex problems.

The El Paso Collaborative provides an opportunity for key sectors in the community to assess educational needs and to identify and commit to their roles in moving El Paso's educational entities toward excellence. Parents and community organizations are involved, along with educational, business, and civic entities. School teams guide change at various educational sites. Information from current research and practice is furnished to faculty, staff, and administrators to upgrade the knowledge and skills they will need to implement constructive educational change. Additionally, the collaborative communicates regularly with parents and with the broad community concerning current achievement levels, the progress being made toward academic improvement, and the role that parents and community can play in supporting the process.

Although the collaborative has only been in existence since the spring of 1992, it has already conducted a number of beneficial activities to promote school renewal. Since the summer of 1992, it has provided intensive training for school improvement teams from more than seventy El Paso schools, helping them to organize and plan for change. The El Paso Collaborative has sponsored monthly Principal Seminars to educate principals in their roles in school improvement processes, and it has sponsored meetings between national educational leaders and El Paso-area education policy makers to discuss possible new directions for local schools and colleges.

Hawaii School/University Partnership

The Hawaii School/University Partnership, originally formed as a five-year experiment in 1986, includes the Hawaii State Department of Education, the University of Hawaii, Manoa, and the Kamehameha Schools/Bishop Estate. After more than a year of discussion, the participants agreed that the climate of cooperation and mutual support engendered by the partnership is vital in efforts to renew and restructure schools and to strengthen the teacher education programs on which they depend. Thus, the group has recently extended its commitments for another five years, with the intention of expanding to include schools throughout the state. The focus of the renewed partnership is threefold: developing partnership schools as exemplary sites for school renewal, encouraging dialogue on Goodlad's postulates, and expanding to include the university's college of arts and sciences and the schools of public health and social work.

School success has been enhanced by a number of projects in school reform and renewal, focused on promoting success for all students and reducing or preventing at-risk behavior. Initially, two sites piloted a school-within-a-school program, in which learning is centered around smaller groups of teachers and learners so that instruction can be more personalized. At Castle High School, all ninth-grade students are grouped heterogeneously and assigned to four teachers who teach the core subjects. The program has been successfully replicated in a number of schools throughout the state. The third site has developed a model for preventing students from becoming at risk, as part of a guidance program centered on positive self-concepts and social interaction skills. Lessons have been specifically developed to adapt to students' different learning styles and to incorporate aspects of Hawaiian culture into the classroom.

The Preservice Education for Teachers of Minorities (PETOM) program, a cooperative development of the university and the Kamehameha Schools/Bishop Estate, is an alternative within the university's elementary education program which is designed to teach special competencies for working with underachieving minority students, especially in rural settings. Such competencies include use of an interdisciplinary knowledge base and an ability to adapt instruction to varying cultural backgrounds. Attempts to increase commitment among preservice teachers in this program to teach in rural schools with multicultural populations have been successful.

   Principal preparation has been a major focus of the partnership; through its efforts, the principal training program has been completely restructured. The resulting Cohort School Leadership Program places candidates in a working context, providing an internship in which they shadow their mentor principals in addition to completing integrated university coursework. As students are required to enroll full-time in this program, the Department of Education supports them with a full salary during this time. As an outgrowth of this program, the state has developed the LEAD Academy, an inservice training center for current administrators.

   The Masters of Education in Teaching (MET) Program, introduced in the fall of 1991, is a two-year graduate program focused on reflectively integrating theory and practice. This program, which is interdisciplinary and interdepartmental, relies on an inquiry mode of problem solving as its primary teaching and learning methodology. Some of the seminars are conducted at school sites so that mentors who are public school teachers can participate with students and college faculty in problem solving and dialogue. Action research has become a focus of staff development for the students and teachers involved with the MET program in the partner schools.

Institute for Educational Renewal at Miami University

The Institute for Educational Renewal at Miami University is a collaborative partnership centered at Miami University, a state-assisted university in Oxford, Ohio, located on the edge of a metropolitan corridor than includes the major cities of Cincinnati, Hamilton, Middletown, and Dayton. The partnership includes, along with the university, two middle schools and a large high school in the Cincinnati public schools, a large urban district; an elementary school and an alternative high school in the Middletown City Schools, a district located in a mid-size industrial city affected by deindustrialization; two small rural/suburban elementary schools; one rural/suburban middle school; a suburban junior/senior high; and a vocational high school serving a rural/suburban population. In addition to these schools, the partnership includes health and human service agencies that serve the areas of the partner schools. Thus, a wide diversity of student characteristics and student needs is included, along with a variety of educational and social service personnel to work with the students.

The institute seeks systemic change with the twofold purpose of, first, renewing the commitment and ability of partner organizations and their communities to nurture the learning, development, and well-being of all children; and, second, sharing findings and implications of local developments so they can receive critical analysis and thoughtful application by organizations and communities throughout North America. Motivation, sharing, and eventual dissemination are carried out collaboratively by all stakeholders in the partnership.

In meeting these goals, the Institute for Educational Renewal encourages collaboration among the participants in strengthening preservice preparation of school and human service personnel, and in strengthening education and services to children and families. Collaboration is also initiated to provide continued education for professionals currently teaching or working in the human service areas. As schools and organizations undergo change in the processes of renewal, partnership resources are available to encourage and assist.

But the partnership's interest in meeting the needs of children, youth, and families is not limited by school and agency parameters. Primary needs must be met in students' homes also. Thus, the partnership also involves itself with changes in local, state, and national policies and funding patterns as they affect children and families. Partnership participants are also concerned with the underrepresentation of some minority groups in higher education and in the human services professions. Steps are being taken through the partnership to encourage greater multicultural participation.

Collecting and analyzing data and using it in assessment, evaluation, and research are additional focus points of partnership activity. Research activities of the partnership are disseminated to organizations and communities nationwide.

The Teacher Education Program at Montclair State University

The hallmark of the preparation and professional development of teachers at Montclair State University is a thematic school-university partnership that seeks renewal in each setting. The organizational framework for collaboration at Montclair, the New Jersey Network for Educational Renewal, continues to evolve as a principal in the university's association with both Goodlad's Project for Teacher Education in a Democracy and the Teacher Education Initiative of the National Education Association's National Center for Innovation.

Montclair State has been closely associated with the promotion of critical thinking in the schools. In 1987, the Institute for Critical Thinking was established on campus, and teaching for critical thinking is the theme of the university's teacher education program. The need to extend this theme into the clinical (field-based) components of the program was the immediate impetus for the establishment of the New Jersey Network for Educational Renewal. Field-based mentor teachers support the theme and relate it to their classroom practice.

Montclair State and fourteen urban and suburban school districts established the network using the Carnegie Forum's *clinical school* model for collaboration in teacher education. The affiliated school districts are Caldwell/West Caldwell, Cedar Grove, Dumont, East Orange, Hasbrouck Heights, Montclair, Newark, Orange, Paramus, Parsippany-Troy Hills, Passaic, Scotch Plains-Fanwood, Verona, and Wayne. In each district, teachers are invited to apply for formal appointment at the university as clinical adjunct faculty.

Formal appointment brings with it campus privileges and necessitates participation in paid and credit-bearing summer and follow-up workshops on teaching critical thinking and mentoring novice teachers. Related professional development activities for clinical faculty members are also undertaken in their districts. To date, 170 clinical adjunct faculty members have received formal appointments at the university.

In addition to serving as mentors for student teachers, the cadre of clinical faculty have made possible a variety of collaborative activities within the network, not all of which are directly connected to the thinking skills theme. They have co-taught courses on campus, they have served as on-site supervisors for student teachers, and they have worked as planners and trainers for professional development workshops both on campus and in network schools. Three clinical faculty members have received appointments as visiting clinical professors. They work half-time at the university and half-time in their own schools. Conversely, Montclair State faculty have taught classes in network schools and have participated in a variety of teacher development initiatives.

A three-year commitment, financial support, and a willingness to share information and resources are required of each member district in the New Jersey Network for Educational Renewal. The daily operation of network activities is overseen by a director who reports to a policy-making committee composed of representatives from each school district and the University.

Perhaps the most ambitious undertaking within the network has been the establishment of New Jersey's first professional development/partner school, the Harold Wilson Middle School for Professional Development, in the Newark clinical district. Preservice preparation and professional development are undertaken at Wilson. In the latter case, middle-school teachers in Newark spend five weeks at Wilson in full-time study, while their home-school classes are covered by specially trained exchange teachers provided by the Wilson School.

At its core, the Montclair State University Teacher Education

Program represents a collaborative effort with public schools to achieve simultaneous renewal in each setting. In many cases, renewal comes through the infusion of teaching for critical thinking. Most broadly, the program is intended to systematically involve public school personnel in policy formation, instruction, and supervision as each contributes to the preparation and professional development of teachers.

Puget Sound Educational Consortium

The Puget Sound Educational Consortium (PSEC) is a partnership that includes the University of Washington College of Education and eleven school districts in the Puget Sound area. The consortium's overarching goal is to unite school districts and university in expanding the capacity of all members to maximize learning. To meet this objective, it serves as a catalyst in introducing innovative practices into the member organizations, often extending its influence throughout the state. Its program and activities can be classified into four categories: policy, practice, preparation, and communication.

An example of PSEC's policy function can be seen in its series of Policy Initiatives Papers, which are written to inform state policymakers about the critical policy issues facing the state. Currently, the consortium is working with the university's admissions officers to increase awareness and responsiveness of colleges and universities throughout the state to the alternative assessments now being developed in high schools.

One significant way in which the consortium has affected educational practice is through its Foxfire Teacher Outreach Center. Through this center, PSEC has trained more than three hundred teachers in the Foxfire approach. Another far-reaching aspect of practice has been its encouragement and support of research. PSEC has consistently emphasized the use of action research in classrooms, and it has cosponsored the annual International Seminar on Action Research. University faculty have been encouraged to share their work with others throughout the educational professions through various meetings designed for research dissemination. The practice function of the consortium extends into leadership as well: the Leadership Institute has brought teachers and administrators together to explore the challenges and practices associated with site-based management and shared leadership methodology.

In its preparation function, PSEC was the catalyst for the creation of the Puget Sound Professional Development Center. The center has established professional development schools (PDS's) in four middle schools, and recently six elementary schools have been designated as PDSs. The University of Washington College of Education is planning to have all its teacher education students prepared in PDSs. The college is also changing its teacher education program to accommodate the change to a professional development school approach to teacher education. Concerned with preparing principals as well as teachers, the consortium was instrumental in developing the College of Education's Danforth Principal Preparation Program, which is currently serving as a state and national model for administrator preparation.

The consortium is involved in communicating as well as generating and implementing exemplary practices and preparation programs. It brings a variety of speakers to the area. In recent years its list of speakers has included John Abbott from Project 2000 in England, Crystal Kuykendal, Patricia Albjerg Graham of the Spencer Foundation, Elizabeth Cohen and Larry Cuban from Stanford University, John Goodlad, Ted Sizer, and Howard Gardner. The consortium sponsored a conference on decentralization and site-based management featuring speakers from Chicago, England, and New Zealand.

South Carolina Collaborative to Renew Teacher Education

Unique among the NNER sites is the South Carolina Collaborative to Renew Teacher Education, which consists of the state-funded South Carolina Center for the Advancement of Teaching and School Leadership, Benedict College, Columbia College, Furman University, the University of South Carolina, and Winthrop University. The Center for School Leadership was established by the state legislature in 1989 to assist schools and colleges in restructuring and renewing through institutes, training, and technical assistance. Through cross-functional teams of school and college personnel, the center provides leadership and team development in the essential elements of restructuring.

An invitation was extended to all colleges in the state with teacher education programs to form a collaborative to study and implement Goodlad's nineteen postulates. Nine colleges joined the initial discussions in a self-study using the postulates as benchmarks and indicators of commitment. Administrative commitment, faculty unity, collaboration between education faculty and arts and sciences faculty, and partnerships with public schools were obstacles for some institutions. The five colleges that emerged to join with the Center for School Leadership in the South Carolina collaborative agreed to use the postulates as their compact and to function as a unit, with the center as state coordinator.

The most significant outcomes, on the one hand, of the collaborative's effort to implement Goodlad's postulate "to function as a collaborative unit" include a state-funded center for communication and logistics; pooling of resources and expertise in restructuring; collegial support; and sharing of successes and failures. The collaborative serves as a united, six-part voice for funding and for influencing state policy.

On the other hand, inherent in collaboration is the difficulty in sharing great ideas and innovative programs with traditionally rival institutions as funding for higher education decreases each year. Their own individual agendas for renewal are still foremost with each of the five college partners, but a close second agenda is to make the collaborative effective for the benefit of all students— both college and school—in the state.

The Center for School Leadership now works with 108 associate and partner schools in the Restructuring Network. Twenty-one of the twenty-eight colleges with teacher education programs work with associate and partner schools in established and developing partnerships. During its first year, the South Carolina Collaborative decided to concentrate on establishing partner/professional development schools. The relationship between schools and teacher training programs was seen as the most tangible area to develop because it was a microcosm of the relationships necessary for working with the arts and sciences, for forming centers of pedagogy, for working with state policy makers, and for integrating the collaborative into educative communities. The collaborative now has thirty partner/professional development schools in relationships with its five colleges.

The second-year goal was to use the emerging partner/professional development schools to drive changes in teacher education curricula. That goal has been more difficult than the first year's goal, but there is evidence of initial successful efforts at change. The center's role as coordinator is to keep all the partners focused on the big picture of the moral and political agenda, and to push them to avoid bogging down in endless discussions about three hours of credit, changing the site but not the content.

The goal of the collaborative's third year has been to influence state policy on partner/professional development schools as the impetus to changing teacher education curricula. This goal is merely a combination and extension of the first two, but there is still much work to be done. The arts and sciences have not been neglected. Four collaborative conferences have increased their participation.

Each college has established its own agenda for implementing the postulates and for using them as benchmarks for their progress. The collaborative, however, has enabled each to share its progress, experiences, successes, and failures with the others so that each does not have to reinvent the wheel. Pooling of expertise and resources has allowed the collaborative to draw in other colleges in the state that are now interested in partnership work and in reforming teacher education curricula. They are invited to attend conferences and training sessions to witness what the members of the collaborative are learning about implementing the postulates and about managing the necessary implicit and explicit change. The partners have made numerous state presentations to every association and state conference in order to raise the awareness of the institutions outside of the collaborative.

The Center for School Leadership has provided funds and training for colleges and their partner schools. These include training in restructuring and renewal; a state PDS conference; a conference on cultural diversity; Managing Change seminars; and the formation of a statewide college-partner school telecommunications network. In addition, the center has begun to collaborate with the South Carolina Carnegie Project, for which the center has long been the training unit. This year the center gave grants to five colleges to develop new curricula to prepare middle school educators within the context of partner/professional development schools. Two of the public universities in the South Carolina Collaborative stood together to win experimental funds for six partner/professional development schools from formula funding for public universities. It is likely that neither of the universities alone would have won the funds. Funding would not even have been proposed had not the center and the collaborative proved to the state higher education commission that the postulates and partnerships were the wave of the future.

Looking at the collaborative's day-to-day progress, there is still much work to do in renewal and with the postulates. Comparing where the six individual units were in the summer of 1991 with where they are as a collaborative in the spring of 1994 has revealed great changes and much progress. With the center as coordinator and with $100,000 of its operating budget supporting college/school partnerships, the collaborative continues to advance the agenda for teacher preparation in the American democracy.

Southern Maine Partnership

The Southern Maine Partnership, founded in 1985, is an original member of the National Network for Educational Renewal. The partnership links the University of Southern Maine (USM) with twenty-four school districts, three private schools, and the Maine College of Art. More than 150 schools, with 4,300 teachers teaching 57,000 students, are involved. The activities of the partnership are focused on creating learner-centered environments. Structures, projects, and formats are deliberately fluid in order to respond to the individual and changing needs of the participants. The partnership is in the process of becoming. It offers multiple entry points and a variety of opportunities for learning.

Assessment is a major focus of the partnership's activity. For three years, it has given assessment mini-grants to teachers interested in developing alternative methods of assessment. These projects formed the core of the partnership's annual Assessment Conference. The partnership also has an Alternative Assessment Resource Collection—a steadily growing collection of articles, books, tapes, and assessment tasks designed by teachers and students. This collection is housed at the College of Education's Assessment Center on the campus of the University of Southern Maine. Additional contributions to assessment are generated by the Demonstration Schools Project. Three partnership schools (one elementary, one middle, and one secondary) are charged with identifying significant student outcomes, finding strategies by which these can be reached, and designing instruments for their assessments. The schools receive financial and human resources necessary for this research, which is disseminated throughout the partnership.

Teacher education is an area of extensive innovation at the University of Southern Maine. The College of Education has eliminated its undergraduate degree program in favor of an Extended Teacher Education Program (ETEP). ETEP has three components: an educational studies minor taken in conjunction with the baccalaureate program (usually a discipline within the College of Arts and Sciences), an internship in an academic one-year certification program to follow the baccalaureate degree, and a culminating master's program. ETEP students do their internship year in one of five partnership districts as members of cohort groups. Each of the five sites is directed in tandem by a university professor and an experienced teacher.

During the 1994–1995 academic year, the partnership will initiate a new program called the School Quality Review (SQR). Based on a process developed in Great Britain by Her Majesty's Inspectorate, the SQR initiative is designed to establish a culture of review, reflection, and internal accountability on a schoolwide basis. Run on a multi-year cycle, the process focuses on teaching and learning, including an in-depth review by an external review team made up of both educators and non-educators, and a series of internal reviews conducted by the school.

Texas Educational Collaborative (TEC)
Texas A&M University and School Partners

The centerpiece of the NNER work at Texas A&M University involves establishing school-university partnerships. State legislation provided funding to support such partnership efforts. The legislation specified that funded school-university partnerships must restructure their education programs and start implementing the new programs by fall 1994. As a result of this legislation, the Texas Educational Collaborative (TEC) was formed. The partnership includes Texas A&M University, Prairie View A&M University, and Blinn Community College, along with seven school districts and two regional educational service centers. The TEC has four areas of focus: collaborative development of field-based teacher preparation programs, implementation and exploration of innovative technology systems at schools and colleges, provision of new partner schools in which education students could be trained, and connection of family and home experiences for children in the schools.

The teacher preparation component was guided by Goodlad's

postulates during the development of new programs, and accomplished with school-based partners and with input from the liberal arts and sciences educators. Programs and experiences are being planned that socialize future teachers into the culture of teaching, provide opportunities to be reflective about teaching and learning, and help preservice teachers to identify curriculum and instruction that allows all children to learn.

The three comprehensive programs that are evolving include three distinct phases. The first phase is called *children, families, and communities*. It occurs before the student is admitted to teacher education and includes seminars in which potential teacher candidates explore children, communities, and families, and education as a profession. This phase involves fieldwork in the community, with families and in agencies that deal with health and human services. The second phase, which also occurs before admission to teacher education, is called *children, schools, and society*. In this phase future students study the impact of schooling on society and consider what it means to educate children for their roles in democracy. Both phases require potential teacher candidates to collect evidence of experiences that illustrate their awareness of language, socioeconomic differences, and cultural diversity. Students then proceed through their professional development phase, called *children, teachers, and classrooms*. This takes place during the last phase of three or four semesters. Students study the development of learners and the methodology and pedagogy that is appropriate for the age level they have selected. Teacher education students begin working with children in the classroom and gradually move toward more complex classroom instructional situations. They plan and work in teams with both school and university faculty. They have contact with school settings for at least two semesters.

Technology application, a second important component of the school-university partnership, has focused on obtaining, implementing, and evaluating technology in public school curricula and in teacher education. Computers, laser disks, and distance learning are some of the technologies that teachers, faculty, and students explore within partnership activities.

Family and home connections constitute a third component around which significant programs have been structured. A school-family structure has been implemented at Jane Long Middle School, in which twenty-five children are assigned to a family group with eight adults, including student teacher, college faculty, social service professionals, community volunteers, and others whose training enables them to provide social and emotional as well as educational support. As the families meet each week, each adult implements a special relationship with three or four children. Counseling, tutoring, and outside activities are provided through this support structure. Interprofessional collaboration occurs as counselors, administrators, health and human service workers, and adult literacy educators become involved along with the teacher and university personnel.

Texas A&M University considers the partnership model as the crucial component of simultaneous renewal in schools and university systems. In order to work toward establishing the conditions set forth in Goodlad's nineteen postulates, the College of Education is changing the way the college is organized. A new organizational structure is being planned that brings together faculty from across the college and from other colleges in the university to work collaboratively and interdisciplinarily. New programs are emerging that represent the collaborative's efforts to prepare teachers for the challenges of teaching in a complex and diverse society. In the future, the collaborative hopes to expand its knowledge base to include the interrelationships among the many professionals who contribute to the well-being of children, families, and schools.

Wheelock College

Over the past six years, Wheelock College has been involved in a partnership with five public schools in Brookline and Boston, Massachusetts. During this time, the college and the schools have accomplished a number of goals targeted toward teacher education and school renewal. They have developed a student teaching seminar. They have created a teaching team, consisting of a graduate intern, classroom teachers, and specialists to address special needs of learners within the regular classroom. Team flexibility enables one teacher to be released one day a week to pursue professional development. They have also initiated a theme-based, interdisciplinary curriculum that integrates multicultural content.

Recently, Wheelock also established a partnership with two public schools in Cambridge. This partnership has developed a steering committee, broadly representative of the school and the larger community, that makes decisions concerning the school by consensus. Additionally, science has been selected as a focal content area for the partnership, and the partners are currently examining the systems by which the school and the larger system are teaching science. Participants are finding that, through the partnership, they have developed a common language for discussing teaching and learning. This common language has allowed more sharing and discussion to take place among the teachers, which has been enhanced by visits to other sites. Partnership members are also currently conducting evaluation and expansion of the whole language curriculum.

A potential partnership is being developed between Wheelock and the Walker Home, a residential program for boys aged three to thirteen with learning and emotional problems. A steering committee with representatives from both institutions has been meeting monthly to develop a master's program to prepare students to work with children with moderate special needs. A curriculum for graduate interns has been designed and will be jointly taught by Wheelock and Walker faculty. Possible expansion of this model to an additional school is being discussed.

Wright State University: Partners Transforming Education

The motto for the College of Education and Human Services at Wright State University is "Working with others to better understand and improve the human condition." Accordingly, activities of partnership groups that have formed over the years have centered on the interrelated objectives of providing maximum opportunities for learning for children, youth, and adults through strengthening the schools, fostering improvement in human service agencies, enhancing professional growth of teachers and human services workers, and promoting continuous improvement in the college programs that prepare individuals to serve in the fields of education and human services.

As various groups have worked in collaborative relationships, the result has been a series of learning laboratories in which mutual challenges are discussed and new approaches are devised and applied. Examples of these laboratories include the Educational Development Leadership Network K-12 (ED-LINK-12), the Southwest Ohio Vocational Personnel Development Center, the Ohio Consortium for Portfolio Development, the Center for the Arts for the Disabled and Handicapped Persons, the Comprehensive Health Fitness for Life Curriculum Project, the developing Center for Clinical Practice and Research for Counseling Education and Rehabilitation, and a collaborative program with area mental health agencies to train rehabilitation counselors in psychiatric rehabilitation counseling. Although there is much variety in the specific projects, the underlying aspects of meeting human needs and developing human potentials are common and pervasive.

The developing Partners Transforming Education collaboration considers itself a learning laboratory for "rethinking and restructuring professional development in education and human services at Wright State University while simultaneously engaging in the renewal of schools and human service agencies" (College of Education and Human Services, *Milestone One*. Dayton, Ohio: Wright State University, 1993). This partnership has involved the human services professions beyond education in recognition of the growing body of evidence that the needs that must be served for children and youth in today's society go beyond the classroom door. Social changes in recent decades have altered the structures of the family and community; support systems that earlier sustained the moral and social development of children are eroding; and society turns to the schools to provide for the deficits. Among the services now expected from the schools are breakfast programs to provide for nutritional needs; counseling to help with emotional disturbances; extended care to provide safety and recreational opportunities for children with working parents; values and morality education, including sex education and drug abuse prevention; and music, art, and drama programs to provide enriched artistic and aesthetic opportunities. Teachers must be prepared with adequate knowledge for these expanded roles, and community service personnel must be prepared to back up and support the work of teachers as well as to deal with the needs of the children that teachers refer to them for additional services. The knowledge and expertise of the various groups that serve children and families can and should be combined for the benefit of all groups.

In addition to meeting a diversity of current social and human needs, schools need to prepare students to meet a diversity of future needs, particularly those due to changes in today's society and work force. New skills are needed to handle new technology and to work with new human relations as well as administrative structures. With these educational necessities as a base, the partnership is planning initiatives in the following areas: academic goals; vocational goals; social, civic and cultural goals; citizen participation; enculturation; moral and ethical education; personal goals; creativity and aesthetic expression; and self-realization.

Wyoming School-University Partnership

The Wyoming School-University Partnership joins the University of Wyoming with fifteen public school districts and the Wyoming State Department of Education in a collaborative organization dedicated to simultaneously restructuring the education of teachers and renewing the public schools. Close coordination occurs between the College of Education and the College of Arts and Sciences, as well as between campus, school districts, and state representatives.

Centers for Teaching and Learning (CTLs) are schools in the partnership designated as sites for implementing partnership functions. They have been specifically designed to provide field experiences that allow student teachers to connect their course instruction to classroom realities. At the same time, the CTLs enable practicing teachers to observe innovative strategies for teaching and learning and to dialogue with other professionals in exploring practices for improving instruction for all children. A Partnership Training Cadre has been established to facilitate development of these centers.

The Wyoming Teacher Education Program began in September 1992, as cohort groups of preservice teachers joined partner district clinical faculty in clinical faculty teams to implement this new program in the CTLs. The new program features four semesters (phases) of field experiences in CTLs for cohort groups of students beginning in the sophomore year and continuing through the senior year. CTLs are striving to become characterized as places where there is personal renewal, organizational renewal, a supportive climate, and lifelong learning.

The Video Education Interactive Network (VEIN) Project has involved University of Wyoming faculty and partner teachers as collaborative teams in developing instructional modules for both preservice and inservice teachers, to be presented over the Wyoming State Compressed Video Network. For their participation in this project, the partnership received a certificate of merit from the Business Higher Education Forum under the Anderson Business Medal. At this time, the partnership is attempting to obtain compressed video equipment for its school districts, so that all districts can tie into the Wyoming state network and access these modules and other materials available through the university and various community colleges.

Resources for staff development have been written in cooperation with the associate dean for graduate studies and continuing professional education, targeted to help districts develop long-range staff development plans tailored to their personnel needs. Participants have compiled profiles of initiatives and interests for the various districts to facilitate networking as resources are developed and refined.

Major grant proposals have been submitted for innovative projects involving districts and their faculty. At least fifteen have been written, including the New American Schools Development Project, the National Science Foundation Systemic Project, and the FIRST program.

A new administrator preparation program has been implemented, redesigning the educational leadership unit. Funded by the Danforth Foundation, public school educators have worked collaboratively with university personnel on this project. The selection process for the program identifies leadership talent; cohort group participation helps to provide educators with the skills necessary for restructuring schools. Candidates for the administrative degree serve a full-semester internship in which they work closely with student teachers to hone the skills necessary to facilitate teacher participation on the instructional leadership team.

Wyoming Governor Mike Sullivan has used the partnership as an example before the National Governor's Association to highlight Wyoming's attempts to meet national educational goals.

Index

Lewis & Clark College - Watzek Library

3 5209 00645 6517